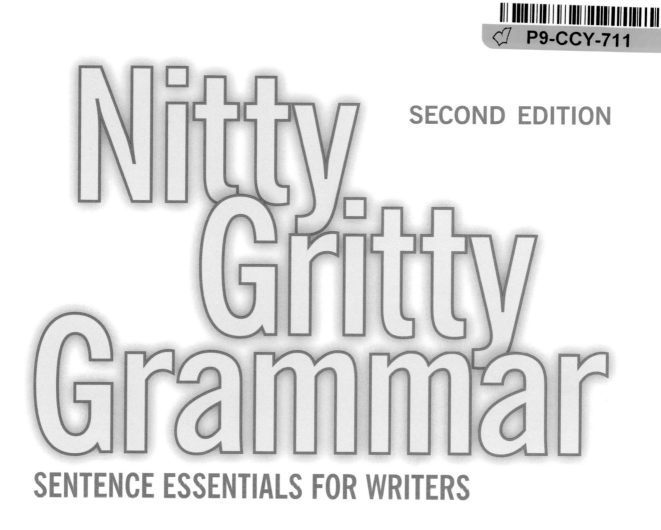

Nitty Gritty Grammar

SECOND EDITION

SENTENCE ESSENTIALS FOR WRITERS

A. Robert Young
Ann O. Strauch

CAMBRIDGE UNIVERSITY PRESS
Cambridge, New York, Melbourne, Madrid, Cape Town, Singapore, São Paulo, Delhi

Cambridge University Press
32 Avenue of the Americas, New York, NY 10013–2473, USA

www.cambridge.org
Information on this title: www.cambridge.org/9780521606547

First edition 1998
First published by St. Martin's Press, Inc. 1994
2nd printing 2007

Printed in Hong Kong, China, by Golden Cup Printing Company Limited

A catalog record for this publication is available from the British Library

Library of Congress Cataloging in Publication Data
Young, A. Robert.
Nitty gritty grammar : sentence essentials for writers / A. Robert Young, Ann O. Strauch.—2nd ed.
    p.   cm.
Includes index.
ISBN 978-0-521-60654-7
1. English language–Sentences–Problems, exercises, etc. 2. English language–Rhetoric–Problems,
exercises, etc. 3. English language–Textbooks for foreign speakers. 4. English language–Grammar–
Problems, exercises, etc. 5. Report writing–Problems, exercises, etc. I. Strauch, Ann O. II. Title.
PE1441.Y68 2006
428.2′4–dc22   2005058273

ISBN 978-0-521-60654-7 Student's Book

Cover and Book design and text composition: Adventure House, NYC

Cambridge University Press would like to thank Jane Sturtevant for her significant contribution to this book.

Contents

Plan of the Book

SECTION 2

Chapter 4 Nouns

Part 1 Count Nouns
1 Singular count nouns and determiners
2 Modifiers
3 Plural nouns and determiners
4 Forming regular plural nouns
5 Forming irregular plural nouns

Part 2 Noncount Nouns
6 Count vs. noncount nouns
7 Nouns that can be count or noncount

Part 3 Proper Nouns
8 Identifying and using proper nouns

Writing Assignments
1 An exercise (or weight loss) program
2 A special gift

Chapter 5 Articles

Part 1 Articles with Singular Count Nouns
1 A vs. *an*
2 *A/An*, *the*, and common focus
3 *The* with a synonym, part, or closely related idea
4 *The* with a limiting phrase or clause
5 *The* with superlatives and adjectives of rank order
6 *The* with natural common focus
7 No article with singular nouns in set phrases

Part 2 Articles with Plural and Noncount Nouns
8 *The* with plural nouns and common focus
9 Noncount nouns and common focus
10 Plural proper nouns

Writing Assignments
1 A photograph
2 A pleasant (or distressing) walk

SECTION 3

Chapter 6 The Simple Present and the Present Progressive

Part 1 The Simple Present
1 The form of the simple present
2 Forming the third person singular
3 Irregular verbs
4 Habits and customs
5 Time markers for habits and customs
6 General truths

Part 2 The Present Progressive
7 The form of the present progressive
8 Contractions vs. full forms
9 Using the present progressive to express the moment of communication
10 Stative verbs
11 Temporary situations
12 Time markers for temporary situations

Writing Assignments
1 Household responsibilities
2 Pets

Chapter 7 The Simple Past and the Past Progressive

Part 1 The Simple Past
1 The form of the simple past
2 Irregular past tense verbs
3 Negatives in the simple past
4 Actions completed in the past
5 Time markers for the simple past

Part 2 The Past Progressive
6 The form of the past progressive
7 The past progressive vs. the simple past
8 Stative verbs

Writing Assignments
1 A special celebration
2 A public event

Chapter 8 The Present Perfect and the Present Perfect Progressive

Part 1 The Present Perfect
1 The form of the present perfect
2 Irregular verbs in the present perfect tense
3 The present perfect for unspecified past time
4 Frequency adverbs with the present perfect
5 The present perfect for past to present time
   (and possibly the future)
6 *For* and *since* with the present perfect

Part 2 The Present Perfect Progressive
7 The form of the present perfect progressive
8 Stative verbs
9 The present perfect progressive for emphasizing
   duration

Writing Assignments
1 A disagreement
2 A separation
3 An annoyance

Chapter 9 The Future

Part 1 The Future
1 Forms of the future with *be going to* and *will*
2 The form of future time clauses
3 Predictions with *be going to* and *will*
4 Plans and intentions with *be going to* and
   the present progressive
5 Scheduled and planned events with the simple
   present and the present progressive
6 Future forms in longer passages

Part 2 Future in the Past
7 Meaning
8 Form

Writing Assignments
1 A road trip
2 A planned day

SECTION 4

Chapter 10 Modals

Part 1 Forming Modals
1 Modals: present and future time
2 Modals: past time
3 *Can*
4 Phrasal modal: *have to*

Part 2 Using Modals to Express Ability
5 *Can* and *could*

Part 3 Using Modals to Express Possibility, and Logical Conclusions
6 *Could*, *may*, and *might*
7 *Must*

Part 4 Using Modals to Express Requirements, Recommendations, and Mistakes
8 *Must* and *have to*
9 *Might*, *could*, and *should*
10 *Might have*, *could have*, and *should have*

Writing Assignments
1 September 11, 2001
2 Leaving a job
3 Changes in your family's country
4 Driving
5 An emergency

Chapter 11 Conditionals

Part 1 Clauses in Conditional Sentences
1 Two clauses
2 Condition and result

Part 2 Unreal Conditionals
3 Meaning
4 Form: present and future

Part 3 Real Conditionals
5 General truths and habitual actions
6 Conditional predictions

Writing Assignments
1 Your rich relative
2 Problems with friends

Chapter 12 *Hope* and *Wish*

Part 1 Clauses in Sentences with *Hope* and *Wish*
1 Two clauses
2 *That*

Part 2 Verb Tenses in Sentences with *Hope* and *Wish*
3 Verb tenses after *hope*
4 Verb tenses after *wish*, present/future
5 Verb tenses after *wish*, past

Part 3 Meaning: *Hope* vs. *Wish*
6 Events in the present/future
7 Events in the past
8 Different points of view

Writing Assignments
1 A situation you are unhappy about
2 A hope or wish

Preface

INTRODUCTION TO *NITTY GRITTY GRAMMAR*

Nitty Gritty Grammar, Second Edition, focuses on essential areas of English grammar that cause difficulty for developing writers. It guides students through the learning process by exploring grammar in context, providing controlled practice, and giving students thought-provoking writing assignments in which they can practice grammar in a more open-ended format.

The grammar points are illustrated in reading passages from a variety of genres, from comic strips to an excerpt from the 9/11 Commission Report. After each grammar point is thoroughly explained, it is presented in summary form in a Nitty Gritty box that serves as a handy reference tool for students and teachers. A Chapter Review at the end of each chapter lists all of the grammar points in the chapter and offers exercises that give students the opportunity to practice and consolidate what they have learned.

This book addresses the specific grammar problems common in student writing, such as run-on sentences, sentence fragments, and incorrect article usage. It truly covers the "nitty gritty*." In keeping with this focus on grammar for writers, some grammar structures that are traditionally included in a general grammar text are not covered or are mentioned only briefly in this book. For example, in the chapters on verb tenses, significantly more attention is paid to statements than to questions because questions are relatively uncommon in academic writing.

Nitty Gritty Grammar can be used as the main text in a grammar class or as a grammar supplement in a writing class. It teaches grammar in the context of writing and includes several writing assignments in every chapter. However, because *Nitty Gritty Grammar* does not teach composition per se, teachers may want to supplement the material in this book with a composition text as needed.

It is not necessary to teach the chapters in order and it is not necessary to cover all of them. Students and teachers should select the chapters that are relevant to their needs.

ORGANIZATION OF THE BOOK

The basic unit of the book is the chapter. There are 15 chapters in the book grouped into sections of several chapters each. Each chapter is divided into two or more parts that present specific aspects of a broader topic. For example, Chapter 5, *Articles,* covers Articles with Singular Count Nouns and Articles with Plural and Noncount Nouns. Each chapter ends with a Chapter Review that combines material from all of the parts, stepping up the challenge. Each section ends with a Section Review in which grammar points from all of the chapters in the section are brought together in review exercises.

✱ *Nitty gritty* is most commonly used as a noun meaning "the basic, essential facts of a situation." *Nitty Gritty Grammar* refers to the basic, essential grammar points.

CHAPTER STRUCTURE

Introduction

Every chapter begins with these two features:

Introduction to the Topic

This introduction gives a brief description of what will be covered in the chapter.

Exploring the Topic

Exploring the Topic presents the chapter's grammar topic in context, usually in a literary passage. It stimulates the student to begin thinking about the grammar topic by asking inductive questions about the structures seen in the passage (with answers in the Teacher's Manual). This exercise lends itself well to group or pair work.

Where needed, some chapter introductions also include an exercise called Refreshing Your Memory. This exercise reminds students of material presented in previous chapters that will be needed to understand the material in the current chapter. If you are teaching chapters (or even specific grammar points) out of sequence, this activity highlights anything you might need to pre-teach.

Chapter Parts

The remainder of the chapter is divided into two or more related parts. Each part introduces a grammar topic and then develops it in a series of steps called Grammar Points. A typical Grammar Point has three parts:

Exploring the Grammar Point

This inductive exercise introduces the grammar point. It asks the student to read example sentences and consider a few questions about form and/or meaning. For some grammar points, an inductive introduction is unnecessary; in such cases Exploring the Grammar Point is omitted.

Understanding the Grammar Point

Understanding the Grammar Point is a deductive exercise that answers the questions posed in Exploring the Grammar Point, and goes on to present an explanation of the grammar. This exercise ends with a Nitty Gritty box, an easy-to-find blue box with a concise summary of the grammar point that students can use as a reference tool as they work through the rest of the chapter.

Practice

Practice exercises follow nearly every Grammar Point. The number and placement of these exercises vary according to the nature and complexity of the grammar topic. Exercises can be done in class as group or pair work, or they can be assigned for homework. A few Practice exercises are open-ended, but nearly all of them have answers in the Teacher's Manual.

To emphasize induction, have students keep their books closed for Exploring the Grammar Point, and write the example sentences on the board. In many cases, you may also want to teach Understanding the Grammar Point with books closed, allowing students to read it after you have taught it, or assigning it for homework or review.

Writing Assignments

In every chapter, Writing Assignments appear at intervals where a reading passage or Practice exercise triggers an appropriate and stimulating topic. These are personal-experience topics requiring no research on the part of the student and little classroom preparation by the instructor. In many cases, writing assignments naturally generate the grammar structures presented in the chapter. They can be assigned where they appear in the chapter (when any necessary grammar points have been covered) or reserved for later use.

Chapter Review

A Chapter Review concludes each chapter. It begins with a list of the chapter's Nitty Gritty boxes. This provides a review and ready reference for students while they do the exercises. The Chapter Review continues with Review Practice exercises that bring together the grammar from the whole chapter.

Many of the Review Practice exercises are editing tasks in which students identify and correct a variety of errors in a text. These should generally be done individually. The first Review Practice exercise is often a traditional short-answer or sentence- completion exercise that reminds students of key points and grammar terms. This exercise can be done in class as pair work or taught with books closed. Answers to all review exercises are provided in the Teacher's Manual.

SECTION REVIEWS

The five Section Reviews supply additional practice of the grammar points from several chapters combined. Each Section Review begins with a Refreshing Your Memory exercise with a series of questions that focus students' attention on the most important grammar points of the preceding group of chapters. Questions often refer to specific grammar terms and elicit specific facts or generalizations about form and meaning. These questions lend themselves to instructor-led discussion by the whole class; however, some classes may be able to handle them in small groups.

Review Practice exercises are typically passages that students edit by correcting mistakes in grammar. The mistakes involve specific points covered in the chapters. The exercises may be done as pair work during class time or assigned as homework.

NEW FEATURES OF *NITTY GRITTY GRAMMAR, SECOND EDITION*

- This new edition of *Nitty Gritty Grammar* includes more practice of specific grammar points and more review exercises.
- Inductive learning, a popular feature of the first edition, is now supported by explanation — something for every learning style.
- There is additional instructor support in the Teacher's Manual, including suggestions for varying and streamlining lessons, as well as grammar "trouble spots" to watch out for.
- The new Teacher's Manual includes a comprehensive Answer Key.
- *Nitty Gritty Grammar* now has a more consistent, more transparent organization showcased in an inviting and functional two-color design. New art contextualizes literary passages and inspires more creativity in the writing assignments.

Sentence Essentials

Flat or round?

Introduction to the Topic

The subject of a sentence is what the sentence is about. The verb says something about the subject. Every English sentence has at least one subject and one verb that go together.

In this chapter, you will learn about some of the different kinds of subjects and verbs. You will also review the importance of capital letters and end punctuation in written English.

EXPLORING THE TOPIC

Read the passage on the next page about the common misconception shown in the illustration above. In the passage, the subject of each sentence is underlined once. The verbs are underlined twice.

Flat or Round?

You know this story.

In 1492, Christopher Columbus took three small ships and sailed westward from Europe to find a route to the Indies, east of Europe. Scholars and geographers of his day believed that the earth was flat. In their view, sailing west was insane. The ships would fall off the edge of the earth. However, Columbus had a revolutionary idea. He believed that the earth was round.

Don't believe it! In Columbus's day, and going back as far as ancient Greece, most educated people believed that the earth was round.

1. Which subject is two words joined by *and*?
2. Which verb is two words joined by *and*? (There may be some extra words in between.)

Imperative sentences like *Don't believe it!* have no visible subject, but the subject *you* is understood.

 Subjects

Noun Subjects

UNDERSTANDING THE GRAMMAR POINT

The subject of a sentence is often a noun*. Nouns name people, places, physical things, concepts, or activities. Consider the following examples:

NOUNS		
	From *Flat or Round?*	**From a school setting**
People	Columbus, geographers	teacher, student
Places	Europe, the Indies, earth	Miami Dade Community College, library, classroom
Physical things	ships, route, edge	notebook
Concepts	idea, story	education, knowledge
Activities	sailing	repetition, writing

NOUN SUBJECTS
Columbus had a revolutionary idea.
The ships would fall off the edge of the earth.
Sailing west was insane.

❋ *For more information about nouns, see* Chapter 4, Nouns.

The subject of a sentence is often a noun. Nouns name people, places, physical things, concepts, or activities.

Practice 1.1

Read these proverbs. Underline the subject of each sentence.

1. <u>Variety</u> is the spice of life.
2. Honesty is the best policy.
3. Still waters run deep.
4. A friend in need is a friend indeed.
5. Absence makes the heart grow fonder.
6. Two wrongs don't make a right.
7. Things are not always what they seem.
8. Actions speak louder than words.

Grammar Point 2 | **Pronoun Subjects**

UNDERSTANDING THE GRAMMAR POINT

A *pronoun* stands for a noun. A pronoun can be the subject of a sentence as long as the reader knows what noun it stands for.

noun   pronoun
 ↓   ↓
Columbus had a revolutionary idea. *He* believed that the earth was round.

The following chart shows the subject pronouns in English.

SUBJECT PRONOUNS	Singular	Plural
First person	I*	we
Second person	you	you
Third person	he, she, it	they

The subject of a sentence can be a pronoun.

✱ *The pronoun I is always a capital letter.*

Practice 2.1

Underline the subjects. Write *N* above the subject nouns and *P* above the subject pronouns.

Harriet Tubman

1. <u>Harriet Tubman</u> ^N was a slave in Maryland in the 19th century.
2. <u>She</u> ^P escaped from her owner.
3. Later, she became the most famous "conductor" on the Underground Railroad.
4. She helped hundreds of other slaves escape to freedom.
5. The Underground Railroad was not an actual railroad.
6. It was a secret network of safe places called "railroad stations."
7. Escaping slaves traveled from station to station on their way to the North and freedom.
8. The conductors were free blacks and white abolitionists.

Writing Assignment 1

Imagine that you are a slave who has escaped on the Underground Railroad. Write a short letter to a friend or relative. Tell them that you have escaped and give a few details of your trip to safety. Use your imagination to invent the details.

Harriet Tubman

Grammar Point 3 **Compound Subjects**

UNDERSTANDING THE GRAMMAR POINT

Sometimes a subject consists of more than one noun or pronoun. This is called a *compound subject*. The word *and* joins the parts of a compound subject. In the following sentences, the compound subjects are shown in bold.

1. **Scholars and geographers** believed that the earth was flat.
2. Today, **you and I** know better.

> **THE NITTY GRITTY** *A sentence can have a compound subject: two or more nouns and/or pronouns joined by* and.

Practice 3.1

Read the following sets of sentences about Christopher Columbus. Combine each set into one sentence with a compound subject. Make any other necessary changes in the new sentence.

Christopher Columbus

1. The king of Spain paid part of the cost of the voyage.

   The queen of Spain paid part of the cost of the voyage.

   The king and queen of Spain paid part of the cost of

   the voyage.

2. The Santa María was one of Columbus's three ships.

   The Niña was one of Columbus's three ships.

   The Pinta was one of Columbus's three ships.

3. Columbus left Spain on August 3, 1492.

   His 104 crewmen left Spain on August 3, 1492.

4. On October 8, ducks flew near the ships.

   On October 8, other land birds flew near the ships.

5. On the island of Guanahaní, Taino men greeted Columbus.

   On the island of Guanahaní, Taino women greeted Columbus.

6. Their peaceful manner impressed him.

   Their handsome appearance impressed him.

EXPLORING THE GRAMMAR POINT

Read the sentences below. What does the word *it* mean in sentence 1? What does *it* mean in sentence 3? Is *there* the subject of sentence 2? In which sentence does *there* refer to a place?

1. The Home Center has opened a new store. **It** is on River Street.
2. They sell plants and flowers **there**.
3. **It** is Saturday morning.
4. **There** are a lot of people buying plants this morning.

UNDERSTANDING THE GRAMMAR POINT

In sentence 1, *it* means "the store." In sentence 3, *it* is a *filler subject* that means something like "today."

As a filler subject, *it* takes a singular form of the verb *be*. As a filler subject, *it* does not refer to anything previously mentioned. Readers understand its meaning because they are accustomed to filler subjects and because the context makes the meaning clear. The main uses of the filler *it* are to express time, day, date, distance, weather, and temperature.

FILLER SUBJECT *IT*	
Meaning	**Example**
time	It was 2:00 A.M.
day	It was Friday.
date	It was October 12, 1492.
distance	It is about 2500 miles from New York to Los Angeles.
weather	It was cloudy and rainy last weekend.
temperature	It was very hot yesterday.

There can also be a filler subject, as in sentence 4 above. In sentence 4, *there* does not refer to a place. It signals the existence of something. When *there* is a filler subject, the verb is always *be*. The real subject follows the verb, and the verb agrees with the real subject. In the following sentences, the real subjects are underlined.

5. **There were** strong winds here yesterday.
6. **There is** a fallen tree in our driveway today.

- A filler subject (*it* or *there*) appears in the normal subject position, but its meaning is different from its usual meaning.
- As a filler subject, *it* often stands for time, day, date, distance, weather, or temperature. The verb is *be*.
- As a filler subject, *there* fills the place of the subject in the sentence, and the real subject follows the verb. The verb is *be*, and it agrees with the real subject.

Practice 4.1

Rewrite these sentences. Use the filler subject *it*.

1. The time was 9:20. _It was 9:20._

2. The day was Tuesday. _____

3. The date was November 2. _____

4. The weather in spring is cold and rainy. _____

5. The distance from my home to my office is about thirty miles. _____

_____

6. The time necessary to go from my home to my office is about forty-five minutes. _____

_____

Practice 4.2

Complete the sentences. Use the filler subject *there* and the verb *was/were*.

1. After the party, _there was_ a terrible mess in the living room.

2. _____ dirty glasses on every table.

3. _____ used napkins and leftover food everywhere, even on the floor.

4. _____ an overturned soda bottle in one corner.

5. _____ two broken chairs.

6. _____ a stranger asleep on the sofa.

Practice 4.3

Complete the sentences with a filler subject: *it* or *there*.

1. _____It_____ is mid-August.

2. _____ is early in the morning.

3. _____ isn't a cloud in the sky.

4. _____ is still cool.

5. _____ is dew on the grass.

6. _____ are only a few people in the park.

7. _____ is a perfect day for a run.

8. _____ is just enough time for a run before class.

Verbs

Grammar Point 5 ▸ Verbs and Verb Phrases

UNDERSTANDING THE GRAMMAR POINT

A verb* may consist of one word, or it may consist of one or more auxiliary verbs plus the main verb, forming a *verb phrase*. In the following sentences, the verb is one word.

1. Last month, I **read** *So Far from the Bamboo Grove*.
2. *Wedding Song* **is** the story of a young man in Cairo, Egypt.

The following sentences use verb phrases:

3. I **am reading** *Wedding Song* now.
4. Before that, I **was reading** *Gone With the Wind*, but I didn't finish it.
5. I **have read** several excellent novels this year.
6. I **am going to read** more books for pleasure.

> THE NITTY GRITTY *Verbs can consist of one word or a verb phrase.*

Practice 5.1

Underline the verbs and verb phrases in the following passage about Easter Island.

> **Rapa Nui**
>
> Rapa Nui, or Easter Island, <u>is</u> 1400 miles from the nearest neighboring population. Polynesians have lived on the island for about 2500 years. The island is famous for its nearly 900 carved stone heads or *moai*. The tallest one reaches 70 feet. Many of them were standing when the first Europeans arrived in 1722. However, over the next hundred years, the islanders pulled them all down. Their descendants say the reason was anger and despair over the island's ecological and economic decline. Today, some moai have been erected again by archeologists. In addition to the famous moai, Rapa Nui had the only written language in Oceania. Today, very few examples of the writing survive, and scientists are studying them. So far, however, no one has been able to read them.

Grammar Point 6 ▸ Compound Verbs

EXPLORING THE GRAMMAR POINT

Underline the verbs in these sentences. How many verbs does each sentence have?

✳ *For more information about verbs, see* Chapters 6–12.

1. In the 17th century, Dutch traders arrived on Manhattan Island and bought it from some Native Americans for goods worth about $700 in today's money.

2. Unfortunately for the traders, those particular Native Americans didn't live on Manhattan and didn't have the right to sell the island.

3. They accepted the traders' goods and went on their way.

UNDERSTANDING THE GRAMMAR POINT

A sentence may contain just one main verb, or it may contain two or more main verbs. A sentence that contains more than one main verb has a *compound verb*. The verbs are usually joined by *and*. Each of the three sentences above about Manhattan has a compound verb consisting of two verbs or verb phrases joined by *and*.

> **THE NITTY GRITTY** *Many sentences have compound verbs. Compound verbs are made up of two or more verbs or verb phrases joined by* and.

Practice 6.1

Read the following pairs of sentences about the original Olympic Games. Combine each pair into one sentence with a compound verb.

The First Olympic Games

1. According to historic records, the Olympic Games began in 776 B.C. They occurred every four years until 393 A.D. _According to historic records, the Olympic Games began in 776 B.C. and occurred every four years until 393 A.D._

2. At their height, the Games lasted for five days. They ended with a sacrifice of 100 oxen. _____

3. Athletes and officials walked to Olympus together. They stopped on the way to make sacrifices. _____
_____

4. The fighting events were very bloody. They caused many deaths. _____
_____

5. Olympic events honored the gods. They tested skills needed in war. _____
_____

6. Winners wore crowns of olive leaves. They received special privileges in their home cities.
_____

Writing Assignment 2

Reread the sentences in Exploring the Grammar Point. Imagine that you are one of the Dutch traders or one of the Native Americans. Write a description of the incident. Tell how you met the other group, what happened, and what you think about it.

3 Sentence Beginnings and Endings

Grammar Point 7 Capital Letters and End Punctuation

UNDERSTANDING THE GRAMMAR POINT

In speech, your voice tells your listener where your sentences begin and end. In writing, visual cues are needed. English uses a capital letter to signal the beginning of a sentence. English sentences end with a period, a question mark, or an exclamation point. Question marks and exclamation points are rare in academic writing.

EXAMPLE	EXPLANATION
You know this story.	A statement ends with a period (.).
Is the earth flat or round?	A question ends with a question mark (?).
Don't believe it!	A sentence with special emphasis may end with an exclamation point (!).

> **THE NITTY GRITTY** *A written sentence begins with a capital letter and ends with a period, a question mark, or an exclamation point.*

Practice 7.1

Read this continuation of the passage about Columbus on page 2. Cross out the small letters at the beginnings of sentences and write capital letters above them. Also cross out all of the exclamation points and write periods or question marks above them.

Flat or Round? (Part 2)

The story is false. why does every schoolchild in North America know it! did Columbus invent the story to make himself look good! there is no evidence that he did! this misconception is the fault of Washington Irving, a popular American writer of the 19th century! in his widely read book *The Life and Voyages of Christopher Columbus*, Irving told a long, detailed, and fascinating story about scholars' opposition to Columbus's theory and Columbus's heroic insistence that he was right! why did people believe Irving's story! at that time, more than three hundred years after the voyages, Columbus was a hero in this country! people wanted to believe the story was true! in fact, Irving simply made it up!

Writing Assignment 3

Write about an event in history that every schoolchild in your country knows. Give enough details to make the story clear and interesting. Write a concluding sentence.

Subjects

- *The subject of a sentence is often a noun. Nouns name people, places, physical things, concepts, or activities.*
- *The subject of a sentence can be a pronoun.*
- *A sentence can have a compound subject: two or more nouns and/or pronouns joined by* and.
- *A filler subject (*it *or* there*) appears in the normal subject position, but its meaning is different from its usual meaning.*
- *As a filler subject,* it *often stands for time, day, date, distance, weather, or temperature. The verb is* be.
- *As a filler subject,* there *fills the place of the subject in the sentence, and the real subject follows the verb. The verb is* be, *and it agrees with the real subject.*

Verbs

- *Verbs can consist of one word or a verb phrase.*
- *Many sentences have compound verbs. Compound verbs are made up of two or more verbs or verb phrases joined by* and.

Sentence Beginnings and Endings

A written sentence begins with a capital letter and ends with a period, a question mark, or an exclamation point.

Review Practice 1.1

Read the pairs of sentences below and on the next page. They are about one family's vacation in Vancouver, British Columbia. Write new sentences that combine the pairs by using compound subjects or verbs. Make any other necessary changes.

Three Exciting Days in Vancouver

1. Christine saw a lot on her vacation in Vancouver last summer. Paul saw a lot on his vacation in Vancouver last summer. _____

   _____

2. They spent three days in this interesting city. Their teenagers Molly and Charley spent three days in this interesting city. _____

   _____

3. On their first day, they flew into Vancouver International Airport. They took the bus downtown. _____

_____

4. Later that day, Paul explored the city on foot. Molly explored the city on foot.

_____

_____

5. Christine took a bus to Simon Fraser University. Charley took a bus to Simon Fraser University. _____

_____

6. The next morning, the family got up early. They took a taxi to Stanley Park. _____

_____

_____

7. At the park, Paul visited the aquarium. The kids visited the aquarium. _____

_____

_____

8. Christine went to see the Indian ruins. She met the family later at the zoo. _____

_____

_____

9. On the third day, the four of them rented a car. They drove to a wilderness area outside of town for a picnic. _____

_____

_____

10. Later, they drove to the historic area of Vancouver. They looked around in the stores.

_____

_____

11. That night, they all had dinner in Chinatown. They finished their evening listening to jazz. _____

_____

12. By the time they got home, Christine and Paul were tired. By the time they got home, the kids were tired. _____

_____

Review Practice 1.2

The following sentences describe the writer's classroom. Complete them with nouns, pronouns, or the filler subject *it* or *there*.

1. <u>Our classroom</u> is fairly large.
2. _____ has four large windows for light and air.
3. _____ is a large desk for Ms. Ball's books and materials.
4. _____ usually arrives a few minutes early.
5. _____ takes attendance as soon as the bell rings.
6. _____ is a whiteboard on the wall behind her desk.
7. _____ often writes on the board to show us the important points.
8. _____ sit at smaller desks.
9. _____ are twenty of them arranged in rows.
10. _____ all sit down at the beginning of class.
11. _____ often move around during class to work with classmates.
12. _____ is at night, on Mondays, Wednesdays, and Fridays.
13. _____ is late when we get out.
14. _____ is usually 10:00 P.M.

Review Practice 1.3

Read the timeline of the life of a famous Native American. Then complete the following passage with the subjects and verbs from the timeline. Use capital letters where necessary.

TIMELINE: The Amazing Life of Squanto

1580	born in Patuxet (now Plymouth, Massachusetts)
1605	captured with four other Native American men, taken to England
1605–1614	lived in England; learned English
1614	returned to America
1614	captured again, taken to Spain; sold as a slave, bought by Spanish friars who freed him
1614–1618	lived with the friars
1618	traveled from Spain to England
1618–1619	sailed to America with Captain Thomas Dermer, mapped the coast of New England
1619	arrived home at Patuxet, found that all his tribe had died; went to live with another tribe nearby
1620	December: some English colonists called Pilgrims arrived at Patuxet; named it Plymouth; did not have adequate food and shelter; did not know how to hunt—half died
1621	Squanto went to Patuxet, lived with the Pilgrims; taught them to hunt and grow food
1621	November: celebrated the first Thanksgiving with the Pilgrims
1622	caught a fever, died

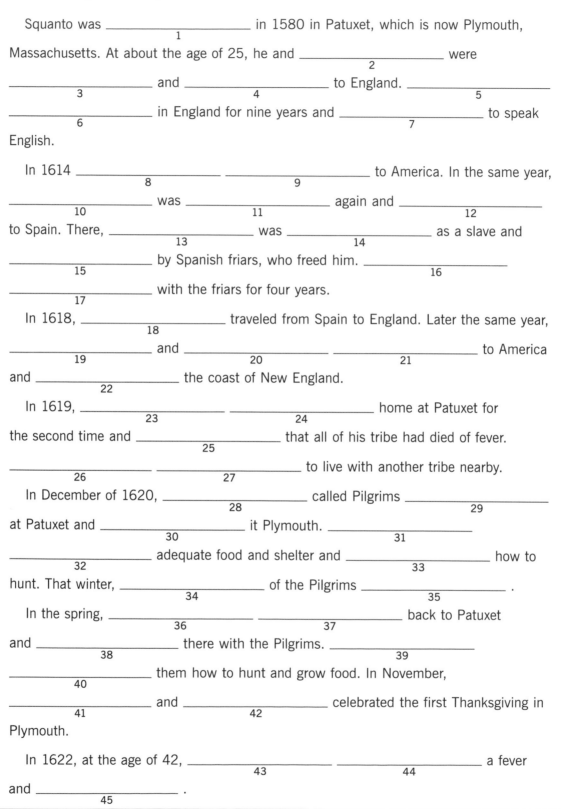

The Amazing Life of Squanto

Squanto was _____ 1 in 1580 in Patuxet, which is now Plymouth, Massachusetts. At about the age of 25, he and _____ 2 were _____ 3 and _____ 4 to England. _____ 5 _____ 6 in England for nine years and _____ 7 to speak English.

In 1614 _____ 8 _____ 9 to America. In the same year, _____ 10 was _____ 11 again and _____ 12 to Spain. There, _____ 13 was _____ 14 as a slave and _____ 15 by Spanish friars, who freed him. _____ 16 _____ 17 with the friars for four years.

In 1618, _____ 18 traveled from Spain to England. Later the same year, _____ 19 and _____ 20 _____ 21 to America and _____ 22 the coast of New England.

In 1619, _____ 23 _____ 24 home at Patuxet for the second time and _____ 25 that all of his tribe had died of fever. _____ 26 _____ 27 to live with another tribe nearby.

In December of 1620, _____ 28 called Pilgrims _____ 29 at Patuxet and _____ 30 it Plymouth. _____ 31 _____ 32 adequate food and shelter and _____ 33 how to hunt. That winter, _____ 34 of the Pilgrims _____ 35 .

In the spring, _____ 36 _____ 37 back to Patuxet and _____ 38 there with the Pilgrims. _____ 39 _____ 40 them how to hunt and grow food. In November, _____ 41 and _____ 42 celebrated the first Thanksgiving in Plymouth.

In 1622, at the age of 42, _____ 43 _____ 44 a fever and _____ 45 .

Simple, Compound, and Complex Sentences

Introduction to the Topic

The structure of the basic English sentence is subject + verb + any additional information. In *Chapter 1, Sentence Essentials,* you learned about subjects and verbs, including compound subjects and verbs. In this chapter, you will learn more about the basic sentence pattern, called the *simple sentence.* You will also learn about two other types of sentences: *compound* and *complex.* You will begin by learning about *clauses,* the building blocks of sentences. This topic is an important one because sentence variety is expected in academic writing.

EXPLORING THE TOPIC

Read the following two versions of a passage from Roald Dahl's novel *Danny: The Champion of the World.* The passage describes life in a trailer like the one shown above. Version 1 is the real one. Do both versions give the same information? Which version is better? Why?

Home, Sweet Home (Version 1)

When I was four months old, my mother died suddenly. I had no brothers or sisters, so there were just us two, my father and me. We lived in an old gypsy trailer behind a gas station, and a square brick building to the right of the office was the workshop. Although we had electric lights in the workshop, we did not have them in the trailer because the electricity people said it was unsafe. There was a wood-burning stove to keep us warm in winter and a kerosene lamp hanging from the ceiling.

I really loved our gypsy trailer. I loved it especially in the evenings when I was in bed and my father was telling me stories. The kerosene lamp was turned low, and it was wonderful to be lying there snug and warm in that little room.

Home, Sweet Home (Version 2)

I was four months old. My mother died suddenly. I had no brothers or sisters. There were just us two, my father and me. We lived in an old gypsy trailer behind a gas station. A square brick building to the right of the office was the workshop. We had electric lights in the workshop. We did not have them in the trailer. The electricity people said it was unsafe. There was a wood-burning stove to keep us warm in the winter. There was a kerosene lamp hanging from the ceiling.

I really loved our gypsy trailer. I loved it especially in the evenings. I was in bed. My father was telling me stories. The kerosene lamp was turned low. It was wonderful to be lying there snug and warm in that little room.

① Independent and Dependent Clauses

Grammar Point 1 Clauses

EXPLORING THE GRAMMAR POINT

Read the word groups from "Home, Sweet Home (Version 1)," in 1, 2, and 3 below. In each pair, either *a* or *b* has both a subject and a verb, and the other does not. Circle the groups of words that have both a subject and a verb.

1. a. there were just us two
   b. my father and me
2. a. although we had electric lights
   b. in the workshop
3. a. it was wonderful
   b. to be lying there snug and warm

UNDERSTANDING THE GRAMMAR POINT

A group of words that has a subject and a verb that go together is called a *clause*. In the examples above, the first group in each pair is a clause. Clauses are the building blocks of sentences.

 A clause is a group of words that contains a subject and a verb that go together.

Practice 1.1

The following groups of words are from "Home, Sweet Home (Version 1)." Write C for *clause* or NC for *not a clause* next to each group.

   __C__   1. when I was four months old

   _____   2. I had no brothers or sisters

   _____   3. a square brick building to the right of the office

   _____   4. was the workshop

   _____   5. because the electricity people said it was unsafe

   _____   6. there was a wood-burning stove

   _____   7. to keep us warm in the winter

   _____   8. a kerosene lamp hanging from the ceiling

   _____   9. when I was in bed

   _____ 10. my father was telling me stories

Grammar Point 2   Independent Clauses

UNDERSTANDING THE GRAMMAR POINT

Some clauses can be sentences on their own. They have a subject and a verb that go together, and they often contain other information as well. They make sense by themselves. These clauses are called *independent clauses*.

A clause that can stand alone as a sentence is an independent clause.

Practice 2.1

The following passage is made up of six independent clauses. Underline the subject of each clause once. Underline the verb twice. Then add capital letters and periods so that the clauses can be read as sentences.

I am proud of my brother and sister. they are taking classes at Bronx Community College in New York they also work my sister works twenty hours a week my brother works twenty-five hours a week it is not easy to work and go to school at the same time

EXPLORING THE GRAMMAR POINT

Read the following examples. How many clauses are in each example? How are the correct examples different from the incorrect ones?

1. **Incorrect:** Danny's mother died. When he was four months old.

   Correct: Danny's mother died when he was four months old.

2. **Incorrect:** Although they had electric lights in the workshop. They did not have them in the trailer.

   Correct: Although they had electic lights in the workshop, they did not have them in the trailer.

3. **Incorrect:** They did not have electric lights in the trailer. Because the electricity people said it was unsafe.

   Correct: They did not have electric lights in the trailer because the electricity people said it was unsafe.

UNDERSTANDING THE GRAMMAR POINT

The correct and incorrect examples contain the same words in the same order, and each example has two clauses. However, the incorrect examples have two sentences, while the correct examples have only one sentence.

In the incorrect examples, one sentence is actually correct. It is an independent clause standing alone as a sentence. The other "sentence" is not really a sentence. It is a *dependent clause* and it cannot stand alone. It must be attached to an independent clause in the same sentence, as in the three correct examples.

Like independent clauses, dependent clauses have a subject and a verb and express something understandable. Unlike independent clauses, they begin with a word that is meant to connect them to another clause.* For this reason, dependent clauses cannot stand alone. In the examples above, the connecting words are *when*, *although*, and *because*. These connecting words are called *subordinators*.**

> **THE NITTY GRITTY**
> • A clause that cannot stand alone as a sentence is a dependent clause.
> • Many dependent clauses begin with a subordinator.

* *Sometimes a connecting word can be omitted, but it is always understood.*

** *In Grammar Point 8, you will learn more about subordinators. In Chapters 3 and 12, you will learn about other kinds of dependent clauses with other connecting words.*

Practice 3.1

The dependent and independent clauses below are from "Home, Sweet Home (Version 1)." Underline the subjects once and the verbs twice. Circle the subordinators. Then write *I* for *independent clause* or *D* for *dependent clause*.

   _D_ 1. (when) I <u>was</u> four months old
   _____ 2. my mother died suddenly
   _____ 3. we lived in an old gypsy trailer behind a gas station
   _____ 4. although we had electric lights in the workshop
   _____ 5. we did not have them in the trailer
   _____ 6. because the electricity people said it was unsafe
   _____ 7. I loved it especially in the evenings
   _____ 8. when I was in bed
   _____ 9. my father was telling me stories

Writing Assignment 1

Describe a place where you lived as a child. Tell what it looked like and how you felt about the place when you lived there.

2 Simple and Compound Sentences

Grammar Point 4 ▸ Simple Sentences

EXPLORING THE GRAMMAR POINT

Read the following sentences. Underline the subjects once and the verbs twice. How many subjects and verbs does each sentence have? Are there any compound subjects or verbs? How many clauses does each sentence have? Are they dependent clauses or independent clauses?

1. Danny was four months old.
2. Danny and his father lived in an old gypsy trailer behind a gas station.
3. Danny's father repaired cars and looked after his son.

UNDERSTANDING THE GRAMMAR POINT

Each sentence above consists of just one independent clause with one subject and one verb (one is a compound subject and one a compound verb).

A sentence that consists of only one independent clause is called a *simple sentence*. In addition to the subject and verb, a simple sentence may also have other information, but not an additional clause. "Home, Sweet Home (Version 2)" on page 16 consists entirely of simple sentences.

Practice 4.1

All of the groups of words below are sentences. Some of them are simple sentences and some are not. Underline the subjects once and the verbs twice. Write *simple* next to the simple sentences. Write *not* next to the sentences that are not simple sentences.

____simple____ 1. There were five children in my family, three girls and two boys.

_____ 2. My brother and I were the youngest, and we were identical twins.

_____ 3. The family could recognize us, but no one else could.

_____ 4. My brother was good at math.

_____ 5. In high school, he sometimes went to my math classes and almost always took my tests for me.

_____ 6. They never caught us.

_____ 7. Now, in college, I am having a terrible time trying to pass my required math course.

_____ 8. Unfortunately for me, my brother is going to a different college, so he can't help me.

Grammar Point 5 ▶ **Compound Sentences**

EXPLORING THE GRAMMAR POINT

Look again at sentences 2, 3, and 8 in Practice 4.1. How many clauses does each sentence have? What words join the clauses?

UNDERSTANDING THE GRAMMAR POINT

Sentences 2, 3, and 8 consist of two independent clauses joined by *and*, *but*, or *so*. They are *compound sentences*.

A compound sentence is two independent clauses joined by a *coordinator*. The coordinator is preceded by a comma. *And*, *but*, and *so* are the most common coordinators. (These words do not always join clauses, but when they do, they are called coordinators.) In a compound sentence, the two independent clauses are of equal importance, and the coordinator shows the logical relationship between them. Ideas combined into one sentence should always be logically related.

Practice 5.1

Read the following passage from Alice Taylor's memoir *To School Through the Fields: An Irish Country Childhood*.

There are nine numbered words in italics: *and*, *but*, and *so*. Some of them join two independent clauses in compound sentences. Some of them join other things. Circle the ones that join clauses. (Remember that a clause has both a subject and a verb.)

A Child's Nest

Our parents were a blend of opposites. My mother was kind ¹*and* gentle. She had a far-seeing wisdom ²*and* expected only the best from her fellow human beings. My father was a man with a high level of intelligence, ³*but* he had a low level of tolerance. Patience was not one of his qualities. He loved trees, birds, ⁴*and* all his farm animals. He appreciated nature, ⁵*but* he viewed his fellow human beings with a suspicious eye. He never expected too much from them.

There were seven children in the family, ⁶*and* we grew up free as birds. We were far away from the outside influence of the city, ⁷*so* we grew up in a world of simplicity. Our farm was our world, ⁸*and* nature was our teacher. We absorbed the natural order of things ⁹*and* were free to grow up at our own pace in a quiet place close to the earth.

Writing Assignment 2

Write about your father and mother as parents. How are they different? How are they alike? What influence did they each have upon your family when you were growing up?

Practice 5.2

Combine these pairs of simple sentences into compound sentences with *and*, *but*, or *so*. Add commas where appropriate.

1. My father had a quick sense of humor. The family loved his jokes.

   <u>My father had a quick sense of humor, and the family loved</u>
   <u>his jokes.</u>

2. He was smart and funny. He was not a patient man.

   _____

   _____

3. My father had a degree from UCLA. My mother did not finish college.

   _____

   _____

4. My mother valued education. She took night classes.

   _____

   _____

5. My father always had a new car. He washed it every Saturday.

   _____

   _____

6. My mother didn't like to drive. My father did most of the driving.

   _____

   _____

Practice 5.3

Write *OK* for sentences with two clauses that are logically related. Write *no* for the others.

<u>no</u> 1. My mother is an attorney, and my sister is a teenager.

<u>OK</u> 2. My mother is an attorney, and she's very good at her work.

_____ 3. My sister is in the tenth grade, and she went to Sea World last year.

_____ 4. My sister is in the tenth grade, and she goes to Lincoln High School.

_____ 5. My sister is interested in marine animals, so she went to Sea World last year.

_____ 6. My brother raises chickens, but he won't eat any kind of meat.

_____ 7. My brother plays the piano, but he won't eat any kind of meat.

_____ 8. My brother is a vegetarian, so he won't eat any kind of meat.

UNDERSTANDING THE GRAMMAR POINT

Compound sentences can have three or four independent clauses or even more. However, long strings of independent clauses can sound awkward and be hard to understand.

1. I waited a long time, but no one came.
2. I waited a long time, but no one came, so I left.
3. I waited a long time, and my sister waited with me, but no one came, so I told her to leave, and she did, and then I did too.

The sentences above are grammatically correct and are acceptable in informal speech. However, you should be cautious about using sentences with three or more clauses in writing.

> **THE NITTY GRITTY** *Too many independent clauses in a single written sentence can be awkward or confusing, even if grammatically correct.*

Practice 6.1

Rewrite these long compound sentences as shorter sentences so that they are appropriate for academic writing. You may add or delete words, but do not change the meaning.

1. I waited a long time, and my sister waited with me, but no one came, so I told her to leave, and she did, and then I did too.

   <u>My sister and I waited a long time, but no one came. Finally, I told her to leave, and she did. Then I left too.</u>

2. My mother did not finish college, but she valued education, so she took night classes for six years, and last month we all went to her graduation.

   _____

   _____

3. My brother is a vegetarian, so he won't eat any kind of meat, but he raises chickens and sells them for meat, so a lot of people think this is very funny.

   _____

   _____

4. One Saturday, as a joke, my twin brother and I went out with each other's girlfriend, but the girls figured it out, and they were really mad, so they broke up with us, and we felt bad about it, so we promised never to do it again, but they wouldn't forgive us.

   _____

   _____

③ Complex Sentences

EXPLORING THE GRAMMAR POINT

Read the following sentences. How many clauses does each sentence have? Are they independent or dependent clauses?

1. When my parents moved to Los Angeles, they lived with my grandparents for a few months.
2. They then moved to the suburbs because they did not like the city.
3. After they settled in Altadena, I was born.

UNDERSTANDING THE GRAMMAR POINT

Sentences 1–3 above each contain an independent clause and a dependent clause. Such sentences are called *complex sentences*.

As you have seen, dependent clauses cannot be sentences on their own. They depend on an independent clause to support them. The independent clause in a complex sentence carries the main meaning, but either clause may come first. When the dependent clause comes first, it is always followed by a comma.

> *A complex sentence is one independent clause with a dependent clause attached to it. Either clause may come first. The independent clause is more important in the sentence than the dependent clause.*

Practice 7.1

Complete the following complex sentences with clauses from the box. Use commas if necessary, and add periods.

> because they convert the sun's energy into food
> ~~they think of animals~~
> animal life will cease
> they send large amounts of oxygen into the air
> when plants are endangered
> because they move and breathe and have families

1. When most people think of endangered species *, they think of animals.*
2. We sympathize with animals _____
3. No one seems concerned _____
4. Plants are important _____
5. When the leaves of trees in rain forests breathe _____
6. If we kill too many of our plants _____

UNDERSTANDING THE GRAMMAR POINT

Complex sentences add variety to writing. They also offer an excellent way to combine and express ideas because dependent clauses give additional information about independent clauses in a concise way. Dependent clauses can give information about the *time*, *purpose*, or *cause* of the action in the independent clause; or they can give information that *contrasts* with the information in the independent clause.

Subordinators indicate the relationship between the two clauses. The chart below shows the most common subordinators and the relationships they indicate, with example sentences.

COMMON SUBORDINATORS		
Time	when	**When** I was single, I didn't think about children.
	while	**While** we were engaged, my wife and I disagreed about having children.
	whenever	**Whenever** my wife saw a baby, she wanted one of her own.
	after	**After** I got married, I wanted children.
	as	I almost had an accident **as** I was speeding to the hospital.
	as soon as	**As soon as** the baby was born, I called everyone to tell them.
	before	Life was very simple **before** we had children.
	until	We had plenty of free time **until** we had our first child.
	since	Life has been very hectic **since** our first child was born.
Cause/ Effect	because	My wife wants another child **because** she loves babies.
	since	**Since** children are expensive, we have very little money saved.
Condition	if	**If** we had a girl, we would name her Danielle.
	unless	Kids can get into all kinds of trouble **unless** you keep an eye on them.
	as if	Children put everything in their mouth **as if** it were candy.
Contrast	although	**Although** we wanted a girl, we have three boys.
	even though	**Even though** my wife still wishes for a daughter, she's very happy with our boys.
	though	**Though** it's hard to raise children, I'm glad we did it.
Purpose	so that	My wife stayed at home **so that** she could devote herself to our children.

Practice 8.1

Complete the passage with subordinators from the box. Use each subordinator once.

although	so that	before
~~right after~~	because	when
as soon as	unless	if

Wedding Plans

Jack and I are going to get married _____right after_____ we finish college.
                                              1

_____ Jack is able to finish his senior project in time, we
         2

will both graduate this year, and the wedding will be in June. We want to have

children _____ we can, but we may have to wait a while
                    3

_____ we can both work and make some money. We both have college
         4

loans to pay back, and we want to buy a house _____ we start a
                                                         5

family. Luckily, I have a great job lined up already _____ my father
                                                               6

wants me to join him in his business. He owns a big hardware store, and I have always

liked working there, _____ it may be different _____ I
                              7   8

am a manager instead of one of the workers. Anyway, _____ something
                                                              9

goes wrong, we should be able to start a family in a couple of years.

Writing Assignment 3

Do you think it is important for a couple to have a house and a good income before they have children? Give reasons for your opinion. If you agree, why is this important? If you disagree, how should people decide when to start a family? Write a concluding sentence.

EXPLORING THE GRAMMAR POINT

Circle the coordinators and subordinators in the following sentences. How many clauses are in each sentence? Are they independent or dependent clauses?

1. My father was an elementary school teacher, and he liked his job, even though it was hard work and he never made much money.
2. Although my parents loved each other very much, their ideas were very different, and they argued whenever they disagreed.

UNDERSTANDING THE GRAMMAR POINT

Sentence 1 has three independent clauses and one dependent clause. Sentence 2 has two independent clauses and two dependent clauses.

Compound-complex sentences contain at least three clauses, including at least one independent and one dependent clause.

> **THE NITTY GRITTY** *Compound-complex sentences have at least three clauses, including at least one independent and one dependent clause.*

Practice 9.1

There are several examples of compound-complex sentences in this chapter. Go back to the passages listed below; find the compound-complex sentences and copy them. Underline the coordinators and circle the subordinators.

1. Page 16, "Home, Sweet Home (Version 1)," second paragraph (one sentence)

   I loved it especially in the evenings (when) I was in bed and my father was telling me stories.

2. Page 26, "Wedding Plans" (four sentences)

   _____

   _____

   _____

   _____

A Common Mistake: Coordinator and Subordinator

EXPLORING THE GRAMMAR POINT

Read the following sentences.

1. **Correct:**   My grandfather loved me, **but** I was afraid of him.
2. **Correct:**   **Although** my grandfather loved me, I was afraid of him.
3. **Incorrect:** **Although** my grandfather loved me, **but** I was afraid of him.

Which correct sentence shows that the writer feels the two clauses are of equal importance? Which shows that the independent clause is more important than the dependent clause?

UNDERSTANDING THE GRAMMAR POINT

A common mistake is to use both a coordinator and a subordinator to connect two clauses. In sentence 1, the coordinator *but* signals that the clauses it joins are equally important in the sentence. In sentence 2, the subordinator *although* signals that the independent clause is more important than the dependent clause. Using both a coordinator and a subordinator, as in sentence 3, seems to say that the two clauses are both equal and unequal.

> **THE NITTY GRITTY** *Do not use both a coordinator and a subordinator to connect two clauses.*

Practice 10.1

Correct the following sentences. Cross out either the coordinator or the subordinator. Make any other necessary corrections.

1. ~~Because~~ M~~y~~ grandfather was very tall and had a long beard, so I thought he looked like God.
2. Although his beard was white, but I didn't think of Santa Claus.
3. Since I thought he looked like God, so I was afraid of him.
4. Although my parents tried to reason with me, but I refused to kiss him or sit on his lap.
5. Because my grandfather loved me dearly, so this must have hurt his feelings.
6. Even though I always cried when I saw my grandfather, but he was always kind to me.
7. Unfortunately, since I didn't see him very often, so I couldn't get used to him.
8. Even though I wasn't able to enjoy my grandfather's visits when I was small, but I came to love him when I was older.

CHAPTER 2 REVIEW

Independent and Dependent Clauses

- *A clause is a group of words that contains a subject and a verb that go together.*
- *A clause that can stand alone as a sentence is an independent clause.*
- *A clause that cannot stand alone as a sentence is a dependent clause.*
- *Many dependent clauses begin with a subordinator.*

Simple and Compound Sentences

- *One independent clause standing alone is a simple sentence.*
- *A compound sentence is two independent clauses joined by a coordinator. The two clauses express related ideas that are equally important.*
- *Too many independent clauses in a single written sentence can be awkward or confusing, even if grammatically correct.*

Complex Sentences

- *A complex sentence is one independent clause with a dependent clause attached to it. Either clause may come first. The independent clause is more important in the sentence than the dependent clause.*
- *Subordinators indicate the relationship between a dependent clause and the independent clause it is attached to.*
- *Compound-complex sentences have at least three clauses, including at least one independent and one dependent clause.*
- *Do not use both a coordinator and a subordinator to connect two clauses.*

Review Practice 2.1

The following passage is adapted from a student composition. It contains simple, compound, and complex sentences. Edit the passage by adding capital letters and periods to show where the sentences begin and end.

The Day the Ground Fell Beneath My Feet

M
~~my~~ most frightening experience was a big earthquake in Japan. at that time, I was in the second grade my friend and I were about halfway home from school when the earthquake occurred we were walking through a rice field my friend was whistling, and I was trying to copy her tunes

all of a sudden, the ground under my feet dropped about five inches at first, I was too surprised to be scared as soon as I felt the earth again, my feet were taken to the right

---

Simple, Compound, and Complex Sentences   **29**

and then jerked to the left I staggered something struck my knee hard, but I couldn't feel any pain

after I fell to the ground, the shaking stopped I stood up as fast as I could and hurried home along the way, I came across a crying woman her knees were bleeding because she had fallen into a ditch when I looked up at the sky, I noticed a dark gray cloud floating heavily above me it gave me an uncanny feeling, and I almost began to cry

in my city, many people got hurt I can remember that bleeding woman and that gray cloud clearly even now it was a very frightening experience, and I hope I never have to go through anything like it again

Review Practice 2.2

This passage from Alice Taylor's memoir contains simple, compound, complex, and compound-complex sentences. Edit the passage by adding capital letters and periods.

Bedtime Dolls

There were no dolls because these were the war years and such luxuries were non-existent. even though my little brother and I had no dolls, our resourceful mother gave us two little statues, one of Saint Theresa and the other of Baby Jesus there was no shortage of statues in Irish homes at that time, so every night we took our much-loved statues to bed

once a week my mother went to visit my grandmother a few miles down the road if she was not home by our bedtime, my oldest sister Frances would put us to bed this happened one winter's night, so Frances changed us into our night-clothes and led us upstairs to bed just as we were falling asleep, I realized that we had no statues to keep us company we knocked on the floor to call Frances, and when she appeared, we explained about our statues she went in search of them, and as soon as she came back, she tucked the statues under the bedclothes beside us

in the morning, instead of our two statues, we were cuddling two glass bottles Frances had not been able to find the statues and had given us the bottles so that we would go to sleep

Run-On Sentences and Sentence Fragments

Introduction to the Topic

Run-on sentences and sentence fragments are mistakes that people sometimes make in their writing. They cause confusion for the reader. In this chapter, you will learn how to avoid or correct run-ons and fragments.

REFRESHING YOUR MEMORY

Recall what you learned in Chapters 1 and 2 about independent clauses, dependent clauses, and sentences.

1. What do all clauses have?
2. Which type of clause can stand alone as a sentence? Which type needs to be attached to another clause?
3. What signals the beginning of a written sentence? What signals its end?

EXPLORING THE TOPIC

Read the two versions of the passage on the next page about nontraditional students, like the ones shown above, in community colleges. Compare the italicized parts. Which version is better? Why?

Helping Nontraditional Students Succeed (Version 1)

Community college programs were originally designed for full-time students in their late teens, single, living at home, and maybe working part time. However, today, in many community colleges, the majority of students are nontraditional. They may be older, and many are studying part time while working full time. *They may get little support from their families, or they may be supporting a family themselves.*

Nontraditional students often find it difficult to fit college into their very full lives. *They need support if they are going to succeed.* Many community colleges now reach out to nontraditional students throughout their college careers. *Colleges provide orientation programs that let students know exactly what is expected of them and where to get help.* They assign students to study groups with others of similar age and circumstances and in similar academic programs. *They give them advisors who work with them until graduation, providing personal, ongoing support.* With such support, nontraditional students can maintain their commitment to college and are likelier to succeed.

Helping Nontraditional Students Succeed (Version 2)

Community college programs were originally designed for full-time students in their late teens, single, living at home, and maybe working part time. However, today, in many community colleges, the majority of students are nontraditional. They may be older, and many are studying part time while working full time. *They may get little support from their families, they may be supporting a family themselves.*

Nontraditional students often find it difficult to fit college into their very full lives. *They need support. If they are going to succeed.* Many community colleges now reach out to nontraditional students throughout their college careers. *Colleges provide orientation programs. That let students know exactly what is expected of them. And where to get help.* They assign students to study groups with others of similar age and circumstances and in similar academic programs. *They give them advisors who work with them until graduation. Providing personal, ongoing support.* With such support, nontraditional students can maintain their commitment to college and are likelier to succeed.

① Run-On Sentences

Grammar Point 1 Identifying Run-On Sentences

EXPLORING THE GRAMMAR POINT

Read the following incorrect sentences. How many clauses does each incorrect sentence have? Are they dependent or independent clauses? How are the clauses joined together?

1. **Incorrect:** The class meets twice a week it starts at 10:00 and ends at 12:20.
2. **Incorrect:** We arrive a little early, the instructor arrives at 10:00.
3. **Incorrect:** We are ready she starts the class.

UNDERSTANDING THE GRAMMAR POINT

The incorrect sentences above are *run-on sentences*. Each one has two independent clauses incorrectly joined together in a single sentence. In run-on sentences, independent clauses are joined by nothing or by just a comma.

> **THE NITTY GRITTY** *A run-on sentence contains two or more incorrectly joined independent clauses.*

Practice 1.1

In the following paragraph, some sentences are correct and others are run-ons. Underline the places where two independent clauses are incorrectly joined together to make a run-on sentence.

A Crazy Day

Yesterday was a crazy <u>day I</u> was running around from early morning until late at night. My alarm clock went off at 6:00, I jumped out of bed. I got dressed and ran out the door without having breakfast. I couldn't find a parking place on campus I parked eight blocks away. I ran to class I was late anyway. After my classes, I raced back to my car, I had to go to work at MacBuns. At work, the boss told me to work overtime. For the next nine hours, I fried hamburgers and unloaded delivery trucks. I got home my body ached all over. I was disappointed, it was too late to go swimming. I really needed a swim after running around all day.

Grammar Point 2 **Correcting Run-On Sentences**

UNDERSTANDING THE GRAMMAR POINT

There are three ways to correct run-on sentences.

1. Separate the two independent clauses to make two simple sentences. Add a period and a capital letter.

Run-on sentence:	The class meets twice a week it starts at 10:00 and ends at 12:20.
Two simple sentences:	The class meets twice a week. It starts at 10:00 and ends at 12:20.

2. Join the two independent clauses with a coordinator to make a compound sentence. *And*, *but*, and *so* are coordinators.

    Run-on sentence: We arrive a little early, the instructor arrives at 10:00.

    Compound sentence: We arrive a little early, and the instructor arrives at 10:00.

3. Add a subordinator* to one independent clause, making it a dependent clause, and join the two clauses to make a complex sentence. If the dependent clause comes first, insert a comma after it.

    Run-on sentence: We are ready she starts the class.

    Complex sentence: As soon as we are ready, she starts the class.

> **THE NITTY GRITTY** *Correct a run-on sentence by making it two simple sentences, a compound sentence, or a complex sentence.*

Practice 2.1

Correct the run-on sentences you identified in Practice 1.1. Try using each of the three ways to correct run-on sentences shown above.

② Sentence Fragments

Grammar Point 3　**Missing Subjects in Simple Sentences**

EXPLORING THE GRAMMAR POINT

Read the following pairs of sentences. What is missing from the incomplete sentences?

  1. **Incomplete:** Frank works a lot of hours at MacBuns. Therefore, has little time to hang out with his friends.

     Complete: Frank works a lot of hours at MacBuns. Therefore, he has little time to hang out with his friends.

  2. **Incomplete:** Jennifer has a great job that she really likes. Unfortunately, can't take a full course load in college.

     Complete: Jennifer has a great job that she really likes. Unfortunately, she can't take a full course load in college.

✱ *For a list of subordinators, see page 25.*

UNDERSTANDING THE GRAMMAR POINT

A complete sentence must have a visible subject.* A sentence that does not have some essential part, such as a subject, is called a *sentence fragment*. The incomplete sentences in 1 and 2 do not have subjects. They are sentence fragments.

> **THE NITTY GRITTY** *Every sentence must have a visible subject.**

Practice 3.1

Edit the following paragraph about a famous soccer player. Add the missing subjects.

> ### Pele
>
> Pele is one of the most famous soccer stars in history. ˄He c Came from a poor family. Was born on October 23, 1940, in a small town in Brazil. All the people in the town were poor. Didn't have enough money to buy food every day. Of course, was not enough money to buy a soccer ball. However, Pele's father was very inventive. Tied some old pieces of cloth together to form a ball. The young Pele and the other boys in the neighborhood joyfully played soccer with this rag ball. Played barefoot every day until the sun went down. Later, Pele played soccer on an organized team. Soon became the best player on the team. Before Pele turned thirty, became a millionaire.

Pele

* *The exception is imperative sentences like* Watch out! *and* Don't do that. *In imperative sentences, the subject (you) is understood but not stated.*

Writing Assignment 1

Pele had little education, but he earned a lot of money playing professional sports. Many blue-collar workers, such as house painters or mechanics, do not need a college education. Is it a good idea for all high school graduates to get a college education anyway? Write a paragraph supporting your answer.

Grammar Point 4 — **Missing Subjects in Dependent Adverbial Clauses**

EXPLORING THE GRAMMAR POINT

As you learned in *Chapter 2,* Grammar Point 8, dependent clauses tell something about the independent clause they are attached to. Some dependent clauses function as adverbs and are called *adverbial clauses.*

Each of the following sentences has an adverbial clause in boldface type. What is missing from the incomplete sentences?

1. **Incomplete:** Pele became a millionaire **before turned thirty**.

   Complete: Pele became a millionaire **before he turned thirty**.

2. **Incomplete:** Pele earned a lot of money **because was an outstanding player**.

   Complete: Pele earned a lot of money **because he was an outstanding player**.

UNDERSTANDING THE GRAMMAR POINT

Like independent clauses, dependent clauses must have visible subjects. In a complex sentence, both clauses must have subjects in order for the sentence to be complete. In the incomplete sentences above, the adverbial clauses lack subjects, so the sentences are sentence fragments.

> THE NITTY GRITTY *Every adverbial clause must have a visible subject.*

Practice 4.1

Edit the following paragraph for missing subjects.

Thoughts of Dropping Out

Although I am fortunate to be in college full time, ^I sometimes feel like dropping out of school for a while. If weren't in college, I could have a real job and make some real money. I think a lot of people are in college because don't want to face real life, and don't want to be one of those people. I know the time to work is after finish college. However, sometimes just don't feel like waiting.

Grammar Point 5 — Missing Subjects in Dependent Adjective Clauses

EXPLORING THE GRAMMAR POINT

Read the following complex sentences from Judy Brady's article "I Want a Wife." Each sentence has a dependent clause in boldface type. In each sentence, circle the word that serves as the subject of the dependent clause.

1. I want a wife **that will pick up after me**.
2. I want a wife **that cooks the meals**.
3. I want a wife **who will keep my house clean**.
4. I want a wife **who takes care of the children**.

UNDERSTANDING THE GRAMMAR POINT

Some dependent clauses function as adjectives. That is, they tell something about a noun in the independent clause they are attached to. The dependent clauses above are *adjective clauses*, and their subjects are *that* and *who*. Like all clauses, adjective clauses must have a visible subject. If the subject is missing, the clause is incomplete and the sentence is a sentence fragment. Compare these examples:

5. **Incomplete:** Susan B. Anthony was a reformer fought for women's rights.
   Complete:　　 Susan B. Anthony was a reformer **who** fought for women's rights.

Use *that*, *who*, and *which* as subjects in adjective clauses, as shown in the chart below.

SUBJECTS IN ADJECTIVE CLAUSES		
Subject	**Refers to**	**Example**
that	people or things	The Ivy League is a group of eight prestigious universities **that** used to accept only men. People **that** go to Ivy League schools are sometimes called Ivy Leaguers.
who	people	Harry S. Truman was the last American president **who** did not have a college degree.
which*	things	An elective is a college course **which** is not required for one's major.

> Like all clauses, adjective clauses must have a visible subject.

Practice 5.1

The following sentences about U.S. history and current events contain adjective clauses. Some of the adjective clauses have missing subjects. Add *that*, *who*, or *which* where necessary to make complete sentences.

1. The only American president who resigned from office was Richard Nixon.
2. Watergate was the incident led to President Nixon's resignation.
3. Franklin Roosevelt is the only American president served four terms.
4. The Peace Corps is an agency sends American volunteers to work in foreign countries.
5. The person initiated the first major action of the civil rights movement was Rosa Parks.
6. A draft is a system registers young people for possible military service.
7. Bill Gates is an American businessman became extremely successful.
8. Ralph Nader is a lawyer with an Arab background was an early activist for consumer rights.

* *Some instructors may recommend against using* which *as a subject in adjective clauses.*

UNDERSTANDING THE GRAMMAR POINT

In conversation, people often use dependent adverbial clauses alone, without joining them to independent clauses. Notice what Bob says in this dialog.

Amy: Why are you looking so sad?

Bob: Because I messed up on my history test.

Amy: How do you know?

Bob: Because Joe, the class genius, said my answers were all wrong.

Amy: When will you know for sure?

Bob: When I get the test back on Monday.

In conversation, adverbial clauses that are not joined to independent clauses can function as complete sentences. This is because the missing independent clause is understood from the questions of the other speaker.

When Amy asks, "Why are you looking so sad?" and Bob answers, "Because I messed up on my history test," his answer is a dependent clause. It is not a complete sentence. However, it functions as a complete sentence because it is understood as, "I am looking sad because I messed up on my history test." In writing, however, a dependent clause cannot stand alone. It must be joined to an independent clause.

> **THE NITTY GRITTY** *An adverbial clause is a dependent clause. In written English, it cannot stand alone. It must be joined to an independent clause.*

Practice 6.1

Are the following groups of words complete sentences or fragments? Write *S* for *complete sentence* or *F* for *fragment*. Then correct each fragment (adverbial clause) by joining it to one of the sentences (independent clauses) next to it to make a logical complex sentence. Rewrite all the sentences in order to form a paragraph.

___F___ 1. When I go on vacation.

___S___ 2. I like to have plenty of money.

_____ 3. Nice hotels are expensive.

_____ 4. When I stay in a cheap hotel, I don't feel comfortable.

_____ 5. Because they are often on noisy streets.

_____ 6. I don't sleep very well.

_____ 7. When I don't sleep well.

_____ 8. I can't enjoy daytime activities such as sightseeing and shopping.

_____ 9. If you don't have plenty of money for your vacation.

_____ 10. Stay at home.

_____ 11. Until you save up enough for an enjoyable trip.

Practice 6.2

Correct the fragments in the following passage.

A Real Vacation?

My wife, Martha, is the Director of Admissions for a large university. She works very hard. In fact, she works too hard. Sometimes she works sixty hours a week. I want us to take a vacation together. Because we need some quality time alone, away from her job. Finally, I convinced Martha to go to Hawaii with me for a week. I made all the arrangements ahead of time. Before she could change her mind. At first, Martha was reluctant to leave her work behind. After I arranged everything. She seemed happy with the plan. I didn't want her to do a thing. Because I wanted this to be a real vacation for her. On the day we left, I even carried all her luggage down to the taxi. Before she had a chance to help. As she left the house, she carried only one little thing with her: her laptop computer.

Writing Assignment 2

Write about one of your best or worst vacations or trips. If you have never been on a vacation, write about a place you would like to visit. Begin your paragraph with a topic sentence that identifies the vacation or trip and tells why you have chosen it. Support your topic sentence with plenty of specific details. End your paragraph with a sentence that makes a general statement or says something about your future vacation plans.

Grammar Point 7 Dependent Adjective Clauses Standing Alone

EXPLORING THE GRAMMAR POINT

Which of the following two sentences is correct? Write *correct* and *incorrect* in the blanks.

_____ 1. Many students get a government loan that they can pay back over ten years.

_____ 2. Many students get a government loan. That they can pay back over ten years.

UNDERSTANDING THE GRAMMAR POINT

As you already know, dependent clauses cannot stand alone as sentences. This requirement also applies to dependent adjective clauses. Version 1 is a complex sentence with an adjective clause. It is correct. Version 2 is written as two sentences. The second sentence is an adjective clause standing alone. It is a sentence fragment and is incorrect.

> **THE NITTY GRITTY** *An adjective clause is a dependent clause. It cannot stand alone. It must be joined to an independent clause.*

Practice 7.1

Rewrite the following sentences to correct the fragments.

1. In community colleges, there are many students. Who work more than 25 hours a week. _In community colleges, there are many students who work more than 25 hours a week._

2. I have a few classmates. Who don't work at all. _____

3. Sachiko has a student loan. That covers all her tuition. _____

4. Our college has a financial aid office. Which helps students apply for scholarships. _____

5. Rafael should go and see a financial aid advisor. Who can help him apply for a scholarship. _____

Practice 7.2

Use the words below to create complete sentences with adjective clauses. Use any other words that are necessary.

1. I / have / calculus class / I / really / like
   I have a calculus class that I really like.

2. Akbar / has / class / requires / essay / week
   _____

3. Manzar / bought / chemistry book / cost / $95
   _____

4. Adrian / wrote / lab report / took / three hours
   _____

5. Marisela / wrote / term paper / required / library research
   _____

EXPLORING THE GRAMMAR POINT

Read the following pairs of sentences. What is missing from the incomplete sentence in boldface type?

1. **Incomplete:** I'm very busy. **Studying for my calculus exam.**

   Complete: I'm very busy studying for my calculus exam.

2. **Incomplete:** I'm very busy. **Especially in my chemistry class.**

   Complete: I'm very busy, especially in my chemistry class.

3. **Incomplete:** I'm very busy. **Taking my kids to ballet lessons and soccer practice four days a week.**

   Complete: I'm very busy. I take my kids to ballet lessons and soccer practice four days a week.

4. **Incomplete:** I'm very busy. **For example, my job, my classes, and my family.**

   Complete: I'm very busy. For example, I have to keep up with my job, my classes, and my family.

UNDERSTANDING THE GRAMMAR POINT

In each of the incomplete examples above, the sentence in boldface type adds details that make the writing more informative. However, it has neither a subject nor a verb, so it is a sentence fragment. When adding details in writing, it is important to make sure they are expressed in complete sentences.

There are two ways to correct added-detail fragments. You can add the detail to a complete sentence (an independent clause with a subject and verb), as shown in 1 and 2, or you can rewrite the fragment as a complete sentence on its own by adding a subject and a verb, as shown in 3 and 4.

- *Added details cannot stand alone without subjects or verbs.*
- *Correct added-detail fragments by (1) adding the information to a complete sentence, or (2) rewriting the fragment as a sentence.*

Practice 8.1

Underline the fragments in the following paragraph.

Muhammad Ali

Muhammad Ali was born Cassius Clay on January 17, 1942. <u>In Louisville, Kentucky.</u> The young Cassius showed an early interest in boxing. For example, by taking boxing lessons when he was twelve years old. In 1960, Clay won a gold medal in boxing at the Olympics in Rome. This success launched him on a career in professional boxing. In 1964, Clay became the world champion heavyweight boxer. Beating Sonny Liston in the sixth round of their fight. Then, in a rematch, he beat Liston again. This time by a knockout in the first round. Soon afterwards, Clay became a Muslim. And changed his name to Muhammad Ali.

Practice 8.2

Rewrite the paragraph in Practice 8.1. Correct each fragment by joining it to a complete sentence or by adding a subject and a verb.

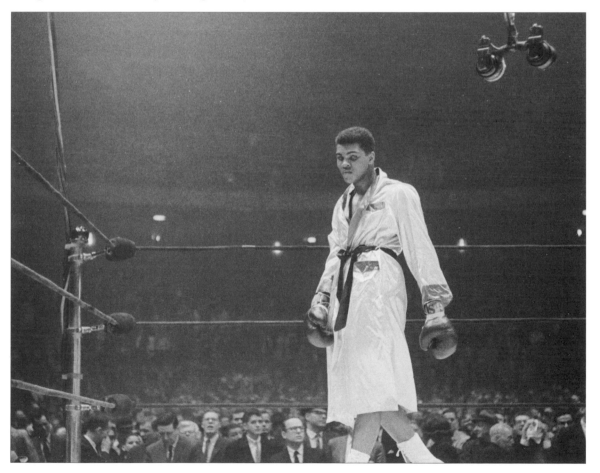

Muhammad Ali

CHAPTER 3 REVIEW

Run-On Sentences

- *A run-on sentence contains two or more incorrectly joined independent clauses.*
- *Correct a run-on sentence by making it two simple sentences, a compound sentence, or a complex sentence.*

Sentence Fragments

- *Every sentence must have a visible subject.*
- *Every adverbial clause must have a visible subject.*
- *Like all clauses, adjective clauses must have a visible subject.*
- *An adverbial clause is a dependent clause. In written English, it cannot stand alone. It must be joined to an independent clause.*
- *An adjective clause is a dependent clause. It cannot stand alone. It must be joined to an independent clause.*
- *Added details cannot stand alone without subjects or verbs.*
- *Correct added-detail fragments by (1) adding the information to a complete sentence, or (2) rewriting the fragment as a sentence.*

Review Practice 3.1

Edit the following paragraph to correct run-on sentences and sentence fragments.

My First Day of College

My first day of classes at Miami Dade Community College was a disaster. Everything was fine. Until I got to the campus. The parking lot on Twenty-Seventh Avenue was full there was no place for me to park. Since I wanted to be on time. I panicked and parked in a staff space. Near the Administration Building. As I ran toward my English class, I looked back and saw the campus police. Giving me a ticket. Next, I discovered that I didn't have my class schedule with me, I didn't remember the room number. The schedule was in my car there were only a few seconds before the class was supposed to start. In a greater panic, I ran back to the car. As fast as I could. When I reached into my pocket for my keys, they were not there. They were in the car. Which was locked! As a result, I missed my first class. In the future, I plan to get to school. With plenty of time to spare.

Review Practice 3.2

Edit the following passage to correct run-on sentences and sentence fragments.

A Folk Tale: The Tiger's Whisker

Yun Ok was unhappy in her marriage. Because her husband did not treat her with consideration. He didn't pay attention to her. When he spoke to her. He was impolite. Yun Ok became so unhappy that she decided to consult a famous wise man had helped many people. For example, marital problems and other types of family problems.

The unhappy young woman explained her situation to the old man, he thought very carefully. And then answered. The old man told Yun Ok that he could solve her problem. If she first brought him the whisker of a living tiger. Yun Ok trembled with fear after a few minutes she agreed to do as he asked.

That night, Yun Ok went out to the mountainside to the cave of a ferocious tiger lived there. She took food with her. That a tiger would like. She put the food at the entrance to the cave. Then she waited at a distance. While the tiger ate. For several months, Yun Ok brought food for the tiger, gradually the tiger got used to Yun Ok. Little by little, she moved closer to the tiger until could almost touch the beast. Finally, Yun Ok asked the tiger for one of his whiskers, he agreed.

As fast as she could, Yun Ok raced back to see the old man. In her hand, she held the tiger's whisker. The cure for her unhappiness. Yun Ok handed the precious whisker to the old man, he immediately tossed it into the fire.

"What are you doing?" she cried. "You've thrown away my last hope!"

"No," answered the old man. "If you know how to tame a vicious tiger, surely can do the same with your husband."

Yun Ok returned home slowly. Thinking about the old man's advice.

Review Practice 3.3

Edit the following passage to correct run-on sentences and sentence fragments.

Fighting Procrastination

One of the most common time management problems is procrastination. Means not doing something until the last minute. Or until it is actually too late. For example, writing a research paper. A student may not begin until the night before the assignment is due. When is not enough time to finish.

Getting started is the most difficult step for procrastinators. Let's suppose that you are procrastinating about doing a writing assignment. Break the assignment down into parts or steps this makes the task more manageable. Even if you work on it only twenty minutes a day. Will make some progress.

Here are some tips for beating procrastination:

1. Start immediately. Before start thinking of reasons to delay. Once you start, is easier to keep going.

2. Don't try to be perfect, can always make revisions later. If you need to. In fact, all good writers revise their material.

3. Guard against temptations to escape. Aren't really hungry and don't really need to make that phone call right now.

4. Work with another person. For example, if you're brainstorming ideas. Do it with a classmate. This will help you keep working, and you may even get some ideas will improve your writing.

SECTION 1 REVIEW

Chapter 1 **Sentence Essentials**

Chapter 2 **Simple, Compound, and Complex Sentences**

Chapter 3 **Run-On Sentences and Sentence Fragments**

REFRESHING YOUR MEMORY

Answer the following questions based on what you learned in *Chapters 1, 2, and 3.*

1. What is the verb of this sentence? What kind of verb is it?
   I arrived in the United States and met my first American on February 8, 2001.

2. What is the subject of this sentence? What kind of subject is it? What does it mean in this sentence?
   It was very cold that day.

3. How many clauses does this sentence have? Are they independent or dependent clauses? What kind of sentence is it: simple, compound, complex, or compound-complex?
   I had a sweater, but I didn't have a winter coat because I came from Belize.

4. The two sentences *in italics* are incorrect. Why? How can you correct them?
   An American woman. Who was standing next to me. She noticed that I was cold.

5. This sentence is incorrect. Why? How can you correct it?
   She had a winter coat and a ski jacket in her luggage, she lent me the ski jacket.

Section Review Practice 1.1

The following passage is a student composition. Mistakes have been added for practice. Edit the composition to correct the mistakes. You may need to change punctuation, capital letters, coordinators, subordinators, and other words.

> ### My Pet Peeves
>
> Two common annoyances in everyday life. They really bother me. The first one is the loudness of TV commercials, television has a lot of commercials. Understand that TV companies need many sponsors. That's OK, I don't understand why the volume is so high. It hurts my ears. Sometimes I grab the remote control in a hurry. And turn the volume down. But this is a big bother. Is stressful to me to hear the loud commercials, is annoying to have to turn the volume down and up again so often.

The other annoyance is the large amount of junk mail that receive. My mailbox is completely filled every day. With mostly useless material. I hate to sort through all the junk to separate out what is important from what is not. Some junk mail pretends that it is very important or official. Is very confusing and time-consuming. For a person like me. Who cannot read English well. I sure that other people feel the way I do, I sure that many people tired of advertisers intruding on their personal lives. And robbing them of their time and energy.

Section Review Practice 1.2

The following passage is a student composition. Mistakes have been added for practice. Edit the composition to correct the mistakes. You may need to change punctuation, capital letters, coordinators, and subordinators.

Not Such a Good Day

When I came here to California. I bought a new car right away, even though I had an international driver's license, but I had never driven in this country. One day, I drove my parents, my daughter, and my son to go shopping at Del Amo. We bought some things, ate pizza, drank coffee, and talked with each other, it was a good day.

When we came out, I had to wait to turn left. From the parking lot. The cars were going by very close to the front of my car I thought maybe I was in the way, I backed up. Without looking in the rearview mirror. I backed into the car in back of me. A new BMW.

Oh, my God! I was so embarrassed. I didn't know what to do, it was definitely my fault. I showed the other driver my insurance papers that was all I could do. A good day was changed to a bad day, after that day, I drove more carefully since that day, I always check the rearview mirror. While driving.

Section Review Practice 1.3

The following passage is a student composition. Mistakes have been added for practice. Edit the composition to correct the mistakes. You may need to change punctuation, capital letters, coordinators, subordinators, and other words.

I Miss Peru

There are three things that I really miss about my country, Peru. The food, my friends, and my family.

Peruvian dishes are made with special seasonings, they have flavors that only Peruvian people know how to make. I really miss all the ingredients. That I used to use to make my favorite dishes. For example, the traditional dish called *cuy frito*. Means "fried guinea pig." Is made with a special sauce and served with rice, potatoes, and Peruvian salad. In this country, guinea pigs are pets. Are no guinea pigs in the supermarket.

Another thing I miss about my country is my friends, we used to enjoy going to each other's houses and spending time talking and joking around together. Also, we often used to go camping at the river, was a special place, the air smelled of flowers and the fresh air and quiet made us feel very free, and we really were free there because no one was watching us or telling us what to do.

The thing I miss most is my family, miss my parents a lot, even though I have a family here, but I always remember their advice about life. Before came to this country. My father told me, "If you believe great things will happen, anything is possible." I know now what he meant by that. I also miss fighting with my sisters, because we always made up and treated each other with a lot of affection afterwards . . . usually.

These are the things I miss the most. When I think about Peru. I hope in the future I can visit my country and experience all these dear things again.

Section Review Practice 1.4

The following passage is a student composition. Mistakes have been added for practice. Edit the composition to correct the mistakes. You may need to change punctuation, capital letters, coordinators, subordinators, and other words.

The Joys of Camping

Camping is my hobby, I do it for fun, have found helpful results from it. First, gives me the experience of working together with others. The spirit of teamwork should be developed more than selfishness. In camping are many opportunities to work in cooperation with others. Second, it cannot be denied that camping is an occasion to live with many kinds of people, therefore is a good chance to practice suitable behavior with others, to know how others see me. Humanity is a mystery to me, I want to learn more about myself and other people. That is my point of view in life. One more good result is making many new friends. Camping has done this for me. When I join in working with people. They see that I am interested in them. They often become friends. Someone once told me that he never wastes a chance to find another half of himself, I have found many new halves of me. By camping. Life is boring. If we have no hobbies or activities at all, each person has his or her own choice, my choice is camping.

Nouns

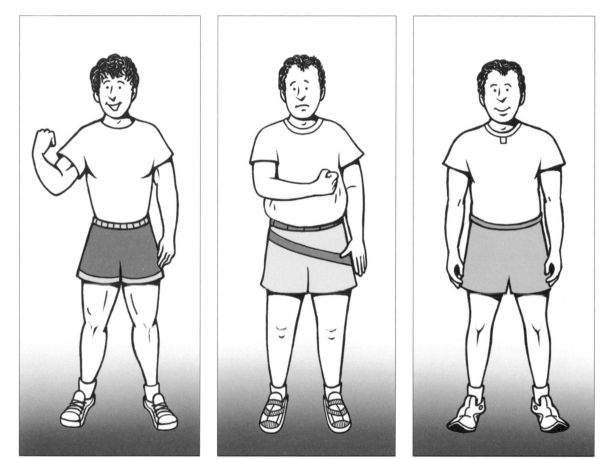

Daniel Blank at age 18   *Daniel Blank at age 35*   *Daniel Blank at age 36*

Introduction to the Topic

Nouns name the things in our lives. Nouns can be *count* or *noncount*. Count nouns can be counted; noncount nouns cannot be counted. In this chapter, you will learn to use count and noncount nouns correctly in your writing. You will also learn how to treat names, which are called *proper nouns*.

EXPLORING THE TOPIC

Read the passages on the next page from *The First Deadly Sin*, by Lawrence Sanders. They introduce Daniel Blank, a man who decided to transform himself. In Part 1, nouns are shown in italics.

Daniel Blank (Part 1)

Daniel Blank was a tall *man*, slightly over six *feet*, and was now slender. In *high school* and *college* he had competed in *swimming, track,* and *tennis.* These physical *activities* had given his *body* well-developed *shoulders* and *thighs.* Shortly after his *separation* from his *wife*, he took a "physical *inventory*" of his *body* in the full-length *mirror* on the *inside* of his *bathroom** door. He saw that *deterioration* had begun.

1. Add at least two more nouns from the paragraph above to each category.

   People: man,
   Places: high school,
   Things: body,
   Concepts: separation,
   Activities: swimming,

2. Underline the nouns in Part 2 of the passage.

Daniel Blank (Part 2)

He at once began a strict program of diet and exercise. He bought several books on nutrition and systems of physical training. He tried to avoid starch, sugar, dairy products, eggs, and red meat. He ate fresh fruit, vegetables, broiled fish, and salads with a dressing of fresh lemon juice. Within three months, he had lost twenty pounds and his ribs and hip bones showed.

① Count Nouns

Count nouns have two forms, singular and plural. The following chart lists some singular and plural count nouns.

SOME COUNT NOUNS	
Singular	**Plural**
man	men
foot	feet
college	colleges
shoulder	shoulders
separation	separations
carbohydrate	carbohydrates

✳ *Here* bathroom *is a noun modifying the noun* door.

EXPLORING THE GRAMMAR POINT

Compare these two versions of a paragraph containing singular count nouns. What is wrong with the second version? What words are missing?

Going to My Son's Swimming Lesson (Version 1)

Yesterday I had to take my son to his swimming lesson. I helped him put on his swimsuit and get a towel. Then we got in the car and drove to the pool. We arrived five minutes before his lesson began. We follow this routine every Saturday. At first he was scared, but now he likes the pool.

Going to Son's Swimming Lesson (Version 2)

Yesterday I had to take son to swimming lesson. I helped him put on swimsuit and get towel. Then we got in car and drove to pool. We arrived five minutes before lesson began. We follow routine Saturday. At first he was scared, but now he likes pool.

UNDERSTANDING THE GRAMMAR POINT

Version 2 of the paragraph has no *determiners*. Singular count nouns need a determiner before them; they rarely stand alone. There are many kinds of determiners in English. The most common ones are articles: *a, an,* and *the.* Below is a chart of some different kinds of determiners, with some examples of each kind.

DETERMINERS FOR SINGULAR COUNT NOUNS	
Articles*	a, an, the
Possessive adjectives	my, your, her
Possessive nouns	Daniel's, a teacher's
Singular demonstrative adjectives	this, that
Singular quantity words	another, every, each
The number *one*	one

> **THE NITTY GRITTY** *A singular count noun almost always needs a determiner.*

✳ Chapter 5, Articles, *discusses the use of articles in more detail.*

EXPLORING THE GRAMMAR POINT

Read the following cartoon. It is funny because a *possessive adjective* has two meanings. What are they?

UNDERSTANDING THE GRAMMAR POINT

The word *possessive* is an *adjective*. An adjective is one kind of *modifier*. A modifier gives information about a noun. Modifiers of singular count nouns usually go between the determiner and the noun. Sometimes there are two or more modifiers, all modifying the same noun. The most common modifiers are adjectives and nouns. Some examples are shown in the chart below.

MODIFIERS: ADJECTIVES AND NOUNS
Adjectives as Modifiers
I bought an **expensive** membership.
I joined an **expensive new** club.
Nouns as Modifiers
I joined a **health** club.
I bought a **health club** membership.
Adjectives + Nouns as Modifiers
I joined a **new health** club.
I joined an **expensive new health** club.
I bought an **expensive new health club** membership.

> THE NITTY GRITTY: *One or more modifiers may appear between a determiner and a singular noun. These modifiers may be adjectives, nouns, or a combination of the two.*

Practice 2.1

Underline the singular nouns and their determiners in the passage below. There may be one or more modifiers between a determiner and its noun. Underline the modifiers too.

Choosing an Exercise Program

Before you begin <u>an exercise program</u>, you should identify your most important needs and choose a plan to meet them. Every plan has its own strengths. One program may be ideal for losing weight, while another program is better for building strength. This plan will give you defined muscles, while that plan will strengthen your cardiovascular system. Your best friend's program may work well for him or her, but it may not be the best plan for you.

An appropriate exercise program also has to fit your schedule. Julia's days were very full. She had two young children at home, and she was taking college courses at night. Even so, she wanted to add some fitness activities to her schedule. She found that she could do a twenty-minute exercise video while the kids were taking their naps.

Writing Assignment 1

Write about a time when you began a program to exercise or lose weight. Begin by stating what you wanted to achieve and why. Then describe the experience. What was your program? Did it work for you?

Grammar Point 3 | **Plural Nouns and Determiners**

EXPLORING THE GRAMMAR POINT

Look again at "Choosing an Exercise Program," above. Underline the plural nouns and their modifiers and determiners (if any) twice. What determiners did you find? Which plural nouns do not have determiners?

UNDERSTANDING THE GRAMMAR POINT

In "Choosing an Exercise Program," two plural nouns have no determiners: *muscles* and *courses*.

Unlike singular nouns, plural nouns do not have to have determiners. However, determiners are often used with plural nouns to give additional information about them. Some common determiners for plural count nouns are listed in the chart on the next page. Note that plural nouns never take the article *a/an*, since it means *one*.

Articles	the* (but not *a/an*)
Possessive adjectives	my, your, her
Possessive nouns	Daniel's, a teacher's
Plural demonstrative adjectives	these, those
Plural quantity words	some, other, both, all
The numbers *two* and higher	two, three, four . . .

> THE NITTY GRITTY
> • *Unlike singular nouns, plural nouns do not have to have determiners.*
> • *Plural nouns do not take the article a/an.*

Practice 3.1

Underline all of the plural nouns in the paragraph below. Then add determiners where they are needed. Use each of the following determiners once.

both	my	other	~~some~~	these

Working It Out

                Some
      ˄ <u>People</u> listen to music while they exercise, although people watch TV. For me, best

ideas come while I'm working out. I'm a writer, and I often get stuck with my writing. I

find that if I wait, ideas will come. But they come faster when I'm exercising. When I'm

really stuck, I spend hours and hours walking, running, and lifting weights. Hours help

my writing and do wonders for my body. Results are welcome.

Grammar Point 4 — Forming Regular Plural Nouns

UNDERSTANDING THE GRAMMAR POINT

Most plural nouns end in -s. Following are guidelines for forming regular plural nouns.

✱ *For more information about* the *with plural nouns, see* Chapter 5, Articles.

1. For most regular nouns, form the plural by adding -s.

SINGULAR	PLURAL
month	months
desk	desks
boy	boys
camera	cameras
holiday	holidays
tree	trees
exercise	exercises

2. For regular nouns ending in -s, -sh, -ch, -z, or -x, form the plural by adding -es.

SINGULAR	PLURAL
class	classes
brush	brushes
lunch	lunches
buzz	buzzes
fax	faxes

3. For nouns ending in a consonant + y, form the plural by changing the y to i and adding -es.

SINGULAR	PLURAL
family	families
pastry	pastries

4. For nouns ending in -ife, form the plural by changing the ending to -ives.

SINGULAR	PLURAL
life	lives
knife	knives

- *For most nouns, form the plural by adding -s.*
- *For singular nouns ending in -s, -sh, -ch, -z, or -x, form the plural by adding -es.*
- *If a singular noun ends in a consonant +y, form the plural by changing the y to i and adding -es.*
- *If a singular noun ends in -ife, form the plural by changing the ending to -ives.*

Practice 4.1

Correct the incorrect plural forms.

Special Gifts

    No elaborate ~~pastrys~~ *pastries*, no boxs and boxs of gifts—my two brothers decided to give their wives something special for their birthdays this year. Both of their wifes have two small children. The kids are not babys, but they don't go to school yet either, and their motheres are tired all the time. My brothers gave the two women six days at a spa in Arizona.

    It's a wonderful place. The rooms are decorated in shades of white with touchs of blue. There are gift baskets of beauty supplys in each room. The days are spent eating delicious and healthy breakfasts, lunchs, and dinners, getting gentle massages, taking classs in yoga, going on long walks, relaxing in the hot tubs, and not much else. My sisters-in-law loved their giftes and dream of going back again someday.

Writing Assignment 2

Write about a special gift that you gave to someone. Describe the recipient (the person who received the gift) and why you chose the gift. Finish with a statement about how the recipient reacted to the gift.

Grammar Point 5 **Forming Irregular Plural Nouns**

UNDERSTANDING THE GRAMMAR POINT

Some count nouns are irregular: their plural form does not end in *-s*. For some irregular nouns, the plural is formed by changing vowels in the middle of the word; for others, the plural form is the same as the singular form, and only the context shows that they are plural. The most frequently used irregular plurals refer to people, but there are many others. The following chart lists some common nouns with irregular plurals.

COMMON NOUNS WITH IRREGULAR PLURALS			
Singular	**Plural**	**Singular**	**Plural**
child	children	foot	feet
person	people	mouse	mice
man	men	fish	fish
woman	women	deer	deer
tooth	teeth	sheep	sheep
goose	geese		

THE NITTY GRITTY *Some count nouns have irregular plural forms that do not end in -s.*

Practice 5.1

Complete the sentences with *a person* or *people*.

1. _____People_____ generally try to avoid loneliness.
2. _____ who is lonely longs for a friend.
3. _____ in my family are pretty outgoing.
4. My sister is in sales and loves to talk to _____ .
5. _____ I can always depend on is my brother.
6. I really appreciate _____ who are open and honest.

Practice 5.2

In each sentence, the noun in italics is singular. Change it to the plural form and rewrite the sentence. Make any other changes needed.

1. The *man* who taught me yoga was a Buddhist monk.

   The men who taught me yoga were Buddhist monks.

2. The *tooth* I broke is right in front.

   _____

3. The *fish* we ate last night was fresh from the sea.

   _____

4. The *woman* I met last night looked much younger than her real age.

   _____

5. The *person* who lives next door to me is an exercise fanatic.

   _____

6. The *child* who left his bike here hasn't come to get it.

   _____

② Noncount Nouns

Noncount nouns have only one form. The following chart lists some noncount nouns.

SOME NONCOUNT NOUNS
deterioration
fish
fruit
juice
meat
swimming

Grammar Point 6 ▸ Count vs. Noncount Nouns

EXPLORING THE GRAMMAR POINT

Compare the following correct and incorrect sentences. Then answer the questions below.

1. **Incorrect:** They bought *a rice.*

   Correct: They bought *a bag of rice.*

2. **Incorrect:** We had to cook *three rices.*

   Correct: We had to cook *three pounds of rice.*

Can you count bags and pounds? Are *bags* and *pounds* singular or plural? Does *rice* have a plural form? Can you count rice?

UNDERSTANDING THE GRAMMAR POINT

You can count bags and pounds; they are count nouns that can be singular or plural. Noncount nouns like *rice* cannot be counted. You can count bags of rice, pounds of rice, or even grains of rice if you want to, but you cannot count just *rice.*

Noncount nouns have only one form: singular. They take singular verbs and the pronoun *it*. However, because they cannot be counted, they never take the article *a/an* (which implies *one*).

Note that some languages do not categorize nouns as count and noncount in the same way as English. A count noun in your language may be a noncount noun in English or vice versa.

There are many noncount nouns in English, and they are commonly used. Many of them fall into recognizable categories that can help you identify them. These categories are shown in the chart below.

COMMON CATEGORIES OF NONCOUNT NOUNS

Solids	bread, fish, rope, ice
Liquids	milk, rain, shampoo, toothpaste
Gases	air, fog, hydrogen, smoke
Particles	flour, rice, sand, sugar
Materials	glass, gold, polyester, paper
Fields of study	art, biology, English, economics
Categories	equipment, clothing, food, luggage
Activities	reading, soccer, swimming, tennis
Feelings	happiness, love, fear, pain
Concepts	independence, knowledge, time, work

THE NITTY GRITTY
- *Many noncount nouns fall into common categories.*
- *Noncount nouns do not have a plural form, and they cannot take the article a/an.*

Practice 6.1

Correct the incorrect noncount nouns. Make any other necessary changes.

A Fishing Trip

Last spring, a friend and I spent a week fishing in the mountains. The ~~sceneries were~~ *scenery was* amazing. The snows had recently melted and the waters in the streams were clear and cold. The weathers were perfect. Every day was full of sunshines and the fishings were great. The only problem was that my friend forgot to bring some of his fishing equipments, so we had to take turns with mine. Oh, well. We remembered all our clothings, we took plenty of foods, and we had lots of times to do everything we wanted.

Grammar Point 7 — Nouns That Can Be Count or Noncount

EXPLORING THE GRAMMAR POINT

Compare the nouns in the following pairs of sentences. How are their meanings different?

COUNT NOUNS	NONCOUNT NOUNS
1a. Can I read your **paper** when you finish?	1b. We're supposed to recycle **paper**.
2a. We'll need five large **pizzas** for the party.	2b. Everyone likes **pizza**.
3a. A large **coffee**, please. No sugar.	3b. **Coffee** doesn't grow in the United States.
4a. I have wonderful **memories** of Brazil.	4b. **Memory** can decline as we get older.

UNDERSTANDING THE GRAMMAR POINT

In sentence 1a, *paper* means a specific newspaper; in 1b, it means the generic material called *paper*. In sentence 2a, *pizza* means individual pizzas, while 2b refers to pizza in general. The other examples are similar. Many nouns have more than one meaning, and some nouns can be either count or noncount, depending on their meaning in a particular context. As count nouns, they refer to individual items. As noncount nouns, they refer to a whole class of items.

> THE NITTY GRITTY *Some nouns can be either count or noncount, depending on their meaning and context.*

Practice 7.1

Complete the sentences. Use all three noun forms: noncount, singular, and plural.

1. (chocolate / a chocolate / chocolates)

   I love _____chocolate_____ . I could eat it all day.

   I have to stop eating these _____ .

   Go ahead, have _____ . One can't hurt.

2. (glass / a glass / glasses)

   I can see much better since I got _____ .

   Get _____ and I'll give you some soda.

   Their new house is almost all made of _____ .

3. (fear / a fear / fears)

   I used to have _____ of heights, but I got over it.

   For the first time, I felt real _____ .

   He has so many _____ that he can hardly function.

4. (football / a football / footballs)

   My nephew got three _____ for his birthday.

   I wish we had _____ so we could play.

   I don't really enjoy watching _____ on TV.

5. (business / a business / businesses)

There used to be successful _____ all along this street.

_____ is slow right now, but it will get better.

I want to start _____ and work for myself.

6. (paper / a paper / papers)

I have to write _____ for my English class.

My father loves news. He reads two _____ every day.

I don't have enough _____ to finish this letter.

 Proper Nouns

Proper nouns have two forms, singular and plural. The following chart lists some proper nouns in singular and plural forms.

SOME PROPER NOUNS	
Singular	**Plural**
Daniel Blank	the Blanks
Saturday	Saturdays
September	Septembers

Grammar Point 8 **Identifying and Using Proper Nouns**

UNDERSTANDING THE GRAMMAR POINT

Proper nouns name specific people, places, and things. They begin with a capital letter. Some common categories of proper nouns are shown in the chart below.

COMMON CATEGORIES OF PROPER NOUNS	
Personal names	Daniel, Danny, Mr. Blank, the Blanks
Names of businesses	IBM, McDonald's, Microsoft Corporation
Certain units of time	Saturday, December
Geographic names	Asia, the Andes, Vietnam, Toronto, Rio de Janeiro
Languages	English, Spanish, Arabic, Portuguese
Holidays	Thanksgiving, Memorial Day, Independence Day
Literary titles	*The Old Man and the Sea, War and Peace*
Course names	Introduction to Psychology, American History 101

Because proper nouns refer to specific people, places, and things, they are most often singular. However, they can sometimes be plural as shown in the chart below.

SINGULAR	PLURAL
Monday is the worst day of the week.	I hate **Mondays**.
Daniel Blank lives alone.	The **Blanks** are separated.
Asia is the largest continent.	Culturally, there are many **Asias**.

Unlike other singular nouns, singular proper nouns typically do not take articles, although there are some exceptions (for example, the Fourth of July, the Hague, the Coliseum).

> **THE NITTY GRITTY**
> - *Proper nouns are usually singular.*
> - *Proper nouns begin with a capital letter.*
> - *Singular proper nouns do not usually take articles.*

Practice 8.1

Capitalize the proper nouns in the following paragraph. Cross out unnecessary articles.

A Run in the Park

~~The~~ L̶ast S̶unday, the day before memorial day, my friend jake and I went for our usual run in the pitt park. The park is becoming very international because it attracts both immigrants and tourists. We heard people speaking languages from the europe and the latin america, but we also heard the japanese, the swahili, and some other languages we didn't recognize. This time we finished our run in a new way. We signed up for a class, introduction to tai chi, which was held right there in the park. There were students from probably ten different countries. It was a great way to end our workout. I don't know if jake will keep going to the class, but I liked it a lot.

Count Nouns

- *A singular count noun almost always needs a determiner.*
- *One or more modifiers may appear between a determiner and a singular noun. These modifiers may be adjectives, nouns, or a combination of the two.*
- *Unlike singular nouns, plural nouns do not have to have determiners.*
- *Plural nouns do not take the article a/an.*
- *For most nouns, form the plural by adding -s.*
- *For singular nouns ending in -s, -sh, -ch, -z, or -x, form the plural by adding -es.*
- *If a singular noun ends in a consonant +y, form the plural by changing the y to i and adding -es.*
- *If a singular noun ends in -ife, form the plural by changing the ending to -ives.*
- *Some count nouns have irregular plural forms that do not end in -s.*

Noncount Nouns

- *Many noncount nouns fall into common categories.*
- *Noncount nouns do not have a plural form, and they cannot take the article a/an.*
- *Some nouns can be either count or noncount, depending on their meaning and context.*

Proper Nouns

- *Proper nouns are usually singular.*
- *Proper nouns begin with a capital letter.*
- *Singular proper nouns do not usually take articles.*

Review Practice 4.1

Edit the following paragraph to correct problems with nouns or related to nouns.

Getting Ready For the Beach

It's june and my two best friend and I are thinking about the beach. We need to do three thing to get in shape for our bikini. First, we need to join a gym. We checked out pumped and we liked it. It has good equipments and it doesn't cost too much monies. I only need to buy a new pair of shoe and lock for my locker. Second, we need an eating plan to help us lose weights. We chose weight managers. It's good program and we all think we can stick to it. You get to eat many different foods including meat, fish, bread, vegetable, and even a few dessert. You have to drink eight glass of waters a day. That's not easy, but I can do it. Third, we have to encourage each other. It's too hard to make change like these alone. But together, we can do it.

Review Practice 4.2

Edit the following paragraph to correct problems with nouns or related to nouns.

> ### My English Class
>
> I am learning a lot in my English class this semesters. One reasons is that the instructor gives us a lot of homeworks. We have to do two writing assignment every weeks. Also, we have learned a lot of new vocabularies. We have to make a lists of all the new word in every books or articles we read. The third and most important reasons why I am learning so much is that I am writing a term paper. Doing the researches for it has helped me learn how to use the library and the Internet to find informations. Even though the classes has given me a lot of extra works, I'm really glad I took my counselor's advices and registered for it.

Review Practice 4.3

Edit the following paragraph to correct problems with nouns or related to nouns.

> ### The Six O'clock News Oral Essays
>
> The six o'clock news often include "oral essay" on various topic. Last night, for an example, the presentation discussed the importance of electronics. It seems that every months a new or improved electronic products comes out that many of us want to buy. It's no wonder that electronic is a leading industry in our economy. The night before last, the topics was economics, and last week they talked about educations. Apparently, mathematics are becoming more popular majors for woman in many college. I appreciate this oral essays because they help me keep up on important issue in our daily lifes.

Articles

A private investigator in his office

Introduction to the Topic

In English the articles are *a/an* and *the*. These words are among the most frequently used words in English. *A/an* is related to the word *one*. *The* is related to the words *this* and *that*.

Many people who are learning English find it difficult to know when to use an article and which one to use. This chapter will help you handle articles with more confidence.

REFRESHING YOUR MEMORY

In *Chapter 4, Nouns,* you learned that articles are part of a larger group of words called determiners. You also learned about the different kinds of nouns: count nouns (singular and plural), noncount nouns, and proper nouns, or names. Answer the following questions based on what you learned in Chapter 4.

1. Which kind of noun almost always has to have a determiner?
2. Which kind of noun rarely takes an article?
3. Which two kinds of noun don't usually take the article *a/an*?

EXPLORING THE TOPIC

In this passage from Raymond Chandler's detective novel *The High Window*, a private investigator is describing his office.

In the two versions of the passage, only the articles are different. Which version is correct? Can you explain why the articles are correct in that version? Or do you just have a feeling that they are?

The Office in the Cahuenga Building (Version 1)

I had *the* office in *a* Cahuenga Building, sixth floor, two small rooms at back. One I left open for *the* patient client to sit in, if I had *the* patient client. There was *the* buzzer on *a* door which I could switch on and off from my private office.

The Office in the Cahuenga Building (Version 2)

I had *an* office in *the* Cahuenga Building, sixth floor, two small rooms at *the* back. One I left open for *a* patient client to sit in, if I had *a* patient client. There was *a* buzzer on *the* door which I could switch on and off from my private office.

1 Articles with Singular Count Nouns

Grammar Point 1 ▶ *A* vs. *An*

UNDERSTANDING THE GRAMMAR POINT

Read the sentence below. Notice the use of *a* and *an*.

> **A man** in **a green suit** was reading **an ad** for cough syrup.

The articles *a* and *an* are regularly used with singular count nouns. Use *a* before a noun that begins with a consonant sound; use *an* before a vowel sound. If there is an adjective between the article and the noun, the choice between *a* and *an* depends on the first sound of the adjective, not the noun.

> **THE NITTY GRITTY** *Use* a *when the next word begins with a consonant sound; use* an *before a vowel sound.*

Practice 1.1

Complete these phrases (often seen in detective fiction) by adding *a* or *an*.

1. _a_ pistol   _____ automatic pistol
2. _____ office   _____ dark office
3. _____ expression   _____ sad expression
4. _____ marriage   _____ unhappy marriage
5. _____ divorce   _____ uncontested divorce
6. _____ room   _____ empty room

Grammar Point 2   *A/An*, *The*, and Common Focus

EXPLORING THE GRAMMAR POINT

Read this continuation of the sentence in Grammar Point 1.

> **A man** in **a green suit** was reading an ad for cough syrup. A few minutes later, **the man** in **the green suit** suddenly stood up and got off the bus.

The first sentence says *a man* and *a green suit*, while the second sentence says *the man* and *the green suit*. Can you explain why?

UNDERSTANDING THE GRAMMAR POINT

A/An is called the *indefinite article*. Writers often use *a* and *an* when they mention a noun for the first time, when it does not yet have a definite meaning for their readers.

The is called the *definite article*. Writers use *the* before a noun when they know the noun has an established meaning for the readers. The writer and reader share knowledge of the noun. When the writer and reader share knowledge of a noun in a particular context, the noun is said to have *common focus*.

Common focus can be established in several ways, described here and in the grammar points that follow. One way is to mention a noun for the first time with the article *a/an*. Then later mentions of the same noun use *the* because now the noun has an established meaning for the reader. There is common focus.

In the two sentences above, the first sentence is the first mention of the man and his suit. There is no common focus, so the writer uses the indefinite article *a/an*. In the second sentence, the reader now knows which man and suit the writer is referring to. There is common focus, so the writer uses the definite article *the*.

> **THE NITTY GRITTY**
> - Common focus *means that the writer and reader share knowledge of a noun. Use* the *before a singular noun when there is common focus.*
> - *In general, use* a/an *for the first mention of a singular count noun to establish common focus. Use* the *for later mentions of the same noun.*

Practice 2.1

In Raymond Chandler's story *The Lady in the Lake*, a private investigator is describing a meeting with a man whose wife has disappeared.

Complete the following passage with *a/an* for the first mention of a noun and *the* for later mentions of the same noun.

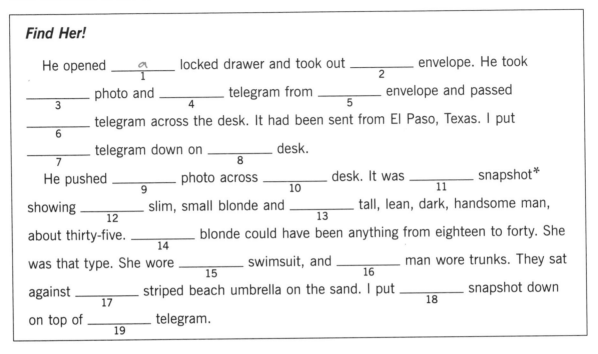

Find Her!

He opened ___*a*___ locked drawer and took out _____ envelope. He took
1   2

_____ photo and _____ telegram from _____ envelope and passed
3   4   5

_____ telegram across the desk. It had been sent from El Paso, Texas. I put
6

_____ telegram down on _____ desk.
7   8

He pushed _____ photo across _____ desk. It was _____ snapshot*
9   10   11

showing _____ slim, small blonde and _____ tall, lean, dark, handsome man,
12   13

about thirty-five. _____ blonde could have been anything from eighteen to forty. She
14

was that type. She wore _____ swimsuit, and _____ man wore trunks. They sat
15   16

against _____ striped beach umbrella on the sand. I put _____ snapshot down
17   18

on top of _____ telegram.
19

Writing Assignment 1

Think of a photograph that is important to you. Describe it and explain what it means to you.

Grammar Point 3 *The* with a Synonym, Part, or Closely Related Idea

EXPLORING THE GRAMMAR POINT

Read the following passage:

> A blonde girl in glasses sat at a table with **a portable typewriter** on it. Her hands were poised over **the machine**, but she wasn't touching **the keys**. Her handbag was sitting on **the typewriter case** next to the table.

The nouns *machine*, *keys*, and *typewriter case* are mentioned for the first time in this passage. Why do they take *the*?

✳ Snapshot *is another word for* photo.

UNDERSTANDING THE GRAMMAR POINT

A noun that has already been introduced may be referred to again with a synonym. The first mention establishes common focus, so the definite article *the* can then be used with the synonym. In the passage above, *typewriter* is mentioned for the first time and so is introduced with the indefinite article *a*. *Machine* is a synonym for *typewriter*, so it takes *the*.

Similarly, when a noun has been introduced, and later a part of this noun is referred to, *the* is used with the part. The part is considered to have common focus, just like the noun itself. Keys are part of a typewriter, so *keys* also takes *the*.

The same is true of a noun that is closely related to a noun already introduced. A typewriter case is closely related to a typewriter, so *typewriter case* also takes *the*.

> **THE NITTY GRITTY**
> • Use the before a synonym for a singular noun that has already been mentioned.
> • Use the before a singular noun that refers to part of a noun that has already been mentioned, or to a closely related noun.

Practice 3.1

Complete the sentences with *a/an* or *the*.

1. She played __a__ Stradivarius violin. _____ anonymous donor gave it to her. I don't know how much _____ instrument was worth. Even _____ bow was probably worth more than I made in a week.

2. I picked up _____ magazine and tried to read, but I couldn't keep my eyes on _____ page.

3. He showed me _____ picture of Stella in _____ ornate frame. At first, I didn't recognize her. Maybe _____ photograph was a bad likeness, but I hadn't seen her for twenty years.

4. I made _____ appointment to see Rogers at _____ downtown hotel at 3:00. I was on time for _____ meeting, but when I got to _____ lobby, _____ elevator was out of service. I started up _____ stairs.

Practice 3.2

Add *a/an* or *the* where they are needed with singular count nouns.

Number 200 was ⌃a tall, dark, old mansion with garage in back. I tried door. It was unlocked. I walked into house, passed through hall, and went downstairs to basement. There was iron bar on floor near large wooden crate. Stain on bar looked like blood. Crate was open.

Grammar Point 4 — *The* with a Limiting Phrase or Clause

UNDERSTANDING THE GRAMMAR POINT

Read the following passage:

> I sit on **the edge of my chair** and glance at **the folder on her desk**. **The look that she gives me** says she knows what I'm thinking. She's right.

Edge, *folder*, and *look* are mentioned for the first time in this passage, but they take *the*.

The can be used with the first mention of a noun when *the* is immediately followed by a phrase or clause that identifies the noun and makes it specific or unique. Limiting the meaning of the noun in this way establishes common focus, so the correct article is *the*, not *a/an*. In the passage above, *the edge of my chair* and *the folder on her desk* are specific because of the phrases that follow *edge* and *folder*. *The look that she gives me* is specific because of the clause that follows *look*.

> **THE NITTY GRITTY** Use the before a singular noun that is followed by a phrase or clause that makes its meaning specific.

Practice 4.1

Underline clauses or phrases that follow singular nouns. Add *the* where necessary.

The
1. Job of my dreams would let me work for six months and then take six months off.

2. Smell of gunpowder was strong in the room.

3. The buzzer was on side of the desk where I could reach it easily.

4. I searched my pockets for phone number I had written down.

5. Car he drove up in was new and expensive.

6. Match I lit didn't help. I couldn't see anything.

7. Window across from the door was open.

8. He never heard shot that killed him.

The with Superlatives and Adjectives of Rank Order

EXPLORING THE GRAMMAR POINT

Read the following passage:

> When I got back to my car, three little kids were washing it. **The oldest boy** rushed over and began explaining why I should pay them for their work. **The next thing** I knew, I had given him five dollars. The kid was right. The car looked better.

The nouns *boy* and *thing* are mentioned for the first time in this passage. Why do they take *the*?

UNDERSTANDING THE GRAMMAR POINT

In the passage above, *boy* and *thing* are made unique by their modifiers. There can be only one "oldest boy" and one "next thing." If there is only one of something, by definition it has common focus and can take *the*, even at first mention. Superlative adjectives like *oldest*, and adjectives of rank order like *next*, give their nouns common focus. Examples of these modifiers are shown in the chart below.

COMMON MODIFIERS THAT PROVIDE COMMON FOCUS	
Superlative Adjectives	best worst oldest youngest most dangerous
Adjectives of Rank Order	first second third next last main top bottom

 Use the before a singular noun that is modified by a superlative adjective or an adjective of rank order.

Practice 5.1

Add *a/an* or *the* as needed with singular nouns. Change capital letters to lowercase where necessary.

> **Going Up**
>
> The f
> ⌃First thing I had to do was find Skye's gun. This was Skye's building, but which was his apartment? Knowing Skye, it would be most expensive one. That meant it had to be the penthouse. I got on elevator and pushed button for top floor. Nothing happened. I pushed it again. Then I noticed that button had keyhole next to it. Floor was locked and I didn't have key. This wasn't worst thing that could have happened, but it was bad enough.

Grammar Point 6 ▸ *The* with Natural Common Focus

EXPLORING THE GRAMMAR POINT

Read the following passage. Notice the use of *the*.

> I got on **the freeway** and drove to **the beach**. **The ocean** was calm and **the sky** was cloudless.

Each of the nouns in boldface type is mentioned for the first time in this passage. Why do they take *the*?

UNDERSTANDING THE GRAMMAR POINT

With some nouns, common focus exists even when the noun is used for the first time, and therefore it can take the article *the*. This *natural common focus* may be because the noun is unique in nature: there is only one in existence. Or it may be because the noun exists in many people's everyday environments and thus is shared knowledge, even though there may be more than one in existence.

Sky is a noun that is unique in nature, and thus has common focus. *Freeway*, *beach*, and *ocean* are part of many people's everyday environments, so they also have common focus (even for people who have never seen them). *The* is used with all of these nouns, even at first mention. The following chart lists some nouns with natural common focus.

Nouns Unique in Nature	weather, horizon, equator, earth, sun, moon, sky, universe
Nouns in the Everyday Environment	*Inside the house:* the kitchen, the bathroom (even though there may be more than one), the floor, the corner *Outside the house:* the yard, the garden, the driveway *Away from the house:* the street, the sidewalk, the curb, the corner *Farther away from the house:* the freeway, the park, the beach, the ocean *Common destinations:* the doctor, the dentist, the hospital, the library, the post office, the bank, the store, the mall

> **THE NITTY GRITTY** *Use the before a singular count noun when it is unique in the world, or when it is common for most people in their everyday environment.*

Practice 6.1

Complete the following passage with *a/an* or *the* where they are needed with singular nouns. Change capital letters to lowercase where necessary.

Interlude

I went into ___the___ kitchen and drank _____ glass of cold water. Samuelson
      1   2

would not call for hours and I was too restless to sit by _____ phone waiting for his
                                                   3

call. I got on _____ freeway and drove to _____ beach. _____ Ocean was
                4   5   6

calm and _____ sky was cloudless. It was too pretty an evening to go looking for
              7

trouble. I almost hoped Samuelson would have nothing to report. I parked on _____
                                                               8

street and strolled along _____ boardwalk for a while. _____ Sun was setting
                        9   10

and _____ moon was already visible in _____ sky. I was hungry, but _____
      11   12   13

hot dog stand was closed. Further on, _____ visitor center was open. There was
                                    14

_____ vending machine in _____ lobby. I went in and got _____ soda from
  15   16   17

_____ machine.
  18

Writing Assignment 2

Describe a walk you have taken that was either especially pleasant or distressing. When was it? Where did you go? What did you see and hear on the walk? What happened? How did you feel?

No Article with Singular Nouns in Set Phrases

EXPLORING THE GRAMMAR POINT

Read the following sentences:

1. We stood **in line** for an hour to buy tickets.
2. They went to Orlando **on vacation**.
3. I'm having some problems **at work**.

The phrases in boldface type do not use articles. Can you explain why?

UNDERSTANDING THE GRAMMAR POINT

In *Chapter 4, Nouns*, you learned that a singular count noun almost always needs a determiner. The sentences above illustrate an exception to this guideline. In English, there are many *set phrases* consisting of a preposition (such as *in*, *on*, *at*, and *for*) + a singular noun. These set phrases do not use articles even when the nouns are singular. In the sentences above, *in line*, *on vacation*, and *at home* are some of these set phrases, so they do not include articles. Below is a chart of some common set phrases of this kind.

COMMON SET PHRASES WITHOUT AN ARTICLE			
At	**In**	**On**	**For**
at breakfast/ lunch/dinner	in bed	on campus	for breakfast/ lunch/dinner
at church	in business	on fire	for example
at college	in college	on sale	for sale
at home	in fact	on schedule	
at night	in line	on time	
at school	in person	on vacation	
at sunrise/sunset	in school		
at work	in shape		
	in uniform		

> *In certain set phrases consisting of a preposition followed by a singular noun, the noun does not take an article.*

Practice 7.1

Cross out the incorrect articles in the following paragraph.

No Sale

Last night at ~~the~~ dinner, my son was teasing me about being fat. Me, fat? I couldn't believe it, but I looked in the mirror, and he's right. In the high school I never had to think about my weight; in the fact, I was thin. Well, I'm forty now, so I guess I'm on the schedule for gaining weight. Anyway, this morning I looked in the newspaper and saw an ad for exercise bicycles on the sale. For a minute, I thought I might buy one, but I changed my mind. In the first place, my bedroom is too small for an exercise bike. But the main reason is that I'll never exercise at the home. I'm going to join a gym. Maybe I'll be in a better shape by the time we go to Florida on a vacation.

---

② Articles with Plural and Noncount Nouns

EXPLORING THE GRAMMAR POINT

Read the following passage:

> **Planes** were taking off and landing every few minutes. **The planes** made so much noise I couldn't hear what Karen was saying. **The trucks** that were delivering **supplies** to planes on the ground finished quickly and pulled away.

Some of the plural nouns in boldface type have articles, and some do not. Can you explain why?

UNDERSTANDING THE GRAMMAR POINT

As you learned in *Chapter 4, Nouns*, plural nouns do not always have to have determiners, and they never take *a/an*. However, plural nouns can take *the* if the context requires it.

In the passage above, *planes* (in the first sentence) and *supplies* have no article because they are the first mention, and plural nouns do not require an article at first mention. However, *planes* (in the second sentence) and *trucks* take *the* because there is common focus. Plural nouns acquire common focus in the same situations as singular nouns, as shown in the following chart, although some situations are very rare.

CONTEXTS THAT OFTEN PROVIDE COMMON FOCUS FOR PLURAL NOUNS

The noun is:	Examples
mentioned for the second (or later) time	**People** were waiting at the bus stop in the hot sun. **The people** were hot and tired.
a synonym for a noun already mentioned	When the snowstorm started, the parking lot was full of **cars**. After the storm, **the vehicles** were almost invisible under the snow.
part of a noun already mentioned	When people tried to get into their **cars**, they found that **the doors** were frozen shut.
closely related to a noun already mentioned	Most of the **cars** stayed in the parking lot until **the owners** could have them towed away.
followed by a phrase or clause that limits its meaning and makes it specific	**The trains on the Number Six line** come every four minutes. All **the trains I took** were new and clean.
modified by a superlative or an adjective of rank order	**The most expensive bicycles** are made of aluminum. Some of **the first bicycles** had very big front wheels.

THE NITTY GRITTY *Plural nouns take* the *when there is common focus.*

Grammar Point 9   **Noncount Nouns and Common Focus**

EXPLORING THE GRAMMAR POINT

Read the following passage:

> We ordered ¹**pizza** last night. The ²**pizza** at Giovanni's is really good, but they don't deliver, so we got six ³**pizzas** from Bella Italia. We got a mushroom ⁴**pizza**, two pepperoni ⁵**pizzas**, and three plain ⁶**pizzas**. They were OK, but Giovanni's ⁷**pizza** is better.

Some of the words in boldface type are count nouns, and some are noncount. Which are which? Numbers 1 and 7 do not have articles. Why? Number 2 has the article *the*. Can you explain why?

UNDERSTANDING THE GRAMMAR POINT

As you learned in *Chapter 4, Nouns*, some nouns (like *pizza*) can be either count or noncount, depending on their context. In the passage above, numbers 3, 4, 5, and 6 are count nouns. Numbers 1, 2, and 7 are noncount nouns.

As you also learned in *Chapter 4*, noncount nouns do not have plural forms, usually don't take *a/an*, and do not have to take *the* except when the context requires it. Number 1 is the first mention of *pizza* in the passage, so there is no common focus and *the* is not required. Number 7 has another determiner, *Giovanni's*, so *the* is not required. However, noncount nouns acquire common focus in some of the same contexts as singular nouns, as shown in chart below. Number 2 requires *the* because of common focus.

SITUATIONS THAT OFTEN PROVIDE COMMON FOCUS FOR NONCOUNT NOUNS	
The noun is:	**Examples**
mentioned for the second (or later) time	Bruce made a lot of **money** working in a restaurant last summer. He spent **the money** on a trip to Europe.
a synonym for a noun already mentioned	The freezer was full of **steaks and ice cream**. We decided to eat some of **the food**.
followed by a phrase or clause that limits its meaning and makes it specific	**The food they serve here** is always good. The daily specials are even better than **the food on the menu**.
modified by a superlative or an adjective of rank order	**The best caviar** is very expensive. **The only real caviar** I've ever had was a gift.

THE NITTY GRITTY *Noncount nouns take* the *when there is common focus.*

Grammar Point 10 **Plural Proper Nouns**

EXPLORING THE GRAMMAR POINT

Read the following sentences:

1. **The Kennedys** are a famous American political family.
2. **Edward Kennedy** has been a United States Senator for decades.
3. **The Maritimes** are three provinces in southeastern Canada.
4. Last summer we visited **Nova Scotia**.

Some of the nouns in boldface type have articles, and some do not. Can you explain why?

UNDERSTANDING THE GRAMMAR POINT

The nouns in boldface type, above, are proper nouns. In *Chapter 4, Nouns*, you learned that singular proper nouns, unlike other singular nouns, almost never take articles. The singular proper nouns in sentences 2 and 4 above have no articles.

Plural proper nouns, however, often take *the* (although never *a/an*). *Kennedys* and *Maritimes* are plural proper nouns, and so they take *the*. Most plural proper nouns are personal names (*the Janes, the Smiths*) or geographical names (*the Balkans, the Great Lakes, the Andes, the Bahamas*).

> **THE NITTY GRITTY** *Plural proper nouns often take* the.

Practice 10.1

Add *the* where necessary before plural common nouns, noncount nouns, and plural proper nouns. Change capital letters to lowercase if necessary.

1. __The__ Tea in the pot is fresh. I just made it.
2. _____ Next music you hear will be _____ Beatles.
3. Mr. Lee showed me an album of _____ photographs. Some of _____ photographs were of his wife.
4. _____ Cars in the driveway were covered with mud and _____ tires were flat.
5. _____ Time that I spend here is always happy.
6. We went camping in _____ Rockies.
7. We found two suitcases on the plane. _____ bags were full of _____ money.
8. _____ Bartletts escaped with their lives. _____ children were frightened, but unharmed.
9. _____ Time flies.
10. This is _____ most beautiful jewelry I have ever seen. _____ earrings are especially fine.

Articles with Singular Count Nouns

- *Use* a *when the next word begins with a consonant sound; use* an *before a vowel sound.*
- *Common focus means that the writer and reader share knowledge of a noun. Use* the *before a singular noun when there is common focus.*
- *In general, use a/an for the first mention of a singular count noun to establish common focus. Use* the *for later mentions of the same noun.*
- *Use* the *before a synonym for a singular noun that has already been mentioned.*
- *Use* the *before a singular noun that refers to part of a noun that has already been mentioned, or to a closely related noun.*
- *Use* the *before a singular noun that is followed by a phrase or clause that makes its meaning specific.*
- *Use* the *before a singular noun that is modified by a superlative adjective or an adjective of rank order.*
- *Use* the *before a singular count noun when it is unique in the world, or when it is common for most people in their everyday environment.*
- *In certain set phrases consisting of a preposition followed by a singular noun, the noun does not take an article.*

Articles with Plural and Noncount Nouns

- *Plural nouns take* the *when there is common focus.*
- *Noncount nouns take* the *when there is common focus.*
- *Plural proper nouns often take* the.

Review Practice 5.1

The following passage is from *The High Window* by Raymond Chandler. You read the first paragraph at the beginning of this chapter. Edit the second and third paragraphs here for mistakes with articles.

The Office in the Cahuenga Building (Continuation)

I had an office in the Cahuenga Building, sixth floor, two small rooms at the back. One I left open for a patient client to sit in, if I had a patient client. There was a buzzer on the door which I could switch on and off from my private office.

I looked into reception room. It was empty of everything but smell of dust. I unlocked communicating door and went into room beyond. Three hard chairs and swivel chair,

---

desk with glass top, five green filing cabinets, calendar on wall, phone, washbowl, and carpet that was just something on floor. Not beautiful, but better than tent on beach.

I hung my hat and coat on hat rack, washed my face and hands in cold water, and lifted phone book onto desk. I wrote down Elisha Morningstar's address and phone number that went with it. I had my hand on instrument when I remembered that I hadn't switched on buzzer in other room. I reached over side of desk and clicked it on. Someone had just opened door of outer office.

Review Practice 5.2

In the following passage from *The Rainmaker* by John Grisham, a law student at Memphis State University is in need of a job after he graduates. Edit the passage, adding articles where they are needed.

Placement

Placement office is on main floor, near front of building. I glance at bulletin board in hallway, but I keep walking. There is not single notice on board. There is no job market at this time of the year.

Madeline Skinner has run Placement here for decades. She's very good at what she does. If Memphis State graduate is in charge of recruiting for big firm, and big firm has too few Memphis grads, then Madeline calls president of university and president visits big firm and takes care of problem.

She's standing by water cooler watching door, as if she's waiting for me. She has cup of water in one hand and she points with cup to her office, "Let's talk in here."

Review Practice 5.3

Edit the following passage to correct mistakes with articles.

A Lie and a Half

A man returned to his hometown after a long trip. He told his neighbor, "On my trip I saw a huge ship with gigantic sails. A ship was bigger than anything anyone could imagine. A young man walked from one end of a ship to other end. His hair and beard turned white before he got there!"

Man's neighbor replied, "That's not so remarkable. I once passed through tremendous forest. A forest had tallest trees in a world. In fact, bird tried to fly to top. It flew for ten years and only made it to halfway point."

"You're the terrible liar," said first man. "That simply can't be possible."

"Why not?" asked his neighbor. "Where do you think a ship you saw got a tree for its mast?"

Review Practice 5.4

Edit the following examples for mistakes with *a/an* and *the*.

1. I had to stop at store to get bread on my way home. I had a time, so I went to Polish bakery on the Tenth Street. In my opinion, bread there is a best bread in town.

2. Weather was terrible. First there was fog, and later there was freezing rain.

3. Oranges are four towns near Newark, New Jersey. I have lived in Oranges all my life—first in Orange and later in East Orange. Orange I live in now is West Orange.

4. I took too much luggage when I went to Africa, and suitcases were too full. I had enough equipment for six-month expedition, and I was only going for month.

5. My best friend in elementary school was Adam McCartney. My name is Adam too, so everyone called us Adams. We spent all our free time together, and McCartneys were like my second family.

6. Love is war.

7. I have to take Advanced Algebra 1 next year. Luckily, I don't have to take Advanced Algebra 2. I hate math.

8. Give me big enough lever and the place to stand, and I can move earth.

SECTION 2 REVIEW

Chapter 4 **Nouns**

Chapter 5 **Articles**

REFRESHING YOUR MEMORY

Answer the following questions based on what you learned in *Chapters 4* and *5*.

1. The plural of *party* is *parties*. Why?
2. Which plural is irregular: *boxes, wives, women*? What are the guidelines for the two that are regular?
3. In which sentence is *food* a noncount noun?
   a. I never say no to food.
   b. I have tried every food I have ever been served.
   c. Some foods are just not good for you.
4. In each of the three sentences above, why doesn't *food* need an article?
5. What is common focus? What article is used for a noun that has common focus?
6. Which phrase is wrong: *on the sale, the last sale, the best sale*? Why?

Section Review Practice 2.1

Read the following paragraph and answer the question.

> ### The Defective Stereo
>
> I bought a new personal stereo and a package of CDs last week. When I got home, *the stereo* didn't work. *The power switch* was defective. I couldn't find *the receipt*, so *the salesperson* wouldn't exchange it for me. Later, I found the receipt under *the box of CDs*.

Why is *the* used with the nouns in italics? Write the letter of the correct answer.

a. The same noun appears earlier.

b. A synonym appears earlier.

c. It is part of a noun that appears earlier.

d. It is a closely related idea.

e. It is common in the everyday environment.

1. _____ the stereo

2. _____ the power switch

3. _____ the receipt

4. _____ the salesperson

5. _____ the box

Section Review Practice 2.2

Edit the following paragraph for mistakes with nouns and articles.

My Sister's Sweet Tooth

My sister's refrigerator is full of the junk food. Top shelf is loaded with can of soda. On next shelf, three box from three bakery are stacked together. They contain a pie and two cake. Next to boxes is carton of milk—chocolate milk. In vegetable bin, several container of pudding crowd out a few old carrot in back of the drawer. Several jar of the jam and the jelly sit next to jar of butterscotch topping. At least in freezer, there is some real foods: two TV dinner. Next to dinner are four pint of ice cream. I'm having dinner at my sister's on Friday. I wonder what menu is going to be.

Section Review Practice 2.3

The following passage is adapted from a student composition. Mistakes with nouns and articles have been added for practice. Edit the composition to correct these problems. You will also need to add the determiners *my*, *her*, and *that*.

This Is Not My Grandmother

I'm not very attentive. That's why I sometimes find myself in awkward situation. One day when I was child, my grandmother and I decided to visit her sister. We didn't have car so we took subway. I was supposed to hold grandmother's hand. We were standing on platform and waiting for train. She gave me piece of candies and I released hand to unwrap it. Just then train came in and I grabbed hand in order not to get lost. There were lot of peoples in car.

After a few minutes, I asked her, "When will we get there?" Man's deep voice answered, "I don't know." Because I was small, my eyes were at level of person's stomach. In astonishment, I looked up, but all I could see was huge stomach. I couldn't see the face. Then I looked at hand. It was not grandmother's hand! Instead I was holding hand of stranger. In a panic, I looked around for grandmother. She was standing right behind me and smiling. I still remember how I felt day. After that, I was always careful to stay with person who accompanied me.

Section Review Practice 2.4

The following passage is a student composition. Mistakes with nouns and articles have been added for practice. Edit the composition to correct the mistakes. You will also need to add the determiners *my*, *her*, *their*, and *that*.

A Dizzy Day

I still remember a worst day of frustration in my lifes. I was frustrated by my own failure. Almost two year ago, one day I felt dizzy because of influenza, but I went to the school anyway. I had the computer class, and I was making home page with classmate. I felt short of breath, but it was raining, so I couldn't open window in computer lab.

Classmate said, "You look pale! Are you OK? You should go home."

I appreciated her concern, but we had to submit assignment by a next week, so I couldn't go home. In those days, I worked at restaurant part time. When we finished in computer lab, time was 4:00 P.M. It was time to start work at restaurant. I went to restaurant in a hurry, and I still felt dizzy because I had run a lot. Anyway, while I was working, I spilled a tea on a customer and dress got wet.

I said, "Sorry," but in fact, I didn't understand what had happened. I just felt dizzy. The manager came and apologized to her. I just watched conversation. Then he said to me, "You should go home today." So I went home. Very next day, I recovered, so I went to restaurant and apologized to boss. "I am so sorry. I made big mistake."

"It's OK. Everyone makes mistakes. Don't worry about it."

Since experience, I have taken care of health. If I get sick, I may cause the trouble for other people. I think the good health is a most important thing of all. And I want to forget experience as soon as possible.

The Simple Present and the Present Progressive

Lilac-crowned Amazon parrots

Introduction to the Topic

In English, the *simple present tense* and the *present progressive tense* are both commonly used to talk about the present. In this chapter, you will learn how to use these tenses to express present time.* *Chapter 9, The Future*, discusses using these tenses to express future time.

EXPLORING THE TOPIC

Read the following two passages and answer the questions that follow them. The first passage is from the story "Mr. Green" by Robert Olen Butler. A woman describes her life in the U.S. and the parrot she brought with her from Vietnam. The second passage is a news item from a publication of the World Parrot Trust.

✱ *For other ways to express present time, see* Chapters 8, 10, 11, and 12.

Mr. Green

Here in New Orleans, he *sits* on my screened-in back porch, near the door, and he *speaks* in the voice of my grandfather. When he *wants* to get onto my shoulder and go with me to the community garden, he *says*, "What then?" And when I first *come* to him in the morning, he *says*, "Hello, kind sir."

Sometimes Mr. Green *comes* with me to the garden. He *rides* on my shoulder and he *stays* there for a long time. Then finally, he *climbs* down my arm, and *drops* to the ground, and he *waddles* around in the garden, and when he *starts* to bite off the stalk of a plant, I *cry*, "Not possible," and he *looks* at me like he *is* angry. I always *bring* twigs with me and I *throw* him one to chew on so that neither of us has to back down.

Parrot Project in Mexico

Katherine Renton *is carrying out* parrot conservation work in Mexico. Recently, a public TV station there produced a program about the Lilac-crowned Amazon parrot which has been broadcast at least four times.

Dr. Renton and her colleagues *are conducting* a nationwide evaluation of the status and distribution of this parrot species in Mexico. An agency of the Mexican government *is funding* the work.

1. Which passage is about current events? Which is about events that happen repeatedly over time?
2. Look at the italicized verbs in the two passages. How are the verbs in "Parrot Project in Mexico" different from the verbs in "Mr. Green?"

① The Simple Present

Grammar Point 1 ▸ The Form of the Simple Present

UNDERSTANDING THE GRAMMAR POINT

In "Mr. Green," the verbs in italics are in the simple present. Some verbs are in the *base form*: come, cry, bring, throw. Others are in the *third person singular* form: sits, speaks, wants, says, etc.

In sentences in the simple present, the base form of the verb is used with all subjects except the third person singular, as shown in the chart below. The third person singular takes -*s* in regular verbs.

	SINGULAR		PLURAL	
First person	I talk	I do not talk	we talk	we do not talk
Second person	you talk	you do not talk	you talk	you do not talk
Third person	he talks she talks it talks Pat talks the parrot talks	he does not talk she does not talk it does not talk Pat does not talk the parrot does not talk	they talk	they do not talk

> **THE NITTY GRITTY** *For the simple present, use the base form of the verb, except for the third person singular, which takes -s in regular verbs.*

Practice 1.1

Complete the sentences with *talk* or *talks*.

1. You ___talk___ too much.
2. Bradley _____ to himself all the time.
3. Some domesticated parrots _____ .
4. You've got to hear this bird. It _____ !
5. My little sister _____ constantly.
6. My mother and I _____ every day.
7. I _____ on the phone at least three hours a day.
8. My parents never _____ about money in front of me.
9. My family always _____ a lot at dinner.
10. Rachel _____ too fast. I can't understand her.

Grammar Point 2 **Forming the Third Person Singular**

UNDERSTANDING THE GRAMMAR POINT

Most third person singular verb forms end in *-s*. The guidelines for forming the third person singular follow. Notice that they are almost the same as the guidelines for forming regular plural nouns (see *Chapter 4, Nouns*, page 51).

1. Most verbs form the third person singular by adding -s to the base form.

BASE FORM	THIRD PERSON SINGULAR
talk	talks
sing	sings
need	needs
include	includes
agree	agrees
mean	means
buy	buys
play	plays

2. For verbs ending in -s, -sh, -ch, -z, or -x, form the third person singular by adding -es.

BASE FORM	THIRD PERSON SINGULAR
stretch	stretches
wash	washes
kiss	kisses
mix	mixes
buzz	buzzes

3. For verbs ending in a consonant + y, form the third person singular by changing the y to i and adding -es.

BASE FORM	THIRD PERSON SINGULAR
study	studies
carry	carries
try	tries

- *Most regular verbs form the third person singular by adding -s to the base form of the verb.*
- *If the base form of the verb ends in -s, -sh, -ch, -z, or -x, form the third person singular by adding -es.*
- *If the base form of the verb ends in a consonant + y, form the third person singular by changing the y to i and adding -es.*

THE NITTY GRITTY

UNDERSTANDING THE GRAMMAR POINT

Some commonly used verbs in English are irregular* in their forms, as shown in the following chart. This can be troublesome, but fortunately no new irregular verbs are entering the language. All new verbs are regular.

COMMON IRREGULAR VERBS IN THE PRESENT TENSE		
Base form	**Singular**	**Plural**
be	am, are, is	are
do	do, does	do
have	have, has	have
go	go, goes	go

Practice 3.1

Read the following paragraph. Fill in the correct forms of the simple present tense for the verbs in parentheses.

> ### Jason and His Parents
>
> Six-year-old Jason (idolize) _____ idolizes _____ his parents, David and
> 1
>
> Hideko. David (own) _____ a computer software business. Hideko
> 2
>
> (study) _____ business management at Florida State University.
> 3
>
> When Hideko (finish) _____ her classes each day, she (go)
> 4
>
> _____ home. After she (greet) _____ Jason and
> 5   6
>
> (have) _____ a snack with him, she (study) _____ for
> 7   8
>
> an hour while Jason plays with his toys. After David (arrive) _____ and
> 9
>
> (greet) _____ his family, he (spend) _____ a short
> 10   11
>
> time at his computer. Later, David (fix) _____ dinner with Hideko. After
> 12
>
> dinner, one parent usually (do) _____ the dishes while the other (help)
> 13
>
> _____ Jason get ready for bed. Jason (wash) _____
> 14   15
>
> his face, (brush) _____ his teeth, and (get) _____
> 16   17
>
> into his pajamas. Later, David usually (tell) _____ Jason a
> 18

✱ *For a longer list of irregular verbs, see* Appendix B.

story or (play) _____ a game with him. Sometimes Jason
                   19

(watch) _____ the news on television with his mother and (fall)
                  20

_____ asleep in her arms. David (carry) _____ Jason
     21   22

to bed and (kiss) _____ him goodnight.
                          23

Writing Assignment 1

Read the comic strip below. In your house, who does what? Are you satisfied with your family's or roommates' arrangements for household duties? If so, why do you think they are fair? If not, how would you like to change them?

Grammar Point 4 Habits and Customs

UNDERSTANDING THE GRAMMAR POINT

In "Mr. Green," on page 88, the woman describes some of her and her parrot's actions at home and at the community garden. These are actions that happen again and again over time. They are routines—habits or customs. This is the most common use of the simple present—to describe habits and customs.

Grammar Point 5 | **Time Markers for Habits and Customs**

EXPLORING THE GRAMMAR POINT

Look again at "Mr. Green." There are three expressions called *time markers* that tell us when or how often a routine action occurs: *in the morning*, *sometimes*, and *always*. Underline the three time markers and notice where they appear in the sentence.

UNDERSTANDING THE GRAMMAR POINT

The use of the simple present is enough to tell us that an action is routine. However, writers often use time markers to further orient the action in time or to tell the reader how frequently the action occurs.

Frequency adverbs, like *sometimes* and *always*, go between the subject and the verb. The exception is with the verb *be*, which precedes a frequency adverb.

The parrot **is always** on his perch near the back door.

Frequently, *often*, *usually*, and *sometimes* can also go before the subject at the beginning of a clause.

Sometimes the parrot comes with me to the garden.

Time phrases (like *in the morning* and the others in the following chart) go either at the end of the clause or at the beginning (at the end is more common).

Some common time markers for the simple present are listed in the chart below.

COMMON TIME MARKERS FOR THE SIMPLE PRESENT	
Frequency adverbs	**Time phrases**
always	every day/week/month
frequently	once a day/week/month
often	twice a day/week/month
usually	three times a day
sometimes	in the morning/afternoon/evening
seldom	at night
rarely	
never	

Practice 5.1

For each verb, write one sentence about yourself and one about another person, using the simple present tense. Use the verbs in parentheses, and select one of the time markers from the chart on page 93.

1. (drink coffee)

   I don't usually drink coffee at night.

   My friend Nelson drinks three or four cups of coffee every morning.

2. (take the bus to work/school)

   _____

   _____

3. (wear black)

   _____

   _____

4. (watch sports on TV)

   _____

   _____

5. (read the newspaper)

   _____

   _____

Grammar Point 6 **General Truths**

EXPLORING THE GRAMMAR POINT

Read these sentences. Which one expresses habitual action? What do the others express?

1. The skin of the hippopotamus **produces** a reddish "sweat."
2. This secretion **protects** the hippo from sunburn and infection.
3. Mature hippos **weigh** from 3500 to 8000 pounds.
4. Hippos **live** for about 45 years.
5. The hippo habitat at the zoo **measures** 400 by 600 feet.
6. My nephew **likes** the hippos better than the monkeys.
7. I **take** him to the zoo several times a year.

UNDERSTANDING THE GRAMMAR POINT

In the examples on the previous page, only sentence 7 expresses a habitual action. The other sentences use the simple present to express general truths. "General truth" is a large category that includes scientific facts, physical descriptions, attitudes, and beliefs.

> **THE NITTY GRITTY** *Use the simple present to write about general truths.*

Practice 6.1

Fill in the correct forms of the verbs in parentheses in the simple present tense.

Better Diets for Parrots

A wild parrot (live) _____ lives _____ in the rain forest. It (spend)

_____ 2 _____ its life in the trees where it (eat) _____ 3 _____ and

is safe from predators. Fresh green foods (make up) _____ 4 _____ most

of the wild parrot's diet. The rain forest (contain) _____ 5 _____ a huge

variety of edible green plants. Parrots (consume) _____ 6 _____ all parts of

these plants, as well as nuts, seeds, fruits and berries. Some of these foods (supply)

_____ 7 _____ small amounts of protein and fat.

The diet of captive parrots (be) _____ 8 _____ very different. Most

birdkeepers (feed) _____ 9 _____ a "parrot mixture" of mostly seeds, nuts,

and grains. Unfortunately, this (produce) _____ 10 _____ a high-fat, high-

protein diet completely unlike the parrot's natural diet. It (lack) _____ 11 _____

essential vitamins, minerals, and fiber. This (be) _____ 12 _____ why we (see)

_____ 13 _____ so many overweight and malnourished parrots in captivity.

2 The Present Progressive

Grammar Point 7 ▶ The Form of the Present Progressive

UNDERSTANDING THE GRAMMAR POINT

In "Parrot Project in Mexico" (page 88), the verbs in italics are in the present progressive tense. The present progressive is formed with the present tense of the verb *to be* (*am/is/are*) + the *-ing* form of the verb.

Here are guidelines for forming the *-ing* forms of verbs.

1. For most verbs, add *-ing* to the base form.

BASE FORM	*-ING* FORM
add	adding
bring	bringing
carry	carrying
listen	listening
remember	remembering
start	starting
study	studying

2. For verbs that end in a consonant + *-e*, drop the *e* and add *-ing*.

BASE FORM	*-ING* FORM
come	coming
ride	riding
waddle	waddling

3. For verbs that (a) end in a single consonant preceded by a single vowel, and (b) are stressed on the last syllable, double the final consonant and add *-ing*.

BASE FORM	*-ING* FORM
nod	nodding
drop	dropping
sit	sitting
forget	forgetting

Do not double the consonant if there are two vowels before it. Do not double the consonant if it is *w*, *x*, or *y*.

BASE FORM	*-ING* FORM
look	looking
remain	remaining

BASE FORM	*-ING* FORM
flow	flowing
relax	relaxing
play	playing

- *Form the present progressive with* am/is/are (not) + *the* -ing *form of the verb.*
- *For most verbs, the* -ing *form is the base form* + -ing.
- *For verbs that end in a consonant* + e, *drop the* e *and add* -ing.
- *For verbs that end in a single consonant preceded by a single vowel, with stress on the last syllable, double the consonant and add* -ing. *Do not double the consonant if:*
    there are two vowels before it;
    the consonant is w, x, *or* y.

Grammar Point 8 Contractions vs. Full Forms

UNDERSTANDING THE GRAMMAR POINT

The verb *be* is often contracted in the present progressive in speaking and informal writing. Contractions are most often used with pronoun subjects (*I'm*, *he's*, etc.) and in negatives (*isn't*, *aren't*, etc.). Full forms are expected in academic writing. The chart below shows some examples of contractions vs. full forms in the present progressive.

CONTRACTIONS WITH *BE* IN THE PRESENT PROGRESSIVE	
Contractions	**Full forms**
I'm trying to find out . . .	**I am** trying to find out . . .
I'm not trying to . . .	**I am** not trying to . . .
It's funding the project.	**It is** funding the project.
It **isn't** developing . . .	It **is not** developing . . .
They're doing some research . . .	**They are** doing some research . . .
They **aren't** reporting . . .	They **are not** reporting . . .

Avoid contractions in academic writing.

Practice 8.1

Complete these sentences about what is happening at the zoo. Use the present progressive tense. Try to use contractions.

1. The sun (shine) ____is shining____ brightly, and it (get) _____ hot.
2. It's afternoon now and the lions (not move) _____ .
3. They (sleep) _____ in the back of their enclosure.
4. One young lion (rest) _____ on her back with her feet in the air.
5. A family on vacation (take) _____ a tour with a guide from the zoo.
6. The guide (explain) _____ about the lions' social behavior.
7. The adults (listen) _____ , but the children (not pay) _____ attention.
8. They (try) _____ to see the monkeys in the next enclosure.

Grammar Point 9 — Using the Present Progressive to Express the Moment of Communication

UNDERSTANDING THE GRAMMAR POINT

The sentences in Practice 8.1 all describe what is happening at the zoo now, at the moment of communication. If you were at the zoo at this moment, this is what you would see. This is the most typical use of the present progressive: to describe what is happening at the moment of communication.

> **THE NITTY GRITTY** Use the present progressive to write about actions taking place at the moment of communication.

Practice 9.1

What is happening around you right now? Write eight sentences: two sentences about yourself, two about another person, two about a group of people, and two about anything else that you see around you.

I am looking at the people around me.

_____

_____

_____

_____

Grammar Point 10 — Stative Verbs

EXPLORING THE GRAMMAR POINT

Read the following two sentences. What is wrong with the first one?

1. **Incorrect:** I'm having a headache because I'm owning three cars and they're all needing repairs.
2. **Correct:** I have a headache because I own three cars and they all need repairs.

UNDERSTANDING THE GRAMMAR POINT

Both sentences describe the moment of communication, but only the second sentence is correct. *Have, own,* and *need* are *stative verbs*: They describe states or conditions rather than actions. The present progressive can only be used with verbs that describe actions. Always use the simple present for stative verbs in present time. The chart on the next page lists some common stative verbs.

COMMON STATIVE VERBS
be, look, look like, sound see, hear, feel cost, weigh have, own, belong include, contain think, know, understand, agree love, hate, need, want

Many verbs can have either active or stative meanings, depending on the context. For example, *have a headache* is stative, but *have dinner* is active. *Think* is stative when it refers to an opinion or a belief, but it is active when it refers to a mental process.

   3. **Stative:** I **think** it would be great to work with animals. (opinion/belief)

   4. **Stative:** I **don't think** it would be hard for me. (opinion/belief)

   5. **Active:** I often **think** about becoming a veterinarian. (mental process)

   6. **Active:** I'm **thinking** of applying to veterinary school. (mental process)

Consider the context when deciding if a verb is stative or active.

> **THE NITTY GRITTY** *Do not use the present progressive with stative verbs to express present time. Use the simple present instead.*

Practice 10.1

Complete the sentences using the verbs in parentheses. Use the present progressive for active verbs. Use the simple present for stative verbs.

   1. I (like) _____like_____ cats a lot.

   2. I (think) _____ cats make the best pets.

   3. I (have) _____ a big, handsome, black cat.

   4. Actually, I (think) _____ about getting another cat.

   5. My cat (not look) _____ out the window right now.

   6. He (sleep) _____ on the desk next to me.

   7. He (look) _____ very relaxed.

   8. He (be) _____ a great cat.

   9. He (understand) _____ me.

   10. Maybe I (not need) _____ another cat.

Writing Assignment 2

How do you feel about pets? Do you like them? Do you have one? Describe one or two experiences with pets that have shaped your reaction to them.

Temporary Situations

UNDERSTANDING THE GRAMMAR POINT

Reread "Parrot Project in Mexico" (page 88).

Currently, Dr. Renton is carrying out research in Mexico. It is possible that she is doing conservation work at this moment, but she also may be eating, shopping, or doing something else. She may not even be in Mexico at the moment. In a larger time frame, she is currently carrying out research in Mexico, but not necessarily at this moment.

The present progressive can express things that are not necessarily happening at the moment of communication but are happening *around* the time of communication.

> **THE NITTY GRITTY** *Use the present progressive to write about actions or activities that are current, but not necessarily happening at the moment of communication.*

Time Markers for Temporary Situations

UNDERSTANDING THE GRAMMAR POINT

Certain time markers are often used with the present progressive when expressing temporary actions or situations. Below is a chart with time markers that are used to express these actions or situations.

TIME MARKERS FOR TEMPORARY SITUATIONS
now, right now, for now
at the moment
currently
today
these days
this summer/winter
this week/month
this semester/quarter/term

> **THE NITTY GRITTY** *Certain time markers are often used with the present progressive to express temporary situations.*

Practice 12.1

What are you doing currently that is unusual for you? Write four sentences with time markers.

This week my dog and I are attending obedience school.

Practice 12.2

Read the information about each person and write one or two sentences using the present progressive to describe a temporary situation.

1.

Sandra

> Fall semester
> Required course: Cell Biology
> Elective: Art History 201

Sandra (take) _is taking Art History 201_____ this term.

She (also take) _____ .

2.

Mark

> Current residence: Oaxaca, Mexico
> Permanent residence: Waltham, Massachusetts

Mark (live) _____ now.

3.

Ruth Ann

> Study partner: Alan
> Engaged to marry: Jake

Ruth Ann (spend a lot of time) _____
these days.

She (not go out) _____ very often.

4.

Rita

> Occupation: Engineer
> Employment status: Unemployed

Rita (work) _____ right now.

She (look for a job) _____ .

The Simple Present

> **THE NITTY GRITTY**
> - *For the simple present, use the base form of the verb, except for the third person singular, which takes -s in regular verbs.*
> - *Most regular verbs form the third person singular by adding -s to the base form of the verb.*
> - *If the base form of the verb ends in -s, -sh, -ch, -z, or -x, form the third person singular by adding -es.*
> - *If the base form of the verb ends in a consonant + y, form the third person singular by changing the y to i and adding -es.*
> - *Use the simple present to write about habits and customs in present time.*
> - *Time markers are often used with the simple present. They cannot go between the verb and the object, except when the verb is* be.
> - *Use the simple present to write about general truths.*

The Present Progressive

> **THE NITTY GRITTY**
> - *Form the present progressive with* am/is/are (not) + *the -ing form of the verb.*
> - *For most verbs, the -ing form is the base form* + *-ing.*
> - *For verbs that end in a consonant* + e, *drop the* e *and add -ing.*
> - *For verbs that end in a single consonant preceded by a single vowel, with stress on the last syllable, double the final consonant and add -ing. Do not double the consonant if:*
>   *there are two vowels before it;*
>   *the consonant is* w, x, *or* y.
> - *Avoid contractions in academic writing.*
> - *Use the present progressive to write about actions taking place at the moment of communication.*
> - *Do not use the present progressive with stative verbs to express present time. Use the simple present instead.*
> - *Use the present progressive to write about actions or activities that are current, but not necessarily happening at the moment of communication.*
> - *Certain time markers are often used with the present progressive to express temporary situations.*

Review Practice 6.1

Change the simple present to the present progressive where necessary.

Laura

Laura has a heavy schedule this semester. She takes a chemistry class, two English classes, an art class, and a business class. Also, she watches her neighbor's house for a month while her neighbor is away, and she babysits for her sister's children. At this moment it is 8:00 on a Thursday evening, and Laura studies for a chemistry test tomorrow. Right now she tries to study and keep an eye on the kids at the same time. The kids watch cartoons. However, Laura doesn't concentrate on her chemistry notes. Instead, she watches the cartoons.

Review Practice 6.2

Change the present progressive to the simple present where necessary.

Louise

This week, Louise is doing something entirely different from what she is usually doing in her daily routine. In her normal routine, she is getting up at 6:00 A.M. on weekdays. She is almost always having breakfast at 7:00 and reading the newspaper while she is eating. She is needing to leave the house before 7:45. She is usually going to work with a co-worker and spending the entire day at the office.

This week, however, Louise's schedule is being entirely different. To start with, she is getting up and having breakfast at 10:00 or later, and she is not reading the newspaper. Instead, she is reading a detective novel. Also, she is spending all her time with her husband and children. They are having time to relax and enjoy each other's company. They are swimming in the ocean every day and going out to dinner every night. You have probably guessed that Louise is being on vacation this week.

Review Practice 6.3

Edit the following passage for problems with present tense verbs.

> ### Second-Hand Smoke
>
> Second-hand cigarette smoke harms nonsmokers. Much of this smoke is rising off the end of a burning cigarette. Scientists are calling it *sidestream smoke*. This type of smoke contain twice as much tar and nicotine as smokers inhale. Smokers are puffing through a filter, but sidestream smoke is not go through a filter. Studies warns against the dangers of second-hand smoke. It is killing about 53,000 nonsmokers in the U.S. each year. It cause about 37,000 deaths a year from heart disease. It is also bringing about 20 percent of all lung cancer in nonsmokers. As a result of these studies, many people wants stricter laws against smoking in public places.

The Simple Past and the Past Progressive

Deng Xiaoping

Introduction to the Topic

The *simple past* and the *past progressive* express past time. The past progressive is less flexible and is used less frequently than the simple past. In this chapter, you will learn how to use these two tenses to write about events in the past.

EXPLORING THE TOPIC

Adam Hessler, an American, taught at a teachers' college in Fuling, Sichuan Province, China. The following passage on page 106, from his memoir, *River Town*, describes how the English department at the college participated in the national memorial ceremony for the Chinese leader Deng Xiaoping.

Most of the verbs in italics are in the simple past. Three are in the past progressive. Read the passage and then answer the following questions: Which are simple past verbs, and which are past progressive verbs? What is different about the verbs in the past progressive?

Memorial for Deng Xiaoping

After Deng Xiaoping *died*, there *was* a memorial service in Beijing's Great Hall of the People. China Central Television *broadcast* the ceremony live, and the government *expected* every work group across the country to watch the broadcast together.

All of the students and teachers in the English department *met* in a lecture hall to watch together. Party Secretary Zhang *led* our ceremony. He *followed* the televised service and *gave* sharp commands to the students and teachers: We *stood* when the dignitaries in the Great Hall of the People *stood*, and we *bowed* when they *bowed*. Then we *sat down* for the memorial speech.

On television, President Jiang Zemin *spoke* for fifty minutes. At the start, he *was wiping* his face and *sobbing*, and I *saw* that some of the students *were* also *crying*. A handful of boys in the back *started* to giggle, but they *kept* quiet, and after ten minutes everybody *was* simply bored.

1 The Simple Past

Grammar Point 1 ▶ **The Form of the Simple Past**

UNDERSTANDING THE GRAMMAR POINT

The past tense of regular verbs ends in *-d* or *-ed*. Here are some guidelines for forming the past tense of regular verbs.

1. Most regular verbs form the simple past tense by adding *-ed* to the base form.

BASE FORM	PAST TENSE
follow	followed
check out	checked out
start	started

2. If the base form of the verb ends in *-e*, add *-d* for the past tense.

BASE FORM	PAST TENSE
die off	died off
notice	noticed
arrive	arrived

3. If the base form ends in a consonant + *y*, change the *y* to *i* before adding *-ed*.

BASE FORM	PAST TENSE
try	tried
study	studied
reply	replied
carry out	carried out

4. If the base form (a) ends in a single consonant preceded by a single vowel, and (b) is stressed on the last syllable, double the consonant before adding *-ed*.

BASE FORM	PAST TENSE
stop	stopped
refer	referred
permit	permitted

Do not double the consonant if there are two vowels before it.

BASE FORM	PAST TENSE
remain	remained

Do not double the consonant if it is *w*, *x*, or *y*.

BASE FORM	PAST TENSE
flow	flowed
relax	relaxed
play	played

Do not double the consonant if the verb has more than one syllable and the last syllable is not stressed.

BASE FORM	PAST TENSE
open	opened
regulate	regulated

THE NITTY GRITTY

- *Form the past tense of most regular verbs by adding* -ed *to the base form.*
- *If the base form ends in* -e, *add* -d *for the past tense.*
- *If the base form ends in a consonant +* y, *change the* y *to* i *before adding* -ed.
- *If the base form ends in a single consonant preceded by a single vowel, and is stressed on the last syllable, double the consonant before adding* -ed. *Do not double the consonant if:*
    there are two vowels before it;
    the consonant is w, x, *or* y;
    the verb has more than one syllable and the last syllable is not stressed.

Practice 1.1

This passage describes the fifteenth birthday celebration of a young woman in Mexico. Complete the passage with the simple past of the verbs in parentheses. (All of the verbs are regular.)

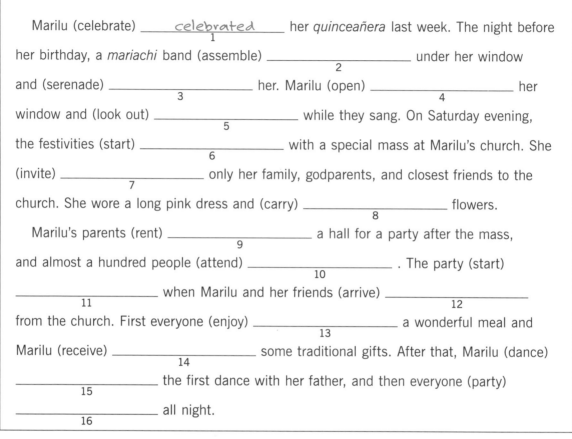

Marilu's Quinceañera

Marilu (celebrate) _____celebrated_____ her *quinceañera* last week. The night before

1

her birthday, a *mariachi* band (assemble) _____ under her window

2

and (serenade) _____ her. Marilu (open) _____ her

3   4

window and (look out) _____ while they sang. On Saturday evening,

5

the festivities (start) _____ with a special mass at Marilu's church. She

6

(invite) _____ only her family, godparents, and closest friends to the

7

church. She wore a long pink dress and (carry) _____ flowers.

8

Marilu's parents (rent) _____ a hall for a party after the mass,

9

and almost a hundred people (attend) _____ . The party (start)

10

_____ when Marilu and her friends (arrive) _____

11   12

from the church. First everyone (enjoy) _____ a wonderful meal and

13

Marilu (receive) _____ some traditional gifts. After that, Marilu (dance)

14

_____ the first dance with her father, and then everyone (party)

15

_____ all night.

16

Writing Assignment 1

Describe a special party or celebration that you have experienced. Explain when and where it was, who it was for, and why it was special. Describe what happened.

UNDERSTANDING THE GRAMMAR POINT

As you learned in *Chapter 6, The Simple Present and the Present Progressive,* some of the most common English verbs are irregular.* Verbs that are irregular in the past tense do not add *-ed* or *-d* to the base form. Instead, they form the past tense in other ways. For a few verbs, the past tense is the same as the base form.

COMMON IRREGULAR VERBS	
Base form	**Past tense**
be	was, were
do	did
have	had
go	went
say	said
write	wrote
put	put
set	set
read	read**

> **THE NITTY GRITTY** *Irregular verbs do not add -ed or -d to the base form for the past tense. Their past tense forms need to be memorized.*

Practice 2.1

Reread "Memorial for Deng Xiaoping" on page 106. Find the ten irregular past tense verb forms. Write the base forms and the irregular past tense forms below.

Base form	Past tense	Base form	Past tense
be	was		

* *For a more complete list of irregular verbs, see* Appendix B.
** *The past tense form is pronounced* red.

Practice 2.2

The following passage is about Amelia Earhart, a pilot in the early years of airplane flight. Complete the passage with the correct past tense forms of the verbs in parentheses. (All of the verbs are irregular.)

Amelia Earhart

Amelia Earhart

In 1928, Amelia Earhart (win) _____ won _____ international recognition
                                          1
as the first woman to cross the Atlantic Ocean by air. After that, people all over

the world frequently (read) _____ about her in the newspaper.
                                    2
In 1932, Earhart (fly) _____ solo across the Atlantic. She (be)
                              3
_____ the first woman and second person to do so (the first person
          4
was Charles Lindbergh). In 1935, she (become) _____ the first person
                                                        5
to fly solo across the Pacific, from Honolulu, Hawaii, to Oakland, California. She also

(set) _____ the women's record for the fastest nonstop transcontinental
              6
flight (from Los Angeles, California, to Newark, New Jersey). Later, she (break)

_____ her own record.
        7
In March, 1935, Amelia Earhart (begin) _____ her first attempt at an
                                                  8
around-the-world flight. However, soon after the plane (take off) _____ ,
                                                                              9
it (go) _____ out of control and (hit) _____ the
                10   11
ground. No one was hurt. In June, 1937, Earhart (leave) _____ on her
                                                                  12
second attempt to fly around the world. On July 2, 1937, when the trip was almost over,

she (get) _____ into trouble. Airport personnel in New Guinea (think)
                  13
_____ that she (have) _____ enough fuel when she
          14   15
took off from there. However, in one of her last radio communications, Earhart (say)

_____ that her gas (be) _____ low. Soon after
          16   17

---

that, the airport (lose) _____ radio contact with her. No one (know)

_____ where she was or what had happened to her.
              19

  Bad weather (make) _____ visibility very poor that day. One theory
                          20

is that the plane (speed) _____ right past its destination at Howland
                              21

Island, northwest of Hawaii. If the plane (run out) _____ of gas, it
                                                          22

probably (fall) _____ into the sea and (sink) _____ .
                    23   24

In any case, no one ever (find) _____ Earhart's plane, and no one
                                    25

knows for sure what happened to Amelia Earhart.

Grammar Point 3 ▶ **Negatives in the Simple Past**

EXPLORING THE GRAMMAR POINT

Read the following sentences. How are the verbs in sentences 1 and 2 different from the verbs in sentences 3 and 4?

  1. Visibility **was not** good that day.
  2. The people at the airport in New Guinea **were not** sure where she was.
  3. Earhart **did not maintain** radio contact after she left New Guinea.
  4. They **did not find** Earhart's plane.

UNDERSTANDING THE GRAMMAR POINT

Sentences 1 and 2 use the past tense of the verb *be*. Sentences 3 and 4 use the base forms of the verbs, but they also use *did*. For negatives with *be* in the simple past, *not* follows *was* or *were*. For negatives with all other verbs, use *did not* + the base form of the verb.

Contractions with *be* and *did* are common in speech and informal writing, as shown in the following sentences.

  5. Visibility **wasn't** good that day.
  6. The people at the airport in New Guinea **weren't** sure where she was.
  7. Earhart **didn't maintain** radio contact after she left New Guinea.
  8. They **didn't find** Earhart's plane.

However, full forms are expected in academic writing, as in sentences 1–4.

> • Form the negative of the simple past with did not + the base form of the verb. The negative past tense of be is was not / were not.
> • The contractions didn't, wasn't, and weren't are common in informal writing. Full forms are expected in academic writing.

Practice 3.1

Change the following sentences to the negative. Use full forms.

1. Amelia Earhart was the first woman to fly solo across the Atlantic.

   Amelia Earhart was not the first woman to fly solo across
   the Atlantic.

2. People heard about Amelia Earhart before 1928.

   _____

   _____

3. Charles Lindbergh flew solo across the Pacific in 1935.

   _____

   _____

4. Earhart's planes were always safe.

   _____

   _____

Change the following sentences to the negative. Use contractions.

5. Earhart's two attempts to fly around the world were successful.

   _____

   _____

6. The second attempt was an easy trip.

   _____

   _____

7. Her last radio communications gave her location.

   _____

   _____

8. She reached her destination.

   _____

   _____

UNDERSTANDING THE GRAMMAR POINT

The simple past expresses actions and events that began and were completed at a specific time in the past, as in the story of Marilu's *quinceañera*.

1. Marilu's parents **rented** a hall for the party.
2. Almost a hundred people **attended**.
3. It **was** a wonderful party.
4. Marilu and her family **were** very happy.

> **THE NITTY GRITTY** *Use the simple past to express actions and events that began and were completed at a specific time in the past.*

Grammar Point 5 ▸ Time Markers for the Simple Past

EXPLORING THE GRAMMAR POINT

Look again at "Amelia Earhart" in Practice 2.2 on page 110. Find the answers to these questions:

1. When did Amelia Earhart win international recognition as the first woman to cross the Atlantic Ocean by air?
2. When did people begin to read about her?
3. When did Earhart say her gas was low?

UNDERSTANDING THE GRAMMAR POINT

The simple past tense refers to a specific time in the past, although the time is not always mentioned. When the specific time is mentioned, it is often indicated with a time marker. See the chart below for common time markers for the simple past.

COMMON TIME MARKERS FOR THE SIMPLE PAST	
yesterday	in 2003
last year/month/night	on July 2
two weeks ago	at 6:00 A.M.
a long time ago	later
	after that

The answers to questions 1–3 on the previous page are all indicated with time markers in the text about Amelia Earhart, as shown in the excerpts from the text given below. Note that the time marker that answers the third question (on July 2, 1937) appears two sentences before the event is mentioned.

4. **In 1928**, Amelia Earhart won international recognition as the first woman to cross the Atlantic Ocean by air.

5. **After that**, people all over the world frequently read about her in the newspaper.

6. **On July 2, 1937** ...Earhart said that her gas was low.

> **THE NITTY GRITTY** *Certain time markers are often used with the simple past to provide more specific information about when the action or event took place.*

Practice 5.1

Underline the eleven time markers in "Amelia Earhart" (Practice 2.2) on page 110.

② The Past Progressive

Grammar Point 6   The Form of the Past Progressive

EXPLORING THE GRAMMAR POINT

Read the following sentences. They are based on *River Town*, the book from which "Memorial for Deng Xiaoping" (page 106) is taken. Examples of the past progressive are shown in bold.

1. At ten o'clock, every horn and whistle in China began to blow. The whole country **was observing** a three-minute period of mourning.
2. Some laborers outside the hall **were not watching** the ceremony on TV.
3. They **were building** a new dormitory.

In the past progressive, when the verb is affirmative, what are the two parts of the verb? What is added when the verb is negative?

UNDERSTANDING THE GRAMMAR POINT

Like the present progressive, the past progressive is formed with *be* and the *-ing* form of the verb. To form the affirmative, use *was* or *were* + the *-ing* form of the verb. For the negative, use *was* or *were* + *not* + the *-ing* form.

In speech and informal writing, you may often notice the contractions *wasn't* and *weren't*. In academic writing, full forms are expected.

Practice 6.1

Complete the following chart of the past progressive for the verb *cry*. Use full forms (no contractions).

	SINGULAR		PLURAL	
	Affirmative	**Negative**	**Affirmative**	**Negative**
First person	I was crying	I	we	we
Second person	you	you	you	you
Third person	he she it	he she it	they	they

Practice 6.2

The passage below describes going to see the fireworks on the Fourth of July (the United States' Independence Day) in New York City. Fill in the correct forms for the past progressive tense of the verbs in parentheses.

Going to See the Fireworks

It rained in the afternoon, but by 6:00 P.M. it (not rain) _____was not raining_____

                                                                1

anymore. There is always a huge crowd for the fireworks, so we had to leave early

to get a good spot. At 6:30, we (walk) _____ along the avenue

                                          2

with thousands of other people. Police (guard) _____ the entrance

                                                  3

points and (check) _____ people's bags, so the crowd (not move)

                          4

_____ very fast. Even so, by 7:00, we (stand) _____

      5   6

near the river where there was a good view out over the water. It was very crowded,

but people (not argue) _____ about space. Everyone (make room)

                              7

_____ for newcomers very cheerfully. Around us, some people (have)

      8

_____ picnics, while others (sit) _____ comfortably

      9   10

in folding chairs and (take it easy) _____ . Four people near us (play)

                                        11

_____ cards. By 8:30, everyone (get) _____ tired of
                12   13
waiting and kids (complain) _____ . It (begin) _____
                              14   15
to get dark, though. By 9:00, it was dark. Everyone (expect) _____ the
                                                              16
first fireworks to go off at any minute when it finally happened—a dozen big bangs! The
rockets whizzed up into the air and burst into fountains of color. Everyone cheered. No
one was tired anymore.

Writing Assignment 2

Think of an event you have experienced that many people attended. What was it?
When and where was it? What was it like? Was it fun, exciting, boring . . .? Give
details to explain how you reacted.

Grammar Point 7 ▶ The Past Progressive vs. the Simple Past

EXPLORING THE GRAMMAR POINT

Compare the following two versions of an extract from "Memorial for Deng Xiaoping"
(page 106). The first is the original version. The second is the same extract with three
of the verbs changed from the past progressive to the simple past.

1. On television, President Jiang Zemin spoke for fifty minutes. At the start, he **was
   wiping** his face and **sobbing**, and I saw that some of the students **were** also **crying**.
2. On television, President Jiang Zemin spoke for fifty minutes. At the start, he **wiped**
   his face and **sobbed**, and some of the students **cried**.

What is the difference in meaning? In which version did Jiang Zemin and the students
cry, stop crying, and then proceed with the speech? In which version did they cry
throughout the beginning of the speech?

UNDERSTANDING THE GRAMMAR POINT

While the simple past describes actions that took place at a specific time in the past,
the past progressive says that the actions were *in progress* at a specific time, and they
may have continued for a while.

In both versions of the extract above, the specific time in the past is the start of the
speech. Both versions are grammatically correct, but their meanings are different. In
version 1 (the original version), the verbs are in the past progressive and the actions
(wiping his face, sobbing, crying) continued for some time. In the second version, the
verbs are in the simple past, and the actions did not continue.

African-American custom from the days of slavery. Slaves were not allowed to marry, so they develop a way of marrying themselves. The couple bring their friends together, promised to love each other, and then lay a broom on the floor and jumped over it. It meaned that they were married. And Tanika and her husband do just that. The maid of honor putting the broom on the floor, they hold hands, everyone count 1-2-3, and they jumped over the broom! Now I understand that many African-American couples jumping the broom at their weddings these days. I was felt really ignorant because I had never heard of this custom before.

Review Practice 7.3

The following passage is based on a letter written in 1849 by a woman named Margaret Munro DeLancey. She was describing the graduation from medical school of Elizabeth Blackwell, the first female doctor in the U.S. Change the past progressive to the simple past where necessary.

Elizabeth Blackwell's Graduation

The commencement ceremony was taking place on a Tuesday morning in January. The sun was shining brightly. We were arriving an hour early, but the seats were filling up already, and we were not getting a seat in front. It was appearing that most of the spectators were women. From the gallery, we were seeing a sea of bonnets. At about eleven o'clock, Miss Blackwell was entering with the other medical students. She was wearing a black silk dress with a lace collar, but she wasn't wearing a hat or shawl. There was some music before the students were getting their diplomas. While the choir was singing, Miss Blackwell sat on the side with old Mrs. Waller. After the music, President Hale was calling the graduates to go up and receive their diplomas. He was speaking Latin and I saw that he was reading the words from a piece of paper! Of course, everyone was waiting for Miss Blackwell, and she was coming last. While she was climbing the steps, Dr. Hale stood up to meet her. He was speaking and giving her the diploma, and bowing. Then he was appearing to expect her to leave. Not so! She was seeming embarrassed, but she was struggling to speak. After a moment, she was thanking him. She said that she hoped to "shed honor on this diploma." Then she was going to sit among the graduates. Everyone was applauding enthusiastically. Miss B. was blushing, but she was becoming calm again while the next speaker, Dr. Lee, was speaking. The program was being over soon. While people were leaving, many of them were stopping to congratulate Miss Blackwell. Finally, she was standing up, putting on her hat and shawl, taking the arm of her brother (who came from New York to be present), and leaving—the first woman M.D.!

The Present Perfect and the Present Perfect Progressive

8

Introduction to the Topic

Developing writers sometimes find the *present perfect tense* difficult to grasp. Part of the difficulty is that this tense can be used to describe two related but different time frames. This chapter will help you understand the present perfect tense so that you can take advantage of its two different uses.

You will also learn the *present perfect progressive tense*. It sometimes means almost the same as the present perfect, but other times its meaning is different. This chapter will help you understand how to use the present perfect progressive appropriately.

EXPLORING THE TOPIC

In the passage on the next page from John Grisham's novel *The Rainmaker*, a lawyer is representing Donny Ray, a young man with leukemia. The insurance company has refused to pay for Donny Ray's treatment, so the lawyer has filed a lawsuit against the insurance company. Leo F. Drummond is the lawyer representing the insurance company.

In the passage, nine verbs are shown in italics. Some are in the present perfect tense and others are in the present perfect progressive tense. Can you tell the difference between them?

Fighting for Donny Ray

Waiting for me when I return to my office is a thick envelope. Leo F. Drummond *has been* busy. He *has filed* two motions. As I read them, I decide that Drummond *has filed* them to prove a point. He is telling me that I'm about to be suffocated with paper.

The phones *haven't started* ringing yet. I have plenty of time to play the motion game. I'm the only lawyer Donny Ray has, and it will take much more than paper to slow me down.

I*'ve been calling* Donny Ray each afternoon. After the first call, his mother mentioned how much it meant to him, and I*'ve tried* to call each day since. We talk about a variety of things, but never his illness or the lawsuit. I know the calls *have become* an important part of his life.

He sounds strong this afternoon. He *has been* out of bed and *has been sitting* on the front porch. He would love to go somewhere for a few hours, to get away from the house and his parents. I pick him up at seven.

① The Present Perfect

Grammar Point 1 The Form of the Present Perfect

EXPLORING THE GRAMMAR POINT

Read the following examples of the present perfect from "Fighting for Donny Ray."

1. He **has filed** two motions.
2. I **have tried** to call each day.
3. The phones **have not started** ringing.

What are the two parts of the verb in the present perfect? In the negative, where does *not* go?

UNDERSTANDING THE GRAMMAR POINT

The present perfect is formed with *have / has* + the *past participle* of the verb. The negative is *have/has* + *not* + the past participle. For regular verbs (like the examples above), the past participle is the same as the simple past tense form, as shown in the chart on the next page.

REGULAR VERBS		
Base form	**Past tense**	**Past participle**
start	started	started
change	changed	changed
study	studied	studied

Have and *has* are often contracted in the present perfect, as in the following sentences from "Fighting for Donny Ray."

   4. **I've** tried to call each day.
   5. The phones **haven't** started ringing yet.

However, full forms are expected in academic writing.

> THE NITTY GRITTY
> • *Form the present perfect with* has/have (not) + *the past participle of the verb.*
> • *For regular verbs, the past participle is the same as the simple past tense form.*

Practice 1.1

Complete the following chart of the present perfect for the verb *start*. Use full forms (no contractions).

THE PRESENT PERFECT		
	Singular	**Plural**
First person	I *have started* I *have not started*	we we
Second person	you you	you you
Third person	he he she she it it	they they

Grammar Point 2 Irregular Verbs in the Present Perfect Tense

UNDERSTANDING THE GRAMMAR POINT

For some verbs with irregular past tense forms, the past participle is the same as the past tense, as shown in the first chart on the next page. For others, however, the past tense form and the past participle are different, as shown in the second chart on the next page.

IRREGULAR VERBS WITH THE SAME FORM FOR PAST TENSE AND PAST PARTICIPLE		
Base form	**Past tense**	**Past participle**
have	had	had
buy	bought	bought
make	made	made

IRREGULAR VERBS WITH DIFFERENT FORMS FOR PAST TENSE AND PAST PARTICIPLE*		
Base form	**Past tense**	**Past participle**
be	was, were	been
go	went	gone
begin	began	begun
take	took	taken

Practice 2.1

Read this case study of a mediation. A mediator is a professional who helps people resolve disagreements without going to court. Complete the sentences with the present perfect of the verbs in parentheses.

August 10: The Problem

Connie Wu (want) _____has wanted_____ to remodel her kitchen for a long time. She
                        1

(hire) _____ Bob Schaeffer, a contractor, to do the work. Bob (buy)
            2

_____ all the materials and (begin) _____ the work.
        3   4

However, Connie (not pay) _____ him for the materials yet. As a result,
                                      5

Bob (stop) _____ working on the kitchen.
                  6

August 24: The Mediation

Connie and Bob (take) _____ their disagreement to a mediator. In
                              7

conversations with the mediator, Bob (come) _____ to understand
                                                      8

that Connie is afraid he will never finish the work if she pays him now. Connie (realize)

_____ that Bob has a right to be paid for the materials.
        9

✳ *For a longer list of irregular verbs, see* Appendix B.

Bob (give) _____ Connie letters from several satisfied customers, so

10

Connie now feels more confident about Bob. Connie (pay) _____ Bob

11

for the materials, and Bob (start) _____ to work on the kitchen again.

12

Writing Assignment 1

Write about a disagreement you have had (or someone you know has had). What was the disagreement about? Did you resolve it? How? If you didn't resolve it, what happened? How did the disagreement affect your life?

Grammar Point 3 ▸ The Present Perfect for Unspecified Past Time

EXPLORING THE GRAMMAR POINT

Read the following sentences.

1. I have taken a course in Web design.
2. Maria has completed her scuba diving certification training.

In sentence 1, is the writer still taking the course now? If not, is it clear when the course ended? In sentence 2, is Maria still working on her scuba diving certification? If not, is it clear when she completed it?

UNDERSTANDING THE GRAMMAR POINT

One common use of the present perfect is to express past time when the exact time of the completed action is not important or it is not necessary to mention it. If the context or a time marker specifies the moment in the past when an action happened, you must use the simple past. If the moment is not specified and doesn't matter, you can use the present perfect.

3. **Correct:**   I **have taken** a course in Web design. (present perfect)
4. **Correct:**   I **took** a course in Web design **last semester.** (simple past)
5. **Incorrect:** I **have taken** a course in Web design **last semester.**

In sentence 3, the precise moment when the action was completed is not specified because it is not important or necessary to mention. Therefore, the present perfect is appropriate.

> **THE NITTY GRITTY**
> - *Use the present perfect for an activity that happened at an unspecified time in the past.*
> - *Do not use the present perfect for a specific past time. Use the simple past.*

Practice 3.1

Complete the paragraph with the correct forms of the verbs in parentheses. Use the present perfect for unspecified past time.

Psychologists and Psychiatrists as Expert Witnesses

Both psychologists and psychiatrists often serve as experts in trials. "Expert testimony" (become) _____has become_____ very common in both civil and criminal trials. However, the training of psychologists and psychiatrists is quite different. Psychologists' training is specifically in the field of psychology. A psychologist (attend) _____ graduate school in psychology and (complete) _____ his or her training in a clinic or counseling office. Psychologists cannot prescribe drugs for their patients. Psychiatrists, on the other hand, have medical training. Psychiatrists (attend) _____ medical school and (obtain) _____ the M.D. (doctor of medicine) degree. They (complete) _____ a training period in a hospital. Due to these differences in training, psychiatrists usually charge more as expert witnesses than psychologists do.

Grammar Point 4 ▸ **Frequency Adverbs with the Present Perfect**

UNDERSTANDING THE GRAMMAR POINT

In *Chapter 6, The Simple Present and the Present Progressive*, you learned to use frequency adverbs, such as *always, usually,* and *never,* with the simple present for habits and customs (page 93, Grammar Point 5). These same adverbs are often used with the present perfect for an unspecified past time. Frequency adverbs go between *have/has* and the past participle, as shown in the following examples.

1. I **have never been** to Europe.
2. I **have always wanted** to spend a few months there.

Another frequency adverb often used with the present perfect is *ever.* It is very common in questions, e.g., "Have you ever been to Europe?" In statements, *ever* can only be used when the subject is *no* + noun, as shown in the following examples.

3. **No one has ever invited** me to go to Europe.
4. **No vacation has ever been** long enough.

> **THE NITTY GRITTY** *Frequency adverbs go between* have/has *and the past participle.*

Practice 4.1

Read this passage about a Japanese prison. Complete it with the present perfect or the simple past of the verbs in parentheses. Use frequency adverbs where necessary.

A Prison in Japan

There (never be) ___has never been___ a hostage crisis in the prison. There
                                    1

(never be) _____ a "prison disturbance." Gang wars (never occur)
                       2

_____ there—in fact, no gangs (ever exist) _____
            3   4

in the prison. No prisoner (ever kill) _____ a guard or another
                                              5

prisoner. Only three prisoners (try) _____ to escape in the last ten
                                            6

years. Guards in all Japanese prisons are highly trained. Last year, two-thirds of the

applicants who (pass) _____ the national test for prison guards (be)
                                7

_____ university graduates. Even so, only one quarter of them (get)
            8

_____ jobs as prison guards.
            9

Grammar Point 5

The Present Perfect for Past to Present Time (and Possibly the Future)

EXPLORING THE GRAMMAR POINT

Read the following examples of the present perfect from "Fighting for Donny Ray."

1. I**'ve tried** to call each day since. (= since the first time I called)

2. He **has been** out of bed. (this afternoon, and he is still out of bed when I call)

Did these actions begin in the past or in the present? Did they end in the past or are they still continuing?

UNDERSTANDING THE GRAMMAR POINT

The present perfect tense can express an activity that began in the past, continues up to the present, and will most likely continue into the future. The time frames are important here—the past, the present, and the (possible) future.

For actions that began in the past and continue up to the present, use the present perfect, not the simple present or the simple past.

3. **Incorrect:** Donny Ray **is** sick for nine months.

   Correct: Donny Ray **has been** sick for nine months.

4. **Incorrect:** Rudy **was** Donny Ray's lawyer since April.

   Correct: Rudy **has been** Donny Ray's lawyer since April.

> **THE NITTY GRITTY**
> Use the present perfect for an activity that began in the past, continues up to the present, and will most likely continue into the future.

Grammar Point 6 ▸ *For* and *Since* with the Present Perfect

UNDERSTANDING THE GRAMMAR POINT

For actions that began in the past and continue up to the present, we often mention the duration of the action with the time marker *for* or *since*.

For refers to a period of time.

1. Donny Ray has been sick **for eleven months.**
2. Rudy has been his lawyer **for a short time.**

Since refers to the point in time at which an action began. This point can be an actual time, like a day, month, season, or hour.

3. Donny Ray has been out of bed **since one o'clock.**
4. He has been sick **since last year.**
5. Rudy has been Donny Ray's lawyer **since April.**

With *since*, the point in time can also be an event in the past expressed as a clause.

6. Rudy has been Donny Ray's lawyer **since he passed the bar exam.***

> **THE NITTY GRITTY**
> • For *refers to a period of time;* since *refers to a point in time.*
> • *The present perfect is often used with* for *and* since *to express the duration of an action.*

Practice 6.1

Complete the sentences with *for* or *since*.

1. Amy has been with her father in Canada _____*for*_____ three years.
2. She has not seen her mother in China _____ 2002.
3. Her parents have lived in separate countries _____ twenty years.
4. Amy's father has sent money home every month _____ he arrived in Canada.
5. Amy's mother has raised their children alone _____ most of their lives.
6. Amy has felt homesick _____ she came to Canada.

✱ *The* bar exam *is an examination that graduates must pass to work as lawyers.*

Writing Assignment 2

Have you (or has someone you know) ever been separated from someone who was important to you? Write about the separation. Describe the circumstances. How did the separation affect you and the other person? How did you deal with it?

Practice 6.2

Look at the chart and the sentences below it. The chart shows some important events in Brian's life. The sentences describe the events. Read the sentences and fill in the missing arrows in the chart. Then look at the chart and write sentences 4, 5, and 8 using *since*.

	1974	1987	1989	1990	1992	1997	1998	2001	NOW
1. be in the U.S.	→————————————————————————————→								→
2. his own business									
3. know his wife									
4. belong to the gym			———————————————————————→						→
5. be married					————————————————→				→
6. vote every year									
7. live in his present house									
8. have his Corvette						————————————→			→

1. _Brian has been in the U.S. since 1974._

2. He has had his own business since 1997.

3. He has known his wife since 1990.

4. _____

5. _____

6. He has voted every year since 1987.

7. He has lived in his present house since 2001.

8. _____

Look at the chart again. Rewrite sentences 2, 3, 6, and 7 using *for*.

2. _____

3. _____

6. _____

7. _____

Practice 6.3

Complete the sentences with the present perfect or the simple past of the verbs in parentheses.

1. According to the New York City Police Department, the city (lead) ____has led____ the U.S. in fighting crime since 1990.

2. The crime rate (fall) _____ 6 percent last year.

3 Last year, there (be) _____ only about 230,000 crimes of all kinds in the city.

4. In 1990, the number of crimes (be) _____ more than 700,000.

5. The city's murder rate (go down) _____ for the last sixteen years.

6. New York (have) _____ fewer murders during the last two years than at any time since the early 1960s.

7. For the last two years, New York (rank) _____ number one for safety among big cities in the country.

8. In fact, last year, New York (be) _____ safer than some American cities with only 100,000 people.

② The Present Perfect Progressive

Grammar Point 7 ▶ **The Form of the Present Perfect Progressive**

EXPLORING THE GRAMMAR POINT

The following two sentences from "Fighting for Donny Ray" on page 124 have verbs in the present perfect progressive.

1. I**'ve been calling** Donny Ray each afternoon.
2. He **has been sitting** on the front porch.

What are the three parts of the verb in the present perfect progressive?

UNDERSTANDING THE GRAMMAR POINT

The present perfect progressive is formed with *have/has* + *been* + the *-ing* form of the verb. Negatives (*not*) and contractions are formed in the same way as in the present perfect.

3. I **have not been visiting** every day. / I **haven't** been visiting every day.
4. He **has not been leaving** the house. / He **hasn't** been leaving the house.
5. He **has been sitting** on the front porch. / He**'s** been sitting on the front porch.

Form the present perfect progressive with has/have (not) + been + *the* -ing *form of the verb.*

Practice 7.1

Complete the following chart of the present perfect progressive for the verb *wait*. Use full forms (no contractions).

THE PRESENT PERFECT PROGRESSIVE		
	Singular	**Plural**
First person	I have been waiting I have not been waiting	we we
Second person	you you	you you
Third person	he he she she it it	they they

Grammar Point 8 ▶ Stative Verbs

EXPLORING THE GRAMMAR POINT

Read the following sentences. What is wrong with the second one?

1. **Correct:**   He **has been lying** in bed.
2. **Incorrect:** He **has been being** in bed.

UNDERSTANDING THE GRAMMAR POINT

Be is a stative verb.* Like all of the progressive tenses, the present perfect progressive is not used with stative verbs.

 Do not use the present perfect progressive with stative verbs. Use the present perfect.

✱ To review stative verbs, see Chapter 6, Grammar Point 10, *on page 98.*

Practice 8.1

Complete the sentences with the present perfect progressive or the present perfect of the verbs in parentheses. Use the present perfect progressive for active verbs, and the present perfect for stative verbs.

1. Ana (practice) <u>has been practicing</u> the piano for an hour.
2. I (listen) _____ to my phone messages. There's one from Leo.
3. She (own) _____ that car for five years.
4. I (not have) _____ a bad headache all year.
5. Li (think) _____ about going back to school.
6. Rex (try) _____ to get away for a vacation, but he's too busy.
7. Jack (weigh) _____ exactly the same since he was in high school.
8. It's so nice to meet you! Niki (tell) _____ me all about you.
9. In the last thirty years, the diamond (belong to) _____ three princes and an actress.
10. We (love) _____ each other since we were children.

| Grammar Point 9 | **The Present Perfect Progressive for Emphasizing Duration** |

EXPLORING THE GRAMMAR POINT

Read the following pairs of sentences. What is the difference in meaning in each pair?

1. a. I've **been calling** Donny Ray each afternoon.
   b. I've **called** Donny Ray each afternoon.
2. a. He **has been sitting** on the front porch all afternoon.
   b. He **has sat** on the front porch all afternoon.

UNDERSTANDING THE GRAMMAR POINT

In the pairs of sentences above, there is no major difference in meaning. Both the present perfect and the present perfect progressive express actions that began in the past, continue in the present, and will most likely continue into the future. However, the present perfect progressive is more expressive and precise because it emphasizes the ongoing nature of the activity.

Because the present perfect progressive emphasizes ongoing activity, it is often used with time phrases of frequency or duration, such as *each afternoon* and *all afternoon* in the examples above. *For* and *since* are also commonly used with the present perfect progressive.

3. Rudy has been practicing law **for a long time.**

4. He has been representing Donny Ray **since April.**

> **THE NITTY GRITTY** *The present perfect progressive describes an action that began in the past, continues up to now, and will most likely continue into the future. It also emphasizes the ongoing nature of an action.*

Practice 9.1

Read the situations. Write a sentence using the present perfect progressive to explain each situation. Use the words in parentheses and any other words you need.

1. *Situation:* People are standing next to a parked car, and they are very annoyed.

   Explanation: (car alarm / go off / for) <u>The car alarm has been going off for</u> <u>over an hour.</u>

2. *Situation:* A woman is standing at a bus stop on a rainy, windy day. She's angry.

   Explanation: (wait for the bus / for) _____

   _____

3. *Situation:* A mother gets home from a hard day at work, and her kids haven't done their homework or chores.

   Explanation: (watch TV / since) _____

   _____

4. *Situation:* Police come into the office and ask for Mr. Ford, one of the accountants. They arrest him.

   Explanation: (steal money from the company / for) _____

   _____

5. *Situation:* Carlos is unemployed. He leaves home in a suit and tie almost every day. He comes home depressed a few hours later.

   Explanation: (look for a job / for) _____

   _____

6. *Situation:* Grady is ten. His family moved to a different city in the middle of the school year. Now Grady doesn't want to go to school.

   Explanation: (tease him / steal his things / since) _____

   _____

Writing Assignment 3

Describe a current situation that has been annoying you or making you angry. What is particularly annoying about it? Do you think the situation will improve? What can you do about it? In the meantime, how is it affecting your life?

Practice 9.2

Complete the sentences. Use the present perfect for completed actions. Use the present perfect progressive for ongoing actions.

1. I (do) __have been doing__ my homework for three hours. I'm sick of it.
2. I (do) _____ my homework. Let's go to the movies.
3. We (paint) _____ the house. Now we can move in.
4. We (paint) _____ the house all day.
5. Rod (never play) _____ tennis.
6. Su Ling (play) _____ tennis two or three times.
7. Roger and Carl (play) _____ tennis since breakfast.
8. Rachel (write) _____ poetry since she was twelve.
9. Many people (write) _____ a poem at some time in their lives.
10. Most people (not write) _____ a good poem.
11. I (eat) _____ some very strange things in different places around the world.
12. They (eat and talk) _____ for three hours.

The Present Perfect

> • *Form the present perfect with* has/have (not) + *the past participle of the verb.*
> • *For regular verbs, the past participle is the same as the simple past tense form.*
> • *Use the present perfect for an activity that happened at an unspecified time in the past.*
> • *Do not use the present perfect for a specific past time. Use the simple past.*
> • *Frequency adverbs go between* have/has *and the past participle.*
> • *Use the present perfect for an activity that began in the past, continues up to the present, and will most likely continue into the future.*
> • *For refers to a period of time;* since *refers to a point in time.*
> • *The present perfect is often used with* for *and* since *to express the duration of an action.*

The Present Perfect Progressive

> • *Form the present perfect progressive with* has/have (not) + been + *the* -ing *form of the verb.*
> • *Do not use the present perfect progressive with stative verbs. Use the present perfect.*
> • *The present perfect progressive describes an action that began in the past, continues up to now, and will most likely continue into the future. It also emphasizes the ongoing nature of an action.*

Review Practice 8.1

Read the six sentences in the box. Answer the four questions about them, and then complete the chart that follows.

> Jack has had his laptop since last week.
> Jack has typed his English term paper.
> Jack has lived in Canada for ten years.
> Jack has been typing his history term paper.
> Jack has been living in Ottawa for two years.
> Jack has read several books for his term paper.

1. Does Jack live in Ottawa?
2. What is already typed?
3. What is not completely typed yet?
4. Is Jack still reading the books?

Complete the chart by writing each of the six sentences in the correct present perfect and/or present perfect progressive box. Not every box will have a sentence.

MEANING		PRESENT PERFECT	PRESENT PERFECT PROGRESSIVE
Unspecified Past Time		(1)	(2)
Past to Present Time	Active verbs	(3)	(4)
	Stative verbs	(5)	(6)

Review Practice 8.2

Edit this passage for problems with the present perfect, the present perfect progressive, and time markers.

> ### The Courtship of Sue and Joe
>
> Things have been getting serious between Sue and Joe recently. Sue has lived in Miami since over four years. She and Joe have been knowing each other for almost two years. They have taken several classes together at Miami Dade Community College. Last year they have taken two English classes together, and they have started dating regularly about six months ago. They didn't date anyone else since then. Lately, they have been talking about getting married.

Review Practice 8.3

Edit the following passage for problems with the present perfect and the present perfect progressive.

> ### A Problem at School
>
> Someone has defined bullying as "doing something to hurt another person or cause him stress." At my daughter's school, bullying has been increase for the last two years. Bullying always been a problem among schoolchildren. However, the bullies have usually been boys, not girls. A couple of months ago, I have seen two older girls who were bullying a younger girl at my daughter's school. They have pushed her down, took her backpack, and threw it into a busy street. When I got out of my car to help the girl, the bullies have run away.
>
> Recently, my daughter acts strangely. She doesn't want to go to school, and I am afraid someone is bullying her. I am trying to get her to talk about it, but she refuses to discuss it. This morning she has said she was sick and I let her stay home. But I have been deciding it's time to get tough. We have to talk.

Review Practice 8.4

Edit the following passage for problems with the present perfect and the present perfect progressive.

Transit Blues

Darius McCollum, 39, has spent more than a third of his life in jail. New York City police arrest him more than twenty times for pretending to be a transit worker. He drive buses and subway trains. He operate signals and switches. He has done almost everything that transit workers do, but he has never worked for the Metropolitan Transit Authority. Time after time, McCollum is able to acquire official MTA keys, tools, uniforms, and documents. He has just spent three and a half years in prison for pretending to be a transit supervisor and stopping a subway train.

When McCollum was eight, he know the entire New York City subway system. Although it is a large and complex system, the boy is able to give directions from any station to any other station from memory. Some medical experts have suggest that McCollum has a condition called Asperger's syndrome. People with Asperger's syndrome often become incredibly expert about specific topics and talk about them endlessly. Many of them do not have good social skills and are not able to hold a job. Recently, McCollum is attending an Asperger's support group. He and his wife are living in Manhattan since he left jail. They met on the subway.

The Future

Guard puppy from Ogata Robotics

Introduction to the Topic

In this chapter, you will learn about using *be going to* and *will* to express the future in written English. In addition, you will see that in some contexts, both the simple present and the present progressive tenses can be used for the future.*

The chapter ends with a way to write about a time in the past when the future was under consideration. It is called *future in the past.*

EXPLORING THE TOPIC

Read the announcement from Ogata Robotics on the next page. Circle verb phrases with *will* and *be going to.* Underline verbs in the simple present and the present progressive. Which verbs refer to a time in the future?

❋ *For more ways to write about the future, see* Chapters 10–12.

New Home Safety Product from Ogata Robotics

Ogata Robotics has announced plans for a new home-safety robot, the Guard Puppy. The new robot will sense intruders or fire. It will automatically call police or firefighters. It will also detect medical emergencies and call for assistance.

Ogata Robotics Vice President for Marketing Miharu Tanaka says, "We are designing the Guard Puppy especially for people who are away all day and for elderly people living alone. It is going to be very easy to operate and very cute. It will actually look like a puppy."

When will the Guard Puppy reach consumers? "We're introducing it next April," says Ogata. "It comes out first in Japan, and we're taking it to the U.S. and Europe in the fall."

1 The Future

Grammar Point 1 Forms of the Future with *Be Going To* and *Will*

EXPLORING THE GRAMMAR POINT

Read the following sentences about the future. In sentences 1 and 2, how does the form of *be going to* change?

1. We **are going to introduce** it in the United States next year.
2. It **is going to be** very easy to operate.
3. It **will look like** a puppy.
4. Elderly people **will like** it.

UNDERSTANDING THE GRAMMAR POINT

The two most common ways of expressing the future are with *be going to* and *will*. To form the future with *be going to*, use the simple present of *be* with *going to* and the base form of the main verb. To form the future with *will*, use *will* with the base form of the main verb.

> THE NITTY GRITTY
> • *Express the future with* be going to *by using* am/is/are + going to + *the base form of the verb.*
> • *Express the future with* will *by using* will + *the base form of the verb.*

Practice 1.1

Complete the sentences with *be going to* and the words in parentheses.

1. (it / rain) __It is going to rain__ before we get home.
2. (Ed and I / meet) _____ after work.

3. (I / start) _____ college in August.
4. (Luisa / buy) _____ a car as soon as she gets a job.
5. (my brother / call) _____ me from the airport.
6. (my neighbors / install) _____ a security system before they leave on vacation.

Complete the sentences with *will* and the words in parentheses.

7. (older people / like)_____the new product.
8. (I / email) _____ you when I get there.
9. (my assistant / fax) _____ the information to you.
10. (the office / close) _____ at 1:00 tomorrow.

Grammar Point 2 **The Form of Future Time Clauses**

EXPLORING THE GRAMMAR POINT

Read the following sentences about the future. Each one contains a dependent clause that specifies the time when something will happen. These dependent clauses are called *time clauses.** What tense are the verbs in the time clauses?

1. Someone is going to meet me **when I arrive in Seattle.**
2. I won't have time to see you **while I'm in the U.S.**

UNDERSTANDING THE GRAMMAR POINT

The future is often specified by time clauses (as well as by time markers like *tomorrow, next week, in a few days*). Future time clauses do not use future verb forms. Instead, they use the simple present.

3. **Correct:** I'm going to move to California as soon as **I find** a job there.
4. **Incorrect:** I'm going to move to California as soon as **I will find** a job there.

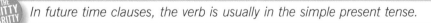

> THE NITTY GRITTY *In future time clauses, the verb is usually in the simple present tense.*

✳ *For a list of common subordinators used in time clauses, see* Chapter 2, Grammar Point 8, *on page 25.*

Practice 2.1

Complete the sentences with future time clauses. Use the correct form of the words in parentheses and an appropriate time clause from the box.

after   as soon as   before   by the time   until   while

1. I'm going to take a road trip ___as soon as my vacation starts___ . (my vacation / start)
2. I won't be able to leave _____ this big project at work. (I / finish)
3. I'll have to make my plans for the trip _____ the project. (I / finish)
4. I'm going to take this trip _____ the money. (I / have)
5. _____ , I'm going to ride every roller coaster between here and Orlando. (my trip / be over)
6. The new roller coaster at Six Flags in New Jersey will be open _____
   _____. (I / get there)
7. I'm going to take a lot of photographs _____. (I travel)
8. I'll show you my photographs _____ . (I / get home)

Writing Assignment 1

Practice 2.1 is about someone planning a road trip. Road trips are part of American popular culture, and there are many songs, movies, and books about them. The purpose of the road trip in Practice 2.1 is to ride roller coasters. Road trips can have many purposes, but many have no special purpose at all. You go somewhere and see what happens on the way.

Describe a road trip that you would like to take. Where do you want to go? How much time will you take? Who will go with you? Will the trip have any special purpose or focus? Why or why not? Give enough details to make your plans interesting.

UNDERSTANDING THE GRAMMAR POINT

Both *will* and *be going to* can express predictions about future events. *Be going to* is more common in speech; *will* is more common in writing.

1. a. The stores **will stay open** late tonight.
   b. The stores **are going to stay open** late tonight.
2. a. The kids **will have fun** tomorrow.
   b. The kids **are going to have fun** tomorrow.

However, when a prediction is based on stated evidence, use *be going to*, not *will*.

3. **Correct:** There are rain clouds forming overhead. It**'s going to rain.**
   Incorrect: There are rain clouds forming overhead. It **will** rain.

> **THE NITTY GRITTY** *Use* will *and* be going to *to express predictions. Use* be going to *for predictions based on stated evidence.*

Practice 3.1

Write sentences with *be going to* or *will*, using the words in parentheses and any other words you need. If both *be going to* and *will* are possible, write two sentences.

1. (my daughter / be in second grade / next year)

   My daughter is going to be in second grade next year.

   My daughter will be in second grade next year.

2. (things / get worse / before / get better)

   _____

   _____

3. Scott is studying hard. (he / pass / this time)

   _____

   _____

4. It's already after 6:00. (we / be late)

   _____

   _____

5. (there / be / a reception / after / the ceremony)

   _____

   _____

6. (I'm sure they / be / very happy)

   _____

   _____

Plans and Intentions with *Be Going To* and the Present Progressive

EXPLORING THE GRAMMAR POINT

Read the following sentences and consider the verbs in boldface type.

1. Someday we**'re going to build** our dream house.
2. We**'re going to build** our dream house next year.
3. We**'re building** our dream house next year.
4. We**'re building** our dream house. It's almost finished.

Which sentence expresses an intention or indefinite plan? Which sentences express definite plans? Which sentence does not express a future meaning?

UNDERSTANDING THE GRAMMAR POINT

Be going to can be used to express intentions or indefinite plans (sentence 1). It can also be used to express plans that are definite (sentence 2).

You learned in *Chapter 6, The Simple Present and the Present Progressive,* that the present progressive is used to describe an action that is ongoing in the present. This is how it is used in sentence 4. However, the present progressive can also be used to express definite plans (sentence 3). In fact, using the present progressive instead of *be going to* can give the feeling that the plans are more definite.

> **THE NITTY GRITTY** Use be going to *for intentions or plans that are not definite. Use* be going to *or the present progressive for definite plans.*

Practice 4.1

1. Write four sentences about intentions you have that are not yet definite plans.

   _____

   _____

   _____

   _____

2. Write four sentences about plans you have that are definite or arranged.

   _____

   _____

   _____

   _____

Scheduled and Planned Events with the Simple Present and the Present Progressive

EXPLORING THE GRAMMAR POINT

Read these statements about a business trip. Which sentences are about scheduled events that cannot change? What verb tense do they use? Which are about personal plans that probably will not change? What tense do they use?

1. **I'm leaving** for the airport at 5:00 A.M.
2. My flight **leaves** at 7:00.
3. I **change** planes in Chicago and **arrive** in Houston at 10:45.
4. I'**m taking** a taxi straight to the meeting.
5. The meeting **runs** until 6:00.

UNDERSTANDING THE GRAMMAR POINT

As explained in Grammar Point 4, the present progressive can be used to express definite plans. The present progressive is used in sentences 1 and 4 to express a traveler's planned activities. To express scheduled events, the simple present is often used. In sentences 2, 3, and 5, the simple present is used to express scheduled airplane departure and arrival times and a scheduled meeting.

Stative verbs, like the verb *be*, cannot be used in the present progressive.

> **THE NITTY GRITTY** *For scheduled events in the future, use the simple present.*

Practice 5.1

Complete the sentences with the simple present or the present progressive.

1. Tomorrow we (get to) ____are getting to____ Yellowstone National Park sometime before lunch.
2. We (take) _____ a picnic and (eat) _____ in the park.
3. We (stay) _____ at a hotel inside the park.
4. There (be) _____ a fireworks show at the hotel tomorrow night.
5. The sun (set) _____ at 8:30 tomorrow, and the fireworks (start) _____ at 9:00.
6. We (have) _____ dinner at the hotel before the fireworks.
7. They (show) _____ *Casablanca* after the fireworks.
8. It (not be) _____ over until 11:30, but we (go) _____ anyway. We love that movie.

EXPLORING THE GRAMMAR POINT

Read the following two passages and then answer the questions below.

1. What future form does Passage 1 begin with? What other future forms does it use?
2. What future forms does Passage 2 use?
3. Which passage is written in more formal English?

Passage 1 (From an e-mail)

My brother **is going to drive** across the country later this summer. He**'s starting** in July and **taking** about six weeks to drive to Los Angeles. He**'ll get there** around the end of August. He**'s stopping off** to see Las Vegas, but beyond that he doesn't have any definite plans for the trip. I've always wanted to take a trip like that, and I know I**'m going to feel** really envious when he leaves.

Passage 2 (From a business proposal)

Our tours **will use** double-decker buses like the famous red buses of London. The buses **will appeal** to tourists and **provide** recognition for the company. The upper level of each bus **will be** open in good weather. However, we **will be able** to enclose the upper deck and control the temperature in bad weather. This **will increase** business during the winter months.

UNDERSTANDING THE GRAMMAR POINT

In informal writing like Passage 1, we often begin with *be going to*, but then switch to shorter future forms to add variety. It's awkward to keep repeating *be going to*, so good writers sometimes use *will* or the present progressive instead.

Note that the shorter forms must be correct in the context. The last sentence of Passage 1 must use *be going to*. It cannot use the present progressive because *feel* is a stative verb. It cannot use *will* because it is a prediction based on evidence, as explained in Grammar Point 3 on page 145.

Formal writing like Passage 2 typically uses *will* instead of a variety of future forms.

THE NITTY GRITTY
- *Informal writing often begins with* be going to, *then continues with shorter future forms.*
- *Formal writing tends to use only* will.

Practice 6.1

Edit the future forms in the following passage to make the passage sound more natural. In some cases, there may be more than one correct answer.

I'm going to spend the day with my two little nieces tomorrow. Before I go, I'm going to make a picnic. I'm going to take my bicycle with me, and when I pick them up, I'm going to put their bikes in my car. First, I'm going to take them to the park, and we're going to ride our bikes for a while. Then we're going to find a nice place and have our picnic. After lunch, I'm going to take them to the movies. It's going to be a great day.

Writing Assignment 2

Describe a day in the near future that you have already planned. What are you going to do? Are you looking forward to the day or not? Why? Give enough details to make your writing interesting.

Practice 6.2

Edit the future forms in the following passage to make the writing more formal.

Hotels of the Future

In the future, we ~~are going~~ *will go* to see hotels in places we can hardly imagine today. Next year, an undersea hotel is going to open in Dubai. Plans already exist for portable hotels, carried by helicopter. They are going to appear almost overnight in the desert, on mountaintops, or in the rainforest. They are going to be self-contained and safe for the environment. Soon, too, travelers are going to find hotels in space. Some are going to be in orbit around the Earth. Others are going to rise on the surface of the Moon, or even Mars.

② Future in the Past

Grammar Point 7 ▸ **Meaning**

EXPLORING THE GRAMMAR POINT

Read the two passages on the following page. Then answer the questions.

Passage 1

My brother **is going to drive** across the country later this summer. He**'s starting** in July and **taking** about six weeks to drive to Los Angeles. He**'ll get there** around the end of August. He**'s stopping off** to see Las Vegas, but beyond that he doesn't have any definite plans for the trip. I've always wanted to take a trip like that, and I know I**'m going to feel** really envious when he leaves.

Passage 2

One summer my brother **was going to drive** across the country. He **was starting** in July and **taking** about six weeks to drive to Los Angeles. He **would get there** around the end of August. He **was stopping off** to see Las Vegas, but beyond that he didn't have any definite plans. I've always wanted to take a trip like that, and I knew **I was going to feel** really envious when he left.

1. What is the time frame of the trip described in Passage 1? Is it before the time of writing, or after it?

2. What is the time frame of the trip in Passage 2? Is it before the time of writing, or after it?

UNDERSTANDING THE GRAMMAR POINT

In the first passage, the trip is in the future. The writer is thinking now (at the time of writing) about her brother's plans for the future, so she uses future forms. In the second passage, the trip is in the past. At the time of writing, the writer is thinking about plans her brother made in the past, so she uses *future in the past*.

 Use future in the past to write about a time in the past when someone had thoughts or plans about the future.

Grammar Point 8 ▸ Form

EXPLORING THE GRAMMAR POINT

Look again at the two passages in Grammar Point 7. Notice the time frame in the two passages: the future in Passage 1 ("later this summer") and the past in Passage 2 ("one summer"). How do the verb forms change in Passage 2? Complete the following chart based on the changes you see.

PASSAGE 1	PASSAGE 2
will do	*would do*
am/is/are going to do	
am/is/are doing	

UNDERSTANDING THE GRAMMAR POINT

In Passage 2, the sister is writing about a time that is now in the past, a time when she and her brother were thinking about the future. With future in the past, future forms become past tense forms. *Will* becomes *would*. *Am, is,* and *are* become *was* and *were*.

As you know, some sentences in the future can use either *will* or *be going to*. In the same way, some sentences in future in the past can use either *would* or *was/were going to*. In Passage 2, both of these sentences would be correct:

1. I knew I **was going to be** really envious when he left.
2. I knew I **would be** really envious when he left.

> **THE NITTY GRITTY** *For future in the past,* will *becomes* would*.* Am/is/are *(with* going to *or in the present progressive) becomes* was/were*.*

Practice 8.1

The following passage is about Pascale Le Draoulec, who wrote *American Pie: Slices of Life (and Pie) from America's Back Roads*. Edit it to change the time frame to the past.

American Pie

    It ~~is~~ ^{was} 2002 and Pascale Le Draoulec is going to move from California to New York. She is going to be a restaurant critic for the *New York Daily News*. She is driving across the country with a friend, a photographer. They are going to look for pie and pie bakers all across the United States. The trip will be a long one because Pascale is going to write a book about it. She believes that people will talk freely to her about pie and about their lives. She hopes they will invite her into their homes and share their recipes with her. She knows she will find both good pie and bad pie, but she is sure it will be a good trip.

Practice 8.2

In 1960, John Steinbeck began a road trip that resulted in his book *Travels with Charley: In Search of America*. Charley was Steinbeck's dog. Imagine that Steinbeck wrote a letter to a friend while he was planning his trip. The passage below is what he might have written.

Edit the passage so that it is about Steinbeck and his plans described by someone in the present, writing about Steinbeck in the past.

> In the fall ~~I'm~~ he was going to explore my own country. I'm buying a pick-up truck with a camper on the back. I'm traveling alone except for Charley. I'll start in the east and drive northwest, zigzagging through the mid-western states and the mountain states. I'm going to avoid cities and stop in small towns and ranches. Then I'll go down the west coast from Washington and Oregon, and back through the southwest and south and up the east coast. Along the way I'll just look and listen.

The Future

> **THE NITTY GRITTY**
> - *Express the future with* be going to *by using* am/is/are + going to + *the base form of the verb.*
> - *Express the future with* will *by using* will + *the base form of the verb.*
> - *In future time clauses, the verb is usually in the simple present tense.*
> - *Use* will *and* be going to *to express predictions. Use* be going to *for predictions based on stated evidence.*
> - *Use* be going to *for intentions or plans that are not definite. Use* be going to *or the present progressive for definite plans.*
> - *For scheduled events in the future, use the simple present.*
> - *Informal writing often begins with* be going to, *then continues with shorter future forms.*
> - *Formal writing tends to use only* will.

Future in the Past

> **THE NITTY GRITTY**
> - *Use future in the past to write about a time in the past when someone had thoughts or plans about the future.*
> - *For future in the past,* will *becomes* would. *Am/is/are (with* going to *or in the present progressive) becomes* was/were.

Review Practice 9.1

Look at "New Home Safety Product from Ogata Robotics" on page 142.

1. The passage is formal writing. Why are there future forms other than *will*?
2. Give an explanation for each of the future verb forms in the passage. Are they predictions, indefinite plans, definite plans or scheduled events?

Review Practice 9.2

Read this extract from an e-mail. A manager in a Japanese company is writing to an American friend. Edit the following informal passage for mistakes with verb tenses.

My company believes that our new product line appeal to the American market, so we exhibit at a trade show in the United States next year. In fact, we've just signed a contract with an American consulting company. The consultants make all the arrangements for the trade show, and I'm being the contact person here in Japan. This is a big responsibility because the show is going to be our first venture outside of Japan. Next week, I'm go to Seattle for my first meeting with the consultants. I leaving on Sunday and return on Saturday. Right now I'm working overtime because I'm getting ready for the trip. I not have time to see you while I'm going to be in the U.S., but I'll call you when I will get home again. The last time we talked, you and Katy are going to start looking for a house outside the city. How is that going?

Review Practice 9.3

Read the following formal office memo. Edit it for problems with verb tenses.

To All Personnel:

Summer hours are going to begin on Tuesday, June 1, and end on Tuesday, September 7. During this time, the office is going to close at 1:00 every Friday.

In order to make this early closing possible, the workday is going to begin at 8:30 A.M. and end at 5:00 P.M. In addition, all personnel are going take 45 minutes for lunch instead of an hour. There is going to be no lunch break on Fridays.

Review Practice 9.4

Read this e-mail about plans for a trip to Washington, D.C. Edit the future forms to make the e-mail more informal.

Randy and I will go to Washington tomorrow. Our plane will leave at 9:00 A.M. and will arrive at 3:20 P.M. We'll stay at a hotel near the Capitol. The next morning, we'll take a tour to Mount Vernon, the home of George Washington. The tour will leave at 9:30 and will return at 4:45 in the afternoon. After we'll get back from Mount Vernon, we'll play it by ear until we'll leave on Saturday. Of course, we'll see the Capitol, the White House, and some of the museums. And we definitely won't miss the Vietnam and Lincoln Memorials. But we'll relax too. This trip will be like a second honeymoon for us.

Review Practice 9.5

Read the following extract from a personal letter. Edit it for problems with verb tenses.

Right now I'm working, but tomorrow is Saturday and I'll go to the country to see my friends Mike and Lynn. They have a house in Rockland County and I'm going to stay with them while the landlord will paint my apartment. I decided to take the bus instead of renting a car. My bus leaves at 8:00 A.M. tomorrow and arrives about 10:30. They pick me up at the bus station. They have a swimming pool! I'm going to swim every day and work in their garden. And we're going to eat well—we always do that. It isn't being exciting, but that's OK with me. I haven't been away from the city all summer and I'm really looking forward to taking it easy for a few days.

Last year when I'm there, we're going to go to the little country fair near their house. It is really going to be fun, but it rains and we didn't go. We thought we'll walk around and look at the farm animals. After that, we were going to have lunch and go on some of the rides. Maybe we'll go this year.

SECTION 3 REVIEW

REFRESHING YOUR MEMORY

Read the following passage about a problem that the astronomer Galileo had. Then answer the questions based on what you learned in *Chapters 6–9*. The numbers in the passage correspond to the questions.

> ### Copernicus and Galileo
>
> [1]Astronomers *study* the stars. [2]Many famous astronomers *have helped* us understand the universe. Most of us *have heard* the names of Copernicus (1473–1543) and Galileo (1564–1642), two great European astronomers. [3]At one time, Europeans *thought* that the Sun and the planets revolved around the earth. First Copernicus, and later Galileo, *said* that the earth and the planets revolved around the Sun. This *seemed* to contradict the Bible, and representatives of the Church *required* Galileo to say nothing more about his conclusions. Some years later, when he *published* additional ideas of this kind, they *forced* him to retract what he had written. Galileo *went* to prison for only a few weeks, but for the rest of his life they *restricted* his visitors and movements.
>
> [4]Copernicus, working before Galileo, *was not going to publish* his ideas, but a student persuaded him to do so. He did not have trouble with the Church for two reasons. First, a friend changed the introduction to his book without Copernicus's knowledge. The new introduction was less controversial than the one Copernicus *was going to use*. Second, Copernicus died just when his book was published. The Church *would not attack* a great thinker who was no longer alive.

1. What is the verb tense in this sentence? Why is it used?
2. What is the verb tense in these two sentences? Why is it used?
3. What is the verb tense in these five sentences? Why is it used? What two time markers determine the tense?
4. What tense are the italicized verbs in these sentences? Why is it used?

The following passage is a student composition. Mistakes with verb tenses have been added for practice. Edit the composition to correct the mistakes.

An Amazing Meeting

I have met my first boyfriend when I was in high school. He was an easygoing and humorous person, so we have a lot of fun whenever we were together. Later, when we were preparing to take the university entrance examinations, we are working too hard to get together. My boyfriend studied hard, but he fails the examination. Then he continues studying in order to repeat it. I was never getting in touch with him while he is studying, and so we lost contact with each other. Sometimes I missed him, but I wasn't knowing how to get in touch with him again. I thought I will never see him again.

Twenty-three years later, my husband and I decide to move to the U.S. for our children's education. Before I move, one day I met with my friends. At that time, my close friend has told me that my ex-boyfriend was in the U.S. She has met him at a medical convention there. He was wanting to see me.

At first I am hesitant. Koreans do not usually accept that married women meet their ex-boyfriends. However, I have thought that I should meet him. I thought that he would have good advice for me, and I was right.

I have had a lot of problems living in the U.S. and educating my children. My ex-boyfriend has been living in the U.S. for twenty years more than me. I have absolutely needing his advice. He recommend that I should learn English in order to adjust to American life. That is why I was in this college and in this class. Now I learn English and getting along much better in this country. Meeting my ex-boyfriend again has been a great help to me, although it is a great shock when it happened. I was afraid that I am going to have problems because of him. Instead, my life is better.

Section Review Practice 3.2

Edit the following passage for problems with verb tenses.

No Fake Earthquake for Me!

I visited most of the major tourist spots in Southern California. When I first arrived, I have been to all of the large theme parks with wild rides. I am visiting Disneyland my first month in Los Angeles. Later, I was going to Knott's Berry Farm and then to Magic Mountain. I am also seeing all the the best-known museums in the area. I have gone to the Los Angeles County Museum a few years ago to see the exhibition of the Impressionists. Shortly after that, I visited the Getty Museum, the Norton Simon Museum, and the Huntington Museum.

There is only one major tourist spot I have not been seeing yet, and that is Universal Studios. I am going there last weekend, but I changed my mind. This theme park had a simulated earthquake ride that is supposed to be very exciting and realistic. But I have already been experiencing a real California earthquake. I really am not needing to pay for a phony earthquake ride. Maybe next weekend, I just stay home.

Section Review Practice 3.3

Edit the following passage for problems with verb tenses and time markers.

Yuri Umansky

Yuri Umansky has lived in the United States since five years. When he first arrived in this country, he has lived in Michigan for six months. Then he and his family were moving to Dallas, Texas, for four and a half years. His first job was in a restaurant. He worked as a waiter. Since then, he has several other jobs, but he has worked as a bookkeeper in a hotel since the last two years. Yuri studied English for the last seven years, and he has still studied it at a community college near his home. He plans to continue taking classes in English and accounting. He meets Lucie three semesters ago in Accounting 1, and they are dating since then. In fact, Yuri and Lucie think about getting married next year. Yuri is going to ask Luci to marry him on her birthday last month, but they are both taking exams then. Now he asks her on his birthday next week.

Modals

Members of the New York City Fire Department

Introduction to the Topic

Modals work with verbs. They express an attitude or opinion about an action or condition (in the verb). For example, *will* and *be going to,** which you saw in *Chapter 9, The Future,* are modals that express expectations or intentions about the future.

The modals presented in this chapter are *can, could, may, might, should, must,* and *have to.* Like *will* and *be going to,* they add information to the verbs they are used with. They can say, for example, that an action is possible or impossible, very likely to happen, a good idea, or prohibited. This chapter concentrates on informational uses of modals, which are most needed in academic writing. It does not include social uses, such as requests and offers. You will see that many modals have more than one meaning, and sometimes two modals have the same meaning.

* *For more about* will *and* be going to, *see* Chapters 9 *and* 11.

EXPLORING THE TOPIC

In 2004, a special commission investigated the September 11, 2001, attacks on the World Trade Center in New York. The following passage is adapted from the commission's preliminary report. It describes the response of the New York City Fire Department (FDNY) on the day of the attacks.

Read the two versions of the passage. Version 1 is the original passage, with several different modals. Version 2 uses only *will* and *would*. Both versions are grammatically correct. Which version tells you more about the FDNY's response?

Sizing Up the Situation (Version 1)

The FDNY commanders decided that they *should evacuate* both towers as quickly as possible. Then the commanders *had to decide* whether they *should try* to fight the fires. They quickly decided that this was impossible, so they *should concentrate* on evacuating trapped civilians.

The FDNY commanders did not have good information about the situation in the buildings. When firefighters going up the stairs discovered information, *they could not always communicate* it to their commanders. In any case, there was no procedure for putting information together and getting it to all the fire commanders. As civilians came down the stairs, there was no procedure for finding out what floor they came from, what the conditions were like on that floor, and how they got down. Such procedures *could be* valuable in large and complex incidents in the future, although they *might not be* necessary for more ordinary situations.

Sizing Up the Situation (Version 2)

The FDNY commanders decided that they *would evacuate* both towers as quickly as possible. Then the commanders considered whether they *would try* to fight the fires. They quickly decided that this was impossible, so they *would concentrate* on evacuating trapped civilians.

The FDNY commanders did not have good information about the situation in the buildings. When firefighters going up the stairs discovered information, they *would not always communicate* it to their commanders. In any case, there was no procedure for putting information together and getting it to all the fire commanders. As civilians came down the stairs, there was no procedure for finding out what floor they came from, what the conditions were like on that floor, and how they got down. Such procedures *will be* valuable in large and complex incidents in the future, although they *will not be* necessary for more ordinary situations.

① Forming Modals

Modals: Present and Future Time

EXPLORING THE GRAMMAR POINT

Read the following sentences about the present or future.

1. *FDNY commanders:* We **should evacuate** both towers.
2. *FDNY commanders:* We **should not try** to fight the fires.
3. *Commission:* Such a procedure **could be** valuable in the future.
4. *Commission:* Such a procedure **might not be** necessary in all situations.

Where is the modal in the verb phrase? What form of the verb is used? Do modals change form to agree with the subject the way verbs do (as in *they live/she lives*)? Where does *not* go?

UNDERSTANDING THE GRAMMAR POINT

The modal is the first word of the verb phrase, and the verb is in the base form. Modals do not change form to agree with the subject, as verbs do. In negatives, *not* goes between the modal and the verb.

> **THE NITTY GRITTY** *For the present and future, form the verb phrase with modal (+ not) + the base form of the verb.*

Practice 1.1

Rewrite the affirmative sentences as negative and the negative sentences as affirmative.

1. Emergencies should catch people unprepared.

   Emergencies should not catch people unprepared.

2. In an emergency, you should panic.

   _____

3. You should not already know what to do.

   _____

4. An office emergency plan might not be a good idea.

   _____

5. It could be hard to make a plan.

   _____

6. We might not be able to do it in a few hours.

   _____

7. It could not save lives.

   _____

EXPLORING THE GRAMMAR POINT

Read the following sentences about the past.

1. Firefighters **could have had** better radios.
2. There **should have been** a procedure for collecting information.
3. They **might have saved** more civilian lives.
4. Some firefighters **might not have died**.

What word follows the modal? What form of the verb is used? Where does *not* go?

UNDERSTANDING THE GRAMMAR POINT

For past time with modals, the verb phrase begins with the modal. Then comes *have* (not *has*) and the past participle of the verb. For negatives, *not* goes between the modal and *have* (not after *have*).

> **THE NITTY GRITTY** *For the past, form the verb phrase with modal (+ not) + have + the past participle of the verb.*

Practice 2.1

Change the following present/future sentences about September 11th to the past.

1. First, firefighters should report to their commanders.
   <u>First, firefighters should have reported to their commanders.</u>

2. They could have lighter equipment.
   _____

3. They should not try to carry firefighting equipment up the stairs.
   _____

4. They might be able to get more people down the stairs.
   _____

5. They should not lose touch with each other.
   _____

6. They might not be able to see each other.
   _____

7. They could miss the order to leave the towers.
   _____

8. They should receive specific training for such disasters.
   _____

September 11, 2001

Writing Assignment 1

How did you first hear about the attacks of September 11, 2001? What did you think at the time? How did you feel? Have your thoughts and feelings about the attacks changed since that time? How? If they have not changed, why have they stayed the same?

Grammar Point 3 *Can*

UNDERSTANDING THE GRAMMAR POINT

In the present and future, the negative of can is *cannot*. For speech and informal writing, there is a contraction—*can't*.

The past tense forms of *can* are *could** and *could not*. Unlike the other true modals in this chapter, *can* does not use *have* in the past tense.

1. **Present/future:** You **can buy** the commission's final report in bookstores now.
   You **cannot buy** the preliminary report.
2. **Past:** You **could not buy** the final report before July, 2004. However, you **could read** the preliminary report online.

> **THE NITTY GRITTY** *The past tense of* can *is* could.

* *The past tense modal* could *is different from the present/future modal* could *and has a different meaning. See Grammar Point 5 for the meaning of* can *and the past tense modal* could. *See Grammar Points 6 and 10 for* could *as present or future.*

EXPLORING THE GRAMMAR POINT

Phrasal modals include a verb (like *have* or *be*) and the word *to*. Read the following sentences with *have to*, the only phrasal modal in this chapter.

1. The FDNY **has to improve** communications during emergencies.
2. They **have to have** better radios and procedures.
3. On September 11, commanders **had to guess** about conditions in the towers.
4. In the future, commanders **will not have to guess** about conditions.

Do these verbs agree with the subject? Do they show tense? What form does the second verb take? How is the negative formed?

UNDERSTANDING THE GRAMMAR POINT

As you have seen with *be going to* in *Chapter 9, The Future*, phrasal modals agree with the subject and they show tense. For *have to*, the verb after the phrasal modal is in the base form. To form the negative, use the appropriate form of *do + not +* the phrasal modal.

> THE NITTY GRITTY
> - *For* have to *in the present and future, form the verb phrase with* have/has to + *the base form of the verb. The negative is* do/does not have to.
> - *The past of* have/has to *is* had to. *The negative is* did not have to.

Practice 4.1

Complete the sentences with the correct forms of the modals and verbs in parentheses.

1. Someone in this family (have to / think) __has to think__ about safety.
2. We (can / not / assume) _____ that nothing will ever happen.
3. When Mitch woke up, he (can / smell) _____ smoke.
4. He (have to / grab) _____ his dog and his photographs and run out of the house.
5. After the fire, Mitch (can / not / live) _____ in his house for three months.
6. He (not / have to / stay) _____ in a hotel. He stayed with his sister.
7. Usually, when escaping from a fire, people think they (have to / leave) _____ the door open for firefighters.
8. Close the door! This (can / slow down) _____ the fire and save lives.

2 Using Modals to Express Ability

EXPLORING THE GRAMMAR POINT

Read the following sentences. Which express the ability to do something? Which express inability? Which expresses the idea that someone had the ability to do something but did not do it? Which are about the present? Which are about the future or past?

1. People **cannot stop** eating and survive.
2. People **can stop** smoking if they really want to.
3. I wanted to stop smoking, but I **couldn't do** it.
4. I **could stop** for only three days.
5. You **could have stopped**. You didn't really want to.
6. I **can't go** to my mother's birthday party next month. I'll be in Chile.
7. I **can call** her, though.

UNDERSTANDING THE GRAMMAR POINT

Sentences 2, 4, and 7 express ability; sentences 1, 3, and 6 express inability. Sentence 5, with *could have*, says that someone had the ability to stop smoking but did not stop.

Could have can also express the idea of a missed opportunity (someone had the chance to do something, but did not do it).

8. My mother **could have come** to Chile with me, but she didn't want to.

Sentences 1 and 2 are about the present; 6 and 7 are about the future; 3, 4, 5, and 8 are about the past. Remember that the form is the same for the present or future: only the context makes the time frame clear.

> - Can/cannot *expresses ability/inability in the present and future. Use* cannot *as the negative in formal writing. The contraction for informal writing is* can't.
> - Could (not) *expresses ability/inability in the past. Use* could not *in formal writing. The contraction is* couldn't.
> - Could have *says that someone had the ability or opportunity to do something, but did not do it.*

Practice 5.1

Complete the sentences with the correct form of *can* or *could* and the verb in parentheses. All of the sentences are from written sources. Some are formal and some are informal.

1. I had a hard time in Marseilles because I (speak) <u>couldn't speak</u> French.
2. Estie (speak) _____ French, although her accent was terrible.
3. I (try) _____ harder to communicate, but I let Estie do it.
4. Without discipline, we (solve) _____ our problems.
5. With total discipline, we (solve) _____ some of our problems.
6. A child's skill in reading (affect) _____ his or her success in school.
7. Very young children (read) _____ , but they (enjoy) _____ listening to a story.
8. What will I do if I (find) _____ a job after college? I (work) _____ for my father, but I don't want to.
9. The class (be) _____ interesting, but I didn't do the reading.
10. Americans know little about geography. In a study last year, many people (name) _____ the capital of Germany.

③ Using Modals to Express Possibility and Logical Conclusions

Grammar Point 6 *Could, May,* and *Might*

UNDERSTANDING THE GRAMMAR POINT

Read the following sentences about the New York Police Department (NYPD).

1. The NYPD **might** have a problem in the next few years.
2. Many police officers **may** decide to retire or resign.
3. This **could** leave the department with a shortage of experienced officers.

The modals *might, may,* and *could* all express possibility. You can use them interchangeably in your writing.

> THE NITTY GRITTY
> - Could (not), may (not), *and* might (not) *express possibility in the present or future.*
> - May (not) have, might (not) have, *and* could have *express past possibility.* Could not have *expresses past impossibility.*

Practice 6.1

Read the information in italics and complete the paragraphs about five officers of the New York Police Department (NYPD). Use *could* (*not*) (*have*), *may* (*not*) (*have*), *might* (*not*) (*have*), and the verbs in parentheses. In most sentences, more than one answer is correct.

1. (~~accept~~ / offer / feel like)

   Many officers leave the NYPD to work on Long Island, where salaries are higher.
   Evelyn Hong, 38, lives on Long Island. She recently resigned from the NYPD. She <u>could have accepted or may have accepted or might have accepted</u> a job with a police department on Long Island. They _____ her more money. Or she _____ driving two hours to work anymore.

2. (retire / decide / make)

   NYPD officers can retire at half pay after 20 years.
   William Johnson, 45, is thinking about his future. He _____ from the NYPD soon. He _____ to accept another police job in a smaller city. He _____ less money there, but with his half salary from the NYPD, it would be enough.

3. (realize / refuse / know)

   Most police officers never fire their guns while on duty.
   Brad Sturgis, 28, shot a man while on duty, but did not kill him. The man was holding a very realistic-looking toy gun. Officer Sturgis _____ it was a toy. The man _____ to put the gun down. The man was agitated. He _____ that Sturgis was a police officer.

4. (resign / take / be / offer)

   Stowe, Vermont, is a small town with a small police force and very little serious crime.
   Lucy Solano, 35, is thinking about a career change. She _____ from the NYPD and _____ a job in the ski resort town of Stowe, Vermont. It _____ safer than New York City policing. Also, they _____ her the job of Police Chief.

5. (be / decide / want)

   NYPD officers must retire at age 63.
   Patrick Murphy retired last month. He _____ 63 because he just turned 60 last year. He _____ to spend more time with his grandchildren. Or he _____ to get serious about his golf game.

Writing Assignment 2

Have you ever left a job? Write about your experience. Why did you leave? How did you feel about leaving? What happened after that? How did the situation work out in the end? If you have never left a job, write about someone you know who has.

Grammar Point 7 *Must*

EXPLORING THE GRAMMAR POINT

Consider these sentences. What is implied by the modal *must*? How is its meaning different from the meaning of *could, may,* or *might*?

1. That's a bad cut on your finger. It **must** hurt.
2. Chris is still in bed. He **must** not want to go to school today.

UNDERSTANDING THE GRAMMAR POINT

In sentences 1 and 2, *must* expresses a logical conclusion. You could also say, "I'm sure that it hurts" or "I'm pretty sure that he doesn't want to go to school."

The meaning of *must* in the past (*must have*) is very similar to its meaning in the present. It is used to draw conclusions about events or conditions in the past.

3. When I left, the score was 10–0 and there were two minutes left to play. They **must have** won.
4. A week before their wedding, she broke up with him. He **must have** felt terrible. She **must not have** loved him.

> **THE NITTY GRITTY**
> • Must (not) *expresses a logical conclusion about the present, based on evidence or experience.*
> • Must (not) have *expresses a logical conclusion about the past, based on evidence or experience.*

Practice 7.1

Complete the sentences with *must (not)* and an item from the box.

| be familiar | ~~be Hispanic~~ | be planning | be getting | have | speak |

1. Noriko is Japanese, but her last name is Martinez. Her husband <u>must be Hispanic</u> .
2. Noriko has lived in Canada for ten years. She _____ with Canadian culture by now.

3. I saw Noriko talking with Antonio. Antonio just arrived from Colombia recently and he speaks very little English. Noriko _____ Spanish.

4. Antonio showed Noriko some photographs of his children, but Noriko didn't show any photos to Antonio. She _____ any children.

5. Noriko has several travel brochures for South America. She _____ a vacation.

6. Sometimes Noriko falls asleep in class. She _____ enough sleep.

Practice 7.2

Read these statements about life in the U.S. fifty years ago. For each one, write a sentence with *must have* or *must not have* and the words in parentheses, using the appropriate verb froms.

1. There was no e-mail. (people / write letters)

   People must have written letters.

2. Long-distance phone calls were very expensive. (people / make many long-distance calls)

   _____

3. There were only five or six TV channels. (everyone / watch the same programs)

   _____

4. There were no cell phones. (it / hard to stay in touch)

   _____

5. There were portable radios, but there were no headphones for them. (that / be annoying)

   _____

6. There were no VCRs or DVD players. (people / watch movies at home)

   _____

7. There weren't many fast-food restaurants. (people / eat at home more)

   _____

8. There were good jobs that only required a high school education. (a lot of people / go to college)

   _____

Writing Assignment 3

How have things changed in your (or your parents') country of origin in the last fifty years? Think about family life, love and marriage, sports, entertainment, education, work, and technology. Choose one or two topics to write about. What has changed? How do people adjust to the changes? What are your thoughts about them?

4 Using Modals to Express Requirements, Recommendations, and Mistakes

EXPLORING THE GRAMMAR POINT

In these sentences, do the modals express (a) a requirement, (b) something that is not required, or (c) a prohibition?

_____ 1. My car needs an oil change. I **have to do** it this weekend.

_____ 2. You **must not park** here. It's for customers only.

_____ 3. In this state, children **must wear** a helmet when riding a bicycle. It's the law.

_____ 4. Adults **do not have to wear** a helment, but it's a good idea.

_____ 5. My car broke down. I **had to buy** a new one.

UNDERSTANDING THE GRAMMAR POINT

Sentences 1, 3, and 5 express requirements. You could also say: "I'm requiring myself to do it this weekend." "The law requires children to wear a helmet." "The situation forced me to buy a new one." Sentence 2 expresses prohibition. You could also say, "You are not permitted to park here." Sentence 4 expresses something that is not required. You could also say, "Adults are not required to wear a helmet."

For requirements, the past of *must* is *had to*, not *must have*. *Must have* only expresses logical conclusions in the past (see Grammar Point 7). There is no form with *must* that expresses past requirements.

Both *must* and *have to* are used in formal and informal writing. *Must* is preferred in signs or lists of rules.

- Must *and* have to *express requirements in the present or future. For past requirements, use* had to.
- Must not *expresses a prohibition.*
- Do/does/did not have to *says that an action is not required.*

Practice 8.1

Complete the sentences about driving in Florida. Use the correct form of *must* or *have to*. Include *not*, if necessary. For some sentences, there may be more than one correct answer.

1. To get a learner's license, applicants (take) <u>must take or have to take</u> a written test, a vision test, and a hearing test.
2. To drive with a learner's license, there (be) _____ a licensed adult with you.
3. While you have a learner's license, you (receive) _____ a traffic conviction.
4. If you receive a traffic conviction, you (wait) _____ another year to get your license.
5. We (forget) _____ that traffic accidents are the number one killer of teens.
6. My friends and I got our licenses at sixteen. First, we (have) _____ a learner's license for a year.
7. My friend Bud (get) _____ glasses to pass the eye test, but I (get) _____ them. I already had glasses.
8. I (take) _____ the road test three times because I couldn't parallel park.
9. Even after we got our regular licenses, we (have) _____ an adult with us to drive late at night.
10. When you are eighteen, you can drive alone anytime. You (have) _____ an adult in the car anymore.

Writing Assignment 4

Write about one of these topics.

1. How and when did you learn to drive? Was getting your license very important to you? How do you feel about driving today? Do you enjoy it or not? Why?
2. If you do not drive, why not? How do you manage in a car-centered society? Are you happy with your choice or not? Why?

Grammar Point 9 *Might, Could, and Should*

EXPLORING THE GRAMMAR POINT

Read the sentences on the next page about what to do if you live in a hurricane area. Which recommendations seem most important? What modals do they use?

1. You **should develop** a hurricane "action plan" for your family, and practice it.
2. You **should not wait** until the last minute to practice your plan.
3. You **should keep** a supply of dry food, canned food, and water in the house in case you need it.
4. From time to time, you **could check** the batteries in your flashlight and radio.
5. You **might buy** a first-aid kit to have in case someone gets hurt during a storm.

UNDERSTANDING THE GRAMMAR POINT

Recommendations 1, 2, and 3 are important, and they use *should*. Recommendations 4 and 5 are good ideas, but you might be all right if you don't do them. Use *should* for strong recommendations (advice); use *could* and *might* for recommendations that are less strong (suggestions).

Use *should not* as the negative for both advice and suggestions. *Could not* and *might not* do not express suggestions; they only express possibility (see Grammar Point 6).

> **THE NITTY GRITTY** *In the present and future,* should *expresses advice.* Might *and* could *express suggestions.* Should not *is the negative for both advice and suggestions.*

Practice 9.1

Read the following recommendations about what to do during a hurricane. Complete them with a modal and the correct form of the verbs in parentheses. (Include *not*, if necessary.) Choose *should* if the recommendation is important for your safety. Choose either *could* or *might* if it is a good idea, but does not affect your safety.

1. For safety, you (stay) __should not stay__ in a room with windows.
2. You (stay) _____ on the first floor of your house. It is safer.
3. The electricity will probably fail, so you (want to rent) _____ movies to watch during the storm.
4. You (reinforce) _____ the outside doors with plywood.
5. You (cook or heat) _____ with gas. You (turn off) _____ the gas lines.
6. You (buy) _____ some cookies or other snacks to munch on during this stressful time.
7. You (listen) _____ to the radio or TV for official bulletins.
8. If there is an evacuation order, you (leave) _____ immediately.
9. If you leave, you (leave) _____ your pets. You (take) _____ them with you.
10. You (take) _____ some of your pets' toys with you, too.

EXPLORING THE GRAMMAR POINT

Read the following sentences about how a family failed to prepare properly for a hurricane. Which sentences are about things they did? Which are about things they did not do?

1. They **could have gone** to the ATM to get cash. They used up all their cash before the ATMs were working again.
2. They **might have put** gas in the car. They ran out of gas.
3. They **should have bought** food and water right away. When they got to the store, there was nothing left.
4. They **should not have left** things outside in the yard. The wind blew a trash can through a window.

UNDERSTANDING THE GRAMMAR POINT

Sentences 1–3 are about things that the family did *not* do. They did not get cash, buy gas, or go to the store in time. Sentence 4 is about something they *did* do. They left things outside in the yard. All of these actions were mistakes.

In writing about the past, you are not suggesting or giving advice because the time has passed—it is too late for suggestions. Instead, *might have, could have,* and *should have* point out good ideas that people did not think of or act on.

There are no examples with *might not have* or *could not have.* They express past possibility and impossibility, respectively (see Grammar Point 6 on page 166). Use *should not have* to express bad ideas that people acted on.

Might have, could have, and should have say that it was a mistake not to do something in the past. Should not have says that it was a mistake to do something in the past.

Practice 10.1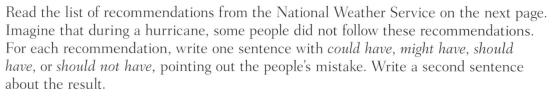

Read the list of recommendations from the National Weather Service on the next page. Imagine that during a hurricane, some people did not follow these recommendations. For each recommendation, write one sentence with *could have, might have, should have,* or *should not have,* pointing out the people's mistake. Write a second sentence about the result.

IF A HURRICANE COMES . . .

1. DECIDE IN ADVANCE WHERE TO GO. DO NOT WASTE TIME THINKING ABOUT THIS WHEN THE STORM ARRIVES.

2. PLAN A SAFE ROUTE TO YOUR DESTINATION. GET THERE SAFELY.

3. DO NOT STAY IN MOBILE HOMES. HIGH WINDS CAN DESTROY THEM.

4. DO NOT STAY NEAR THE COAST. THE STORM SURGE* IS VERY DESTRUCTIVE.

5. DO NOT STAY NEAR RIVERS. FLOODING OFTEN PREVENTS ESCAPE FROM THE AREA.

6. GO IMMEDIATELY. LEAVE BEFORE FLOODING CLOSES THE ROADS.

7. LEAVE EARLY. GO IN DAYLIGHT.

8. DO NOT DRIVE INTO MOVING WATER. IT OFTEN CARRIES CARS AWAY.

1. People could have decided where to go in advance, but they didn't. They wasted time thinking about this when the storm came.

Writing Assignment 5

Have you ever been in a natural disaster or another emergency situation? Describe the event. What did you do? What did others do around you? How did you escape or stay safe? What did you learn from the experience?

✳ A storm surge *is high water caused by hurricane winds.*

Forming Modals

- *For the present and future, form the verb phrase with modal (+ not) +* the base form *of the verb.*
- *For the past, form the verb phrase with modal (+ not) +* have + *the past participle of the verb.*
- *The past tense of* can *is* could.
- *For* have to *in the present and future, form the verb phrase with* have/has to + *the base form of the verb. The negative is* do/does not have to.
- *The past of* have/has to *is* had to. *The negative is* did not have to.

Using Modals to Express Ability

- Can/cannot *expresses ability/inability in the present and future. Use* cannot *as the negative in formal writing. The contraction for informal writing is* can't.
- Could (not) *expresses ability/inability in the past. Use* could not *in formal writing. The contraction is* couldn't.
- Could have *says that someone had the ability or opportunity to do something, but did not do it.*

Using Modals to Express Possibility and Logical Conclusions

- Could (not), may (not), *and* might (not) *express possibility in the present or future.*
- May (not) have, might (not) have, *and* could have *express past possibility.* Could not have *expresses past impossibility.*
- Must (not) *expresses a logical conclusion about the present, based on evidence or experience.*
- Must (not) have *expresses a logical conclusion about the past, based on evidence or experience.*

Using Modals to Express Requirements, Recommendations, and Mistakes

> **THE NITTY GRITTY**
> - Must *and* have to *express requirements in the present or future. For past requirements, use* had to.
> - Must not *expresses a prohibition.*
> - Do/does/did not have to *says that an action is not required.*
> - *In the present and future,* should *expresses advice.* Might *and* could *express suggestions.* Should not *is the negative for both advice and suggestions.*
> - Might have, could have, *and* should have *say that it was a mistake not to do something in the past.* Should not have *says that it was a mistake to do something in the past.*

Review Practice 10.1

Edit the following passage for problems with modals. Then circle the correct answer to the question below.

The San Francisco Earthquake of 1989

There was a major earthquake in San Francisco in 1989. It must ~~has~~ *have* been a frightening experience for the residents. My grandparents were there, and they could have die when their house collapsed, but they escaped. My grandmother's wedding ring disappeared while she was escaping. It might of come off as she struggled to open the door. Their neighbor also escaped from his house, then collapsed on the sidewalk. He may have had a heart attack.

The quake occurred at rush hour, and many more people should of be on the Nimitz Freeway when part of it fell, crushing cars underneath. However, many people left work early that day, so it may have been much worse. They must go home early to watch the World Series on TV. Two local teams were playing, and that coincidence may saved some lives.

The passage uses modals to express:

a. ability

b. possibility and logical conclusions

c. requirements and recommendations

d. mistakes

Review Practice 10.2

Edit the following passage for problems with modals. Then circle the correct answer to the question below.

The April 15th Blues

We all having to pay our income taxes by April 15th. The envelope must to be at the post office before midnight, and I always get there about 11:00 P.M. One problem is that I'm very disorganized. I could kept my records in better order, but I never do. Also, I just don't know enough about taxes. Probably I should an accountant to do them for me. Small business owners like me not have to hire an accountant, but it might will save me money in the long run.

The passage uses modals to express:

    a. ability

    b. possibility and logical conclusions

    c. requirements and recommendations

    d. mistakes

Review Practice 10.3

Edit the following passage for problems with modals. Then circle the correct answer to the question below.

First Fight

Last year was the first year we were married, and we prepared our tax return together. Big mistake! We should of see an accountant. For one thing, our records were incomplete and we shouldn't guessed about some of our expenses. We could have use some professional advice about what to put down. But the main problem was that we made each other crazy. We had our first big fight doing our taxes. Of course, we should not fought about taxes, but with an accountant, we might avoid the fight. We certainly could get over it faster.

The passage uses modals to express:

    a. ability

    b. possibility and logical conclusions

    c. requirements and recommendations

    d. mistakes

Review Practice 10.4

Edit the following passage for problems with modals. Then circle the correct answer to the question below.

> ### Earthquake Country
>
> Scientists believe that California could has a major earthquake at any time in the next thirty years. It should be not hard to imagine what might happen. The next major earthquake could damaging or destroying older buildings. There might could be fires. Electrical service may be lost. Freeways might been blocked and bridges could fallen. All of this is common knowledge. People who live in earthquake country must to know the dangers. Nevertheless, people continue to move to high-risk areas. It just goes to show that people could ignore almost anything.

The passage uses modals to express:

    a. ability

    b. possibility and logical conclusions

    c. requirements and recommendations

    d. mistakes

Review Practice 10.5

For each item, write a new sentence with the same meaning. Use a modal in each new sentence.

1. Based on her driving, I am surprised that she passed the road test.

   Based on her driving, she should not have passed the road test.

2. We are not able to thank you enough.

   _____

3. The twins were able to read when they were four.

   _____

4. I advise that we hurry.

   _____

5. It was a mistake that we didn't hurry.

   _____

6. It is possible that we will be late.

   _____

7. It is possible that we are late.

   _____

8. It is possible that they did not live in Prague.

   _____

9. It is not possible that they lived in Prague.

   _____

10. This probably will not take long.

    _____

11. I'm tired. I conclude that you are tired too.

    _____

12. She left on time. I am surprised that she was not here an hour ago.

    _____

13. Don't smoke here. It is prohibited. (*Begin your sentence with* You.)

    _____

14. He is going to pay his taxes because it is required.

    _____

15. She paid her taxes because it was required.

    _____

16. I suggest that you save this money.

    _____

17. I advise you to save this money.

    _____

18. I suggest that you not spend this money.

    _____

19. I didn't call you on your birthday. I'm sorry; it was a mistake.

    _____

20. I spent all the money. I'm sorry; it was a mistake.

    _____

Review Practice 10.6

Read the following situations. Write sentences based on what you can guess or imagine about the people. Use modals in all of your sentences. Give background information with past tense modals. Also write about what is happening now and what you expect to happen next, using present and future forms.

1. Two small children are standing next to a busy street. They are looking out into the traffic. One child is holding a baseball bat.

   They must have lost their ball. It may have rolled into the street. It could be across the street or in the middle of the traffic. Their mother shouldn't have let them play near a busy street. They must be careful. They shouldn't try to get the ball by themselves. They should ask an adult for help. They might get their ball back.

2. A middle-aged man and a young woman are having dinner at a nice restaurant. The woman is pointing to pictures in a photo album. They are both smiling.

3. Two adults are sitting on a bench in the park. One person is crying. The other person is talking softly to the first person and checking the time frequently.

4. A young man is sitting on a motorcycle that is stopped at the side of the road. A police car is parked behind the motorcycle. The police officer is standing next to the motorcycle and talking to the young man. The officer looks annoyed.

Conditionals

Introduction to the Topic

Sentences with *if* are called *conditionals* because they express a result that depends on a certain condition. There are dozens of different types of conditionals in English. This chapter presents three of the most common ones. They express conditions and results in present or future time.

REFRESHING YOUR MEMORY

Recall what you learned about clauses in *Chapter 2, Simple, Compound, and Complex Sentences.*

1. What is an independent clause?
2. What is a dependent clause?
3. Which kind of clause begins with a subordinator?
4. What does a subordinator do in a sentence?

Also recall what you learned about modals in Chapters 9 and 10.

5. What do the modals *can, may, might, could,* and *should* express in present and future time? Choose from these meanings: ability, advice, possibility, and suggestion. Remember that some modals have more than one meaning.

EXPLORING THE TOPIC

In John Grisham's novel *The Rainmaker*, Rudy, a law student, is talking with an old woman who says she has twenty million dollars. She wants to leave money to four of her grandchildren after she dies, but nothing to the others because they never call her. This passage is what Rudy is thinking. His thoughts are illustrated in the drawing on the previous page.

Multi-Million-Dollar Granny

If I had a grandmother worth twenty million dollars, *I'd send* flowers once a week, cards every other day, chocolates whenever it rained and champagne whenever it didn't. *I'd call* her once in the morning and twice before bedtime. *I'd take* her to church on Sunday and sit with her, hand in hand, during the service. Then off to brunch *we'd go*, and then to an auction, or a play, or an art show, or wherever Granny wanted to go. *I'd take care* of my grandmother.

Complete the sentences according to the passage and the example.

1. ___*If I had*___ a grandmother worth twenty million dollars, ___*I would send*___ her flowers, cards, chocolates, and champagne.
2. _____ a grandmother worth twenty million dollars, _____ her once in the morning and twice before bedtime.
3. _____ a grandmother worth twenty million dollars, _____ her to church on Sunday.
4. _____ a grandmother worth twenty million dollars, _____ to brunch after church.
5. _____ a grandmother worth twenty million dollars, _____ of her.

① Clauses in Conditional Sentences

Grammar Point 1 **Two Clauses**

EXPLORING THE GRAMMAR POINT

Read the following conditional sentences. Each of them has two clauses. What kind of clause are the ones in boldface type: independent or dependent? What kind are the other clauses? What kind of word is *if*?

1. **If you keep your money in a savings account**, it earns interest.
2. I'll be happy **if I can find a good job after college**.
3. **If I had a grandmother worth twenty million dollars**, I would take care of her.

UNDERSTANDING THE GRAMMAR POINT

If is a subordinator.* The *if clause* in conditional sentences is a dependent clause. The other clause, the *main clause*, is an independent clause. Conditional sentences with *if* are complex sentences.

Typically, the *if* clause comes first, but it is also correct to begin with the main clause. As in any complex sentence, if the dependent clause comes first, use a comma before the independent clause.

> THE NITTY GRITTY
> - *A conditional sentence consists of an* if *clause (a dependent clause) and a main clause (an independent clause).*
> - *Either the* if *clause or the main clause can come first in the sentence. If the* if *clause is first, use a comma before the main clause.*

Grammar Point 2 Condition and Result

EXPLORING THE GRAMMAR POINT

Look again at the three examples in Grammar Point 1. In each of the sentences, one clause expresses a condition and the other expresses a result of that condition. Which clauses express the condition and which express the result—the *if* clauses or the main clauses?

UNDERSTANDING THE GRAMMAR POINT

In conditional sentences, the *if* clause expresses a condition and the main clause expresses the result of that condition. The result depends on the condition.

In sentence 1, the condition is keeping your money in a savings account. Savings accounts pay interest. Therefore the result is that the money earns interest. In sentence 2, the condition is finding a good job, and the result is being happy. In sentence 3, the condition is having a grandmother worth twenty million dollars, and the result is taking care of her.

>
> *A conditional sentence expresses a condition (in the* if *clause) and a result (in the main clause). The result depends on the fulfillment of the condition.*

✶ *For a list of common subordinators, see* Chapter 2, *page 25.*

Practice 2.1

Complete the sentences with conditions (*if* clauses) and results (main clauses) from the box. Use each clause once. Use capital letters and periods, and commas if necessary.

~~if I call Evangelina~~	I'd buy a big house by the ocean
if Joe fixes his car	I'd work for myself
if you buy this stock	if the stock market crashes
I usually come in late on Monday	Eileen might study finance

1. _If I call Evangelina,_ we talk for at least an hour.
2. _____ if she went back to school.
3. _____ he can drive us to the conference next week.
4. If I could do anything I wanted _____
5. You might make a lot of money _____
6. If I had a million dollars _____
7. _____ I won't care because I don't own any stock.
8. If I go to the office on the weekend _____

② Unreal Conditionals

Grammar Point 3 Meaning

EXPLORING THE GRAMMAR POINT

Look again at "Multi-Million-Dollar Granny" on page 182. Does Rudy have a grandmother worth twenty million dollars? Is he actually planning to send flowers to his grandmother, call her three times a day, go to church with her, etc.?

UNDERSTANDING THE GRAMMAR POINT

Unreal conditionals express ideas that are untrue, imaginary, or unlikely to happen, in the opinion of the writer. The old woman in the passage is not Rudy's grandmother, and he does not have a rich grandmother. Rudy is not planning to do any of these things for his grandmother. The condition is imaginary, and so the result is also imaginary. Rudy is imagining a situation that he knows is not real.

An unreal conditional expresses conditions that are untrue, imaginary, or unlikely to occur. Therefore the result is also untrue or unlikely to occur.

Form: Present and Future

EXPLORING THE GRAMMAR POINT

Read the following sentences about the present and future, and consider the verbs in boldface type. What is the verb tense in the *if* clauses? Describe the verb phrases in the main clauses. What do you notice about the verb *be* in sentence 1?

1. If my brother **were** a stockbroker, I **would do** business with him.
2. If the stock market **crashed** tomorrow, a lot of people **could lose** their life's savings.
3. If you **could get** an interview with Bill Gates, he **might hire** you.

UNDERSTANDING THE GRAMMAR POINT

Unreal conditionals express the present and future with verbs in the simple past. In the examples, the *if* clauses are in the simple past (including sentence 3, with the past of *can*). The main clauses use a modal (*would, could,* or *might*) + the base form of the verb.

You might expect sentence 1 to use *was* instead of *were* because this is a common misusage in both written and spoken English. However, there is only one form for the past tense of *be* in unreal conditionals: *were*.

PRESENT AND FUTURE UNREAL CONDITIONALS	
***If* clause**	**Main clause**
simple past *or* could + base form	would could might $\Big\}$ + base form

- *In a present or future unreal conditional, the* if *clause is in the simple past or uses* could + *the base form of the verb. The main clause uses* would, could, *or* might + *the base form of the verb.*
- *In the* if *clause of a present or future unreal conditional,* be *has only one form for all subjects:* were.

Practice 4.1

You are watching two people play tic-tac-toe. Answer the questions based on the illustrations. Tell what move you would make if you were playing. Write conditional sentences.

1. It's player X's turn. If you were player X, where would you put your next X?

   If I were X, I'd put it in square 8.
   _____

2. It's player O's turn. If you were O, where would you put your next O?

   _____
   _____

3. It's X's turn. If you were X, where would you put your next X?

   _____
   _____

Practice 4.2

Read the following statements. For each one, write an unreal conditional sentence that describes the opposite situation.

1. I'm not good with money, so I'll never be rich.
   If I were good with money, I might be rich someday.

2. My brother isn't a stockbroker, so I can't do business with him.

   _____

3. I have a lot of credit card debt, so I worry about money all the time.

   _____

4. I don't have a lot of money, so I can't invest in stocks.

   _____

5. People aren't smart, so they overspend on their credit cards.

   _____

6. I always pay my credit card bills on time, so my interest rate doesn't go up.

   _____

Writing Assignment 1

How would you feel if you had a very rich relative, a great-uncle (the brother of your grandfather or grandmother) with no children of his own? What would you do? Would you be influenced by his money? How would you behave toward him?

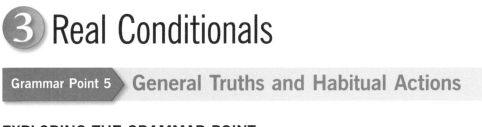

3 Real Conditionals

Grammar Point 5 **General Truths and Habitual Actions**

EXPLORING THE GRAMMAR POINT

Read the following sentences and consider the verbs in boldface type. What verb tense do they use in the *if* clause? What tense do they use in the main clause? Which clause expresses a general truth or a habitual action? Which clause expresses a condition that is necessary for the action to occur?

1. Investors **panic** if the stock market **falls** a lot.
2. If the company **makes** a profit, the employees **get** part of it.
3. If my sister **has** some extra money, she **saves** it.
4. If stock prices **go** up, the price of gold **goes** down.

UNDERSTANDING THE GRAMMAR POINT

In the sentences above, both clauses are in the simple present. The main clause expresses a general truth or a habitual action that depends on the condition expressed by the *if* clause. The sentences express what happens every time the conditions are met.

> **THE NITTY GRITTY** *Real conditionals can express general truths or habitual actions that depend on certain conditions. Both the* if *clause and the main clause are in the simple present.*

Practice 5.1

Write clauses to complete the conditional sentences. All the sentences are about general truths. Use the correct forms of the words in parentheses, and add any other words you need (including *if* and *not*).

1. (it / be / easier / to find / one)

    If you already have a job, <u>it is easier to find a new one.</u>

2. (you / want / a job)

    _____, you have to sell yourself.

3. (he or she / get / a second interview)

    If the interviewer likes a candidate, _____

4. (jobs / be / hard to find)

    _____, employers can be very selective.

5. (people / want / to hire / him or her)

    If someone has a poor reputation in the field, _____

6. (an interviewer / ask / a very personal question)

    _____, a candidate does not have to answer it.

Practice 5.2

Answer the questions by writing conditional sentences. All the answers are about habitual actions.

1. What do you do if you have a problem with your car?

    <u>If I have a problem with my car, I take it to a mechanic.</u>

2. What do you do if you need cash?

    _____

3. What do you do if you're sick?

    _____

4. What do you do if the plumbing breaks in your house (or apartment)?

    _____

5. What do you do if you have trouble spelling a word?

    _____

6. What do you do if you feel sad or depressed?

    _____

7. What do you do if you get hungry in the middle of the night?

    _____

8. What do you do if you forget an appointment?

    _____

Writing Assignment 2

What do you do if you have a problem with a good friend? Do you ignore the problem and hope it goes away? Do you take responsibility for the problem and apologize? Do you try to work it out by talking it over? Do you do something else? Under what circumstances do you do each of these things?

Grammar Point 6 **Conditional Predictions**

EXPLORING THE GRAMMAR POINT

Read the following sentences and consider the verbs in boldface type. What verb tense do they use in the *if* clause? Describe the verbs in the main clauses. Which clause expresses a prediction? Which clause expresses a condition that is necessary for the predicted action to occur?

1. If I **buy** a new car, I **can impress** all my friends.
2. If you **start** reading the financial news, you **should learn** a lot about the stock market.
3. If Elsa **gets** a good raise at work, she**'s going to talk** to a financial advisor.

UNDERSTANDING THE GRAMMAR POINT

In each of the sentences above, the writer makes a prediction based on a condition. The condition is expressed in the *if* clause. The *if* clause is in the simple present, and the main clause uses a modal + the base form of the verb.

MODALS IN CONDITIONAL PREDICTIONS		
	can	impress all my friends.
	may / could / might	have to pay a lot more for insurance.
If I buy a new car, I	**should**	spend less on repairs. / park it in the garage in winter.
	will / am going to	drive across Canada next summer.

"If the crime rate goes up, we'll know it wasn't you."

> **THE NITTY GRITTY**
>
> *Real conditionals can express a prediction that depends on certain conditions. The* if *clause is in the simple present, and the main clause uses a modal + the base form of the verb.*

Practice 6.1

In these short conversations, write the parent's answer. Give a reason for saying no to the child. Make conditional predictions.

1. *Child:* Drive faster!

   Parent: <u>If I drive faster, we might have an accident.</u>

2. *Child:* I want to stay up and watch the movie.

   Parent: _____

3. *Child:* We want to play football in the street. OK?

   Parent: _____

4. *Child:* Can I have an ice cream cone?

   Parent: _____

5. *Child:* I'm not cold. I don't want to wear a sweater.

   Parent: _____

6. *Child:* Why do I have to wash the dishes?

   Parent: _____

Practice 6.2

Read the signs and the information in parentheses. For each sign write a conditional sentence that expresses the same idea.

1. (on a city street)

   If you park here on Monday between 10:00 and
   12:00, you could get a ticket.

2. (on a street corner)

   _____

   _____

3. (at a construction site)

   _____

   _____

4. (in a restaurant)

   _____

   _____

5. (on a soda machine)

   _____

   _____

6. (in a park)

   _____

   _____

Clauses in Conditional Sentences

- *A conditional sentence consists of an* if *clause (a dependent clause) and a main clause (an independent clause).*
- *Either the* if *clause or the main clause can come first in the sentence. If the* if *clause is first, use a comma before the main clause.*
- *A conditional sentence expresses a condition (in the* if *clause) and a result (in the main clause). The result depends on the fulfillment of the condition.*

Unreal Conditionals

- *An unreal conditional expresses conditions that are untrue, imaginary, or unlikely to occur. Therefore the result is also untrue or unlikely to occur.*
- *In a present or future unreal conditional, the* if *clause is in the simple past or uses* could + *the base form of the verb. The main clause uses* would, could, *or* might + *the base form of the verb.*
- *In the* if *clause of a present or future unreal conditional,* be *has only one form for all subjects:* were.

Real Conditionals

- *Real conditionals can express general truths or habitual actions that depend on certain conditions. Both the* if *clause and the main clause are in the simple present.*
- *Real conditionals can express a prediction that depends on certain conditions. The* if *clause is in the simple present, and the main clause uses a modal + the base form of the verb.*

Review Practice 11.1

1. What is the mistake in the sentence below?

   If I had time I would take a vacation.

2. Combine the following two clauses into one conditional sentence using *if*. In one clause, change *water* to a pronoun.
   a. water reaches 100° Celsius
   b. water boils

3. Read the following two sentences. In which one does the writer think it is more likely that the reader will learn some Spanish?
   a. If you learn some Spanish, you'll have more fun in South America next summer.
   b. If you learned some Spanish, you would have more fun in South America next summer.

Review Practice 11.2

Read the following passage about credit cards. Edit it for problems with conditionals.

Managing Your Credit Cards

There are hundreds of credit cards. If you needed a credit card, you should shop around and compare them. Look for a card with no annual fee and a low interest rate. If you will go to the Internet, you will find Web sites that compare dozens of cards.

Always pay your credit card bill on time. If you were late, the bank may charged you a late-payment fee. If you late more than once (or sometimes only once), your interest rate go up. It could double, triple, or more. If you pay the full balance on your credit card every month, you will never get in trouble. However, if you paid only the minimum payment every month, you will soon has a big balance—and a problem. For example, if you carrying a balance of $4,000 on your credit card, and if the interest rate is 25%, and if you paying only the minimum every month, it takes you 27 years to pay off your balance, and it will cost you $12,000. You do not want that to happen. If you cannot pay the full balance, at least you pay more than the minimum payment.

Unfortunately, many people use a credit card to buy things they really cannot afford. If you keep a record of your credit card spending, you always knew where you stand. Have a budget, and when you reach your limit for the month, stop spending!

Review Practice 11.3

Read the following description of a book on how to get rich. Edit it for problems with conditionals.

The Automatic Millionaire

If I can live my life over again, I will do some things differently. I will not buy coffee on the way to work every day. If I needed coffee at my desk, I would take it from home. I will buy my muffins at the supermarket and read the newspaper online. If I do this, I can save at least $4 a day. If I saved $4 every workday, all year, that would be almost $1,000 a year. If I can quit smoking, I can save another $1,500 a year. If I got just 4.5% interest on these savings every year, after ten years I would have more than $35,000! Just from not spending money on coffee and cigarettes!

I found this out by reading a book called *The Automatic Millionaire*, by David Bach. There are many more ideas for saving money easily in this book. If I was 20, and if I follow the advice in this book, I might become a millionaire in time to retire. But I'm 60! It's too late for me to get rich. However, I have sent the book to two young women I know. If they take it seriously, they *can* get rich, and I hope they will.

Hope and *Wish*

Zlata Filipovic

Introduction to the Topic

Hope and *wish* are verbs that express both a feeling and an opinion about an event. In this chapter, you will learn to use *hope* and *wish* to express feelings about events in the present, the future, and the past.

REFRESHING YOUR MEMORY

Recall what you learned about clauses in *Chapter 2, Simple Compound and Complex Sentences.*

1. What is an independent clause?
2. What is a dependent clause?

EXPLORING THE TOPIC

Zlata Filipovic kept a diary of her life in Sarajevo, Bosnia, during the conflict there in 1991–1993, when she was eleven to thirteen years old. It was published in English as *Zlata's Diary: A Child's Life in Sarajevo.* Read the following extracts from Zlata's diary.

> ### Zlata's Diary
>
> *Saturday, May 2, 1992* — The shooting started around noon. . . . Almost every window on our street was broken. . . . I saw the post office in flames. . . . This has been the worst, most awful day in my eleven-year-old life. I hope it will be the only one.
>
> *Sunday, August 15, 1993* — We received a letter from Maja, Bojana, and Nedo. Nedo is getting married on August 26. Maja is going to be the bridesmaid. Oh, I wish I could be there!
>
> *Wednesday, September 29, 1993* — Sometimes I wish I had wings so I could fly away from this hell. And that's impossible, because humans are not birds. That's why I have to try to get through all this. I hope that it will pass and I will not suffer the fate of Anne Frank.* I hope I will be a child again, living my childhood in peace.

1. Underline the sentences with the verbs *hope* and *wish*.
2. Look at this sentence in the last paragraph: "I hope **that** it will pass . . . " In the other sentences you underlined, add *that* in the same place it appears in this sentence.

① Clauses in Sentences with *Hope* and *Wish*

Grammar Point 1 ▶ **Two Clauses**

EXPLORING THE GRAMMAR POINT

Review the sentences you underlined in "Zlata's Diary." They have two clauses, and now all of them include *that*. What kind of clause are the clauses with *that*: independent or dependent? What kind of clause comes immediately before *that*?

UNDERSTANDING THE GRAMMAR POINT

The sentences you underlined have an independent clause with a subject + *hope* or *wish*. The independent clauses are followed by dependent clauses beginning with *that*.**

✳ *Anne Frank was a Jewish child in the Netherlands who kept a diary for two years during World War II. She died in a concentration camp at the age of 15.*

✳✳ *Sentences with both an independent and a dependent clause are* complex sentences; *see* Chapter 2, Simple, Compound, and Complex Sentences.

The dependent clauses are *direct objects* of the verbs *hope* and *wish*.* They answer the question "Hope what?" or "Wish what?" Direct objects are usually nouns. The dependent clauses that follow *hope* and *wish* function like nouns and are called *noun clauses.*

> **THE NITTY GRITTY** *Sentences with* hope *and* wish *have an independent and a dependent clause. The verb of the independent clause (the main clause) is* hope *or* wish. *The dependent clause is a noun clause. It often begins with* that.

Grammar Point 2 > *That*

UNDERSTANDING THE GRAMMAR POINT

Noun clauses do not use the subordinators you studied in Chapter 2. Subordinators are for adverb clauses. A noun clause begins with *that*, which connects it to the main clause and shows its relationship to it. *That* can be omitted if the meaning is clear.

> **THE NITTY GRITTY** *A noun clause after* hope *or* wish *begins with* that. *You can omit* that *if the meaning is clear without it.*

Practice 2.1

Complete each sentence with the best noun clause from the box.

they will wait	~~you feel better soon~~	you can forgive me
you could see her	it were Friday	I turned off the stove
I had not spent so much money	it fits	I had your brains
	I had thought of it	

1. I'm sorry you're sick. I hope _you feel better soon._
2. I had a wonderful time in Cancun, but I wish _____
3. I made this sweater for you. I hope _____
4. This week seems so long! I wish _____
5. Edie came up with a wonderful idea. I wish _____
6. My son and his girlfriend want to get married, but they're only 18. We hope _____
   _____
7. I'm sorry. I didn't mean it. I hope _____
8. The baby is so cute! I wish _____
9. You're so smart. I wish _____
10. I left the house in a hurry this morning. I hope _____

✳ *For more about direct objects, see Chapter 15, Grammar Point 1, page 248.*

2 Verb Tenses in Sentences with *Hope* and *Wish*

EXPLORING THE GRAMMAR POINT

Read the following sentences. A child's grandmother left today after visiting for a week. They are thinking about each other.

Which verbs in boldface type are about present or future time? Which are about past time?

1. *Rickie*:   I hope Grandma **is having** a good trip home.
2. *Rickie*:   I hope she**'ll call** me tomorrow.
3. *Rickie*:   I hope she **misses** me.
4. *Grandmother*: I hope Rickie **wasn't crying** when I left.
5. *Grandmother*: I hope he **has opened** the present I left for him.
6. *Grandmother*: I hope he **played** with it right away.
7. *Grandmother*: I hope I **can visit** again very soon.

UNDERSTANDING THE GRAMMAR POINT

In all of the sentences, the main verb, *hope*, is in the simple present. The second verb, in the noun clause, can be in any of the tenses included in the chart below. Sentences 1, 2, 3, and 7 express hopes about present or future time. Sentences 4–6 express hopes about past time.

TENSES OF VERBS AFTER *HOPE*	
Present/future time	**Past time**
studies is studying can study will study	studied was studying has studied

 To express hopes about the present or future, use hope *in the simple present. The verb of the dependent clause can be in a present, past, or future tense.*

Practice 3.1

In Gabriel García Márquez's story "No One Writes to the Colonel," the author describes the unfortunate lives of a retired colonel and his wife. The colonel performs certain actions in the hope that their lives will get better. Some of these actions are listed below. Complete the sentences showing what you think the colonel hopes for.

1. The colonel shaves by touch because he doesn't have a mirror.

   He hopes he _won't cut himself._

2. The colonel starts to make coffee for himself and his wife. He sees there is very little coffee left. He throws away half of the water and scrapes out the last of the coffee from the can with a knife.

   He hopes there _____

3. He enters his rooster in a cockfight.

   He hopes the rooster _____

4. The colonel goes to the post office when the mail comes in. He watches his own mailbox closely while the postmaster is putting letters in the boxes.

   He hopes someone _____

5. They have no money for food. The Colonel takes his prized clock to Alvaro's shop to sell it.

   He hopes Alvaro _____

6. The colonel doesn't want people to know that they have no money. His wife goes to visit friends in town.

   He hopes she _____

Grammar Point 4 **Verb Tenses After *Wish*, Present/Future**

EXPLORING THE GRAMMAR POINT

Read the comic strip on the next page. Underline the four sentences that have *wish* as the verb in the main clause. What tense of the verb appears in the noun clauses that follow the main clause? What time frame do the sentences refer to, past or present/future? How do you know?

UNDERSTANDING THE GRAMMAR POINT

Although the verbs in the noun clauses are in the past tense, the time frame is the present. This is clear because the character on the left talks about "today" and "this lousy job." *Today* and *this* indicate that they are talking about their present situation.

Read the following sentence from the comic strip.

1. **Informal:** I wish **it was** cooler today.

In conversational English, it is common to use *was* after *wish*. In formal written English, however, use only *were* for all subjects.

    2. **Formal:**   I wish **it were** cooler today.

Also, read the following sentences (these do not appear in the comic strip).

    3. I wish it **would rain**.

    4. I wish we **could take** a break.

After *wish*, the verb in the noun clause can take any of the forms shown in the chart below.

TENSES OF VERBS AFTER *WISH* FOR PRESENT/FUTURE TIME	
Tense	**Example**
past tense *could* + base form *would* + base form	I wish it **were** cooler today. I wish I **had** a big glass of ice water. I wish we **could go** swimming. I wish it **would rain**.

- *To express wishes about the present/future, use* wish *in the simple present. The verb of the noun clause may be in the past tense, or it may use* would *or* could + *the base form of the verb.*
- *In sentences with* wish, *in formal writing, be* has only one past tense form in the noun clause: *were.*

Practice 4.1

Complete the sentences with the correct forms of the verbs in parentheses. Use negatives where appropriate.

1. I wish I (enjoy) _____enjoyed_____ my job more.
2. I wish my boss (be) _____ so hard to satisfy.
3. I wish we (have) _____ more time off.
4. I wish I (quit) _____ tomorrow.
5. I wish they (promote) _____ me to manager.
6. I wish they (give) _____ me a raise.
7. I wish I (call in sick) _____ tomorrow.
8. I wish we (have) _____ so many meetings.
9. I wish it (be) _____ 5:00.
10. I wish there (be) _____ some windows in this office.

Grammar Point 5 ▶ Verb Tenses After *Wish*, Past

UNDERSTANDING THE GRAMMAR POINT

Read the following sentences and consider the verbs in boldface type. The author of these sentences is writing about the year when he lived and worked in West Africa.

1. I wish I **had learned** the language better.
2. I wish I **hadn't spent** so much time with other Americans.
3. I wish I **could have stayed** longer.

Wish is in the present tense, because the author wishes this now, at the time of writing. The verb in the dependent clause can take two forms. It can be *had (not)* + the past participle, which is called the *past perfect*, or it can be *could* + *have* + the past participle.

TENSES OF VERBS AFTER *WISH*	
Name of tense	**Examples**
Past perfect (= *had (not)* + past participle)	I wish I **had not forgotten** my camera. I wish you **had been** there too.
could + have + past participle	I wish you **could have seen** it.

> **THE NITTY GRITTY** *To express wishes about the past,* wish *is in the simple present. The verb of the noun clause is* had (not) + *the past participle or* could have + *the past participle.*

Practice 5.1

Your answer to some of the following questions is probably "no." After every "no" answer, write a sentence beginning with *I wish*.

1. Did you make fifty dollars an hour at your first job?

   No. I wish I had made half that much.

2. Did you begin saving money as soon as you started working?

   _____

3. Did you learn to play the piano before you were five?

   _____

4. Were you popular in school?

   _____

5. When you were a child, did you buy your own clothes?

   _____

6. Was your grade point average 4.0 last semester?

   _____

7. Did your teacher call you up last night?

   _____

8. Did someone give you a BMW for your last birthday?

   _____

③ Meaning: *Hope* vs. *Wish*

Grammar Point 6 ▶ **Events in the Present/Future**

EXPLORING THE GRAMMAR POINT

The following sentences with *hope* and *wish* are from "Zlata's Diary."

1. I **wish** I had wings so I could fly away.
2. I **hope** I will be a child again, living my childhood in peace.

In sentence 1, does Zlata think it is possible to have wings and fly away? In sentence 2, does she think it is possible that the war will pass and her life will return to normal?

UNDERSTANDING THE GRAMMAR POINT

In sentence 1, Zlata knows she can't fly away. She even writes, "that's impossible." She does not hope for wings; she wishes for them. *Wish* expresses a desire for something that is impossible, unreal, or unlikely.

In sentence 2, Zlata feels that she is not living the life of a child, even though she is only 13. On the other hand, she believes it is possible that the war will end and her life will return to normal. She has hope. *Hope* expresses a desire for something that is possible.

> **THE NITTY GRITTY** *About events in the present/future,* hope *expresses a desire for something that is possible;* wish *expresses a desire for something that is unreal, unlikely, or impossible.*

Practice 6.1

Ivan is from a country that is divided by civil war. Ivan lives in Minnesota now, far from his home country. Complete Ivan's sentences with *hope* or *wish*.

1. I ____hope____ the war ends soon.
2. I _____ my relatives are OK.
3. I _____ I could help them more.
4. I _____ that the countries next to mine could solve the problem.
5. Sometimes I _____ I had stayed there to work for peace.
6. I _____ the United Nations can negotiate a lasting peace.

Practice 6.2

Complete the sentences with *hope* or *wish* and the verbs in parentheses. Use correct forms.

Anita and Barbara

My sisters Anita and Barbara differ a lot in their college plans and their career

goals. Both of them are taking classes at Polk Community College. Anita (hope/wish)

_____hopes_____ she (finish) _____ in a few semesters and
       1   2

(transfer) _____ to a four-year college as an accounting major. Barbara
              3

is not sure yet what she wants to do. She (hope/wish) _____ she
                                                              4

(transfer) _____ to a four-year school, but she keeps changing her
              5

major and can't decide on a goal.

When I ask Anita and Barbara how important a career is to them, they give

me different answers. Anita (hope/wish) _____ that she (find)
                                              6

_____ a job in an accounting firm as soon as she graduates. She also
       7

(hope/wish) _____ that she (have) _____ her own
                  8   9

small accounting business in two or three years. She has a lot of confidence in her plans

---

for the future. But Barbara worries about making the wrong decision. She (hope/wish)

_____ she (know) _____ what to do with her life.
         10   11

Some people think that Anita is too optimistic and Barbara is too pessimistic, but I think

they are both realistic about the choices they need to make.

Writing Assignment 1

Think of a situation that you are not happy about. Describe the situation and say why you dislike it so much. What do you wish would or could change? Do you realistically hope that things will get better? Why or why not?

Grammar Point 7 ▶ Events in the Past

EXPLORING THE GRAMMAR POINT

Read the following sentences about past events. They are comments from someone who is reading Zlata's diary.

    1. I **hope** Zlata and her family survived the war.*
    2. I **wish** that this terrible war had never happened.

In sentence 1, does the reader know what happened to Zlata? What is the reader feeling? In sentence 2, what is the reader's feeling about the war?

✴ *They did.*

UNDERSTANDING THE GRAMMAR POINT

In sentence 1, the reader does not yet know what happened to Zlata. The reader is concerned. *Hope* expresses concern about events in the past when the outcome is not known.

In sentence 2, the reader may be angry or sad about the war. *Wish* expresses anger, disappointment, or regret about things that happened in the past.

> **THE NITTY GRITTY** *About events in the past,* hope *expresses concern about an unknown outcome;* wish *expresses anger, disappointment, or regret about a known outcome.*

Practice 7.1

Complete the passage with *hope* or *wish* and the words in parentheses. Use the correct forms, including negatives.

Lost Love

Brad and I dated all through high school. He wanted to get married as soon as we graduated, but I wanted to wait. Now I (I/marry) _wish I had married_ him. I (he/think) _____ that I didn't love him. I just felt too young. I wanted to live a little first. I (I/know) _____ how things were going to work out. But of course that wasn't possible. In all these years, I've never met anybody as sweet as Brad. I (he/change) _____ because of me. No, I'm sure he's still the same. I (I/leave) _____ him, and I (he/forget) _____ me after I left. I've never forgotten him.

Grammar Point 8 **Different Points of View**

UNDERSTANDING THE GRAMMAR POINT

Zlata's diary shows that she is optimistic and hopeful. Zlata believes that her life can change and return to normal. She writes:

1. I **hope** I will be a child again, living my childhood in peace.

A less optimistic child might choose *wish* instead of *hope*:

2. I **wish** I could be a child again, living my childhood in peace.

The choice of *wish* suggests that the writer does not believe that the wished-for thing can really happen. The young writers of sentences 1 and 2 have similar feelings about their childhoods, but they have different opinions.

> **THE NITTY GRITTY** *In some contexts, the choice of* hope *or* wish *depends on the writer's opinion about the possibility of an event.* Hope *expresses optimism that the event will happen;* wish *expresses pessimism.*

Practice 8.1

Mahmood and Parinaz are both thinking about their futures. They have the same ideas, but different attitudes. Mahmood is more optimistic than Parinaz, and he has more confidence that his dreams can come true. Rewrite Mahmood's hopes as Parinaz's wishes.

1. Mahmood hopes he can lose ten pounds.
   Parinaz wishes she could lose ten pounds.

2. Mahmood hopes his girlfriend will stop smoking.
   _____

3. He hopes he can stay in the U.S. for a few more years.
   _____

4. He hopes his younger brother will come to the U.S. too.
   _____

5. He hopes he can get a scholarship next semester.
   _____

6. He hopes he can make more friends who speak English.
   _____

Practice 8.2

On a separate piece of paper, write sentences about your hopes and wishes. Write two things you hope for in the future, two things you wish for, two unknown outcomes in the past that you are worried about, and two events in the past that you are regretful about.

I hope my children will have a better life than mine.
I wish my boss would retire tomorrow.
I hope I didn't upset my mother on the phone last night.
I wish I had worked harder last semester.

Writing Assignment 2

Choose one of your sentences about present or future hopes or wishes from Practice 8.2. Use it as your topic sentence and develop the idea. Why do you have this hope or wish? How would the realization of this hope or wish change things for you or someone else?

Clauses in Sentences with *Hope* and *Wish*

- *Sentences with* hope *and* wish *have an independent and a dependent clause. The verb of the independent clause (the main clause) is* hope *or* wish. *The dependent clause is a noun clause. It often begins with* that.
- *A noun clause after* hope *or* wish *begins with* that. *You can omit* that *if the meaning is clear without it.*

Verb Tenses in Sentences with *Hope* and *Wish*

- *To express hopes about the present or future, use* hope *in the simple present. The verb of the dependent clause can be in a present, past, or future tense.*
- *To express wishes about the present/future, use* wish *in the simple present. The verb of the noun clause may be in the past tense, or it may use* would *or* could + *the base form of the verb.*
- *In sentences with* wish, *in formal writing,* be *has only one past tense form in the noun clause:* were.
- *To express wishes about the past,* wish *is in the simple present. The verb of the noun clause is* had (not) *or could have + the past participle.*

Meaning: *Hope* vs. *Wish*

- *About events in the present/future,* hope *expresses a desire for something that is possible;* wish *expresses a desire for something that is unreal, unlikely, or impossible.*
- *About events in the past,* hope *expresses concern about an unknown outcome;* wish *expresses anger, disappointment, or regret about a known outcome.*
- *In some contexts, the choice of* hope *or* wish *depends on the writer's opinion about the possibility of an event.* Hope *expresses optimism that the event will happen;* wish *expresses pessimism.*

Review Practice 12.1

Answer these questions about sentences with *hope* and *wish*.

1. Write *C* for correct or *I* for incorrect.
    a. _____ We hope can buy a house someday.
    b. _____ We hope we can buy a house someday.
    c. _____ We hope that we can buy a house someday.

2. Write *C* for correct or *I* for incorrect.
    a. _____ I hope I can meet him.
    b. _____ I hope I could meet him.
    c. _____ I wish I can meet him.
    d. _____ I wish I could meet him.
    e. _____ I wish I could have met him.
    f. _____ I wish I would have met him.
    g. _____ I wish I had met him.

3. Match the sentences on the left with the descriptions on the right.
    1. _____ I hope he will be there.
    2. _____ I hope they had a good time.
    3. _____ I wish I had stayed there.
    4. _____ I wish she would call me.

    a. The writer thinks this might happen.
    b. The writer thinks this probably will not happen.
    c. The writer regrets not doing this.
    d. The writer is worried that maybe this did not happen.

Review Practice 12.2

Read the following extracts from a diary. The writer is trying to buy a new sofa for a very small apartment. Edit the extracts for problems with *hope* and *wish*.

September 3rd — I've finally decided to buy a new sofa. I've always liked my old sofa, but I've kept it too long. It is dirty, torn, and faded. I hope I had replaced it a long time ago. I hope I could find a new one quickly. The problem is that my living room is small and most sofas are big. I'm going shopping tomorrow. I hope I'll be lucky.

September 17th — I went to all the furniture stores in town, and I wish I wouldn't have wasted my time. Everything was too big. Finally, I decided to search online, and I found a sofa! It isn't wonderful, but I wish I'll like it well enough. They are delivering the new sofa tomorrow, so I threw out the old one to make room for it. I really wish I would like the new one.

September 18th — When they delivered the new sofa, I saw immediately that it was too big. And it is much too soft. I hope I didn't accept it. I e-mailed Customer Service and I was lucky. They agreed to take it back. They said seven to ten business days. I hope they came sooner. And I hope I can find another sofa before they come.

September 30th — They came a hour ago to pick up the sofa. I wish they couldn't damage it on the way back to the warehouse. I wish I got some proof that it was in perfect condition. I went online again and found a sofa that I like a lot, and it's very small. I wish I can find a store nearby where I can see it and sit on it. I'm not going to buy anything I can't see first.

October 5th — I saw the little sofa today and I like it a lot. I wish I found it at the beginning of this search. But this is custom furniture—they have to make it especially for me. It isn't expensive, but it's going to take fourteen weeks! The salesperson says sometimes they are faster and she wishes they could do it in twelve weeks, but I'm not going to count on that. Anyway, I ordered it today. I wish I chose the right material. I think I like it, but I wish I had brought home samples of the material first. I was in a hurry. I wish I didn't make a mistake.

Review Practice 12.3

Read the following passage and edit it for problems with *hope* and *wish*.

Broadway Bound

My son's sixth-grade class wishes that they can all go to see "The Lion King" on Broadway next June. They have already begun to raise money for the tickets, which are going to cost $100 each. I wish the theater gives them a lower price, but the show is very popular. Some of the kids hope they could have earned the money by selling candy. Others, including my son, are just asking people to give a dollar. My son went to all the apartments in our building yesterday evening. I hope nobody had gotten angry. There are 55 apartments and he made $47. I was impressed. I wish I know how make $47 that easily! I wish this works out for the kids. They are really excited about it. I wish my daughter's class did things like this when she was in elementary school.

SECTION 4 REVIEW

Chapter 10 **Modals**

Chapter 11 **Conditionals**

Chapter 12 *Hope* and *Wish*

REFRESHING YOUR MEMORY

Answer the following questions based on what you learned in *Chapters 10–12.*

1. In these sentences, do the modals express (a) ability/inability, (b) possibility, (c) a logical conclusion, (d) a requirement, (e) a recommendation, or (f) a mistake?

   _____ This could be our lucky day.

   _____ If your son is lonely, you could get him a dog.

   _____ I couldn't hear the announcement.

   _____ These shoes are size eight. They should fit you better.

   _____ I should have called you yesterday.

   _____ I have to go to class now.

   _____ That must have been wonderful.

2. In the following sentence, which is the independent or main clause, (a) or (b)? Which is the dependent clause? Which clause expresses the condition? Which expresses the result?

   a

   b

   If you only have a hammer, everything looks like a nail.

3. Which writer is more optimistic about getting married? Which is more pessimistic?
   Writer A: I wish I could meet someone and get married.
   Writer B: I hope I will meet someone and get married.

Section Review Practice 4.1

The following passage is based on a student composition. Mistakes have been added for practice. Edit the composition to correct the mistakes.

> ### Being a Woman in Korea
>
> A long time ago, Korean women have to use only their last name without their first or middle name. At that time, women were only good for having babies. If a wife didn't bear a son, her husband can take a second or third wife. If she does not accept this, her

husband could divorce her. These days, women's status is higher than in the past, but it is not greatly different. I have felt this in my own marriage. My husband was the oldest son in his family, so he have to had a son to carry on the family line. When I got married, I must have a son. However, I wanted to be in business, and I started my own business before having a son. It was very successful and I made a lot of money.

In the meantime, my husband's business was not doing well. My mother-in-law insisted that if women are successful, their husbands could not succeed. She said my success was blocking his. My husband actually agreed with his mother, and I finally must gave up my business. At the same time, I also agreed to have a son. I thought that if I had a son, my marriage will survive, and it has. But truly, men still dominate women in Korea.

Section Review Practice 4.2

The following passage is based on a student composition. Mistakes have been added for practice. Edit the composition to correct the mistakes.

My Hopes for This Class

I expect a lot from this class. I wish that I will learn how to write English sentences that are clear and understandable. If I learn this, then my employer understands what I write. He will not say, "Vijitha, I got your note and it wasn't clear. Please explain what you mean." Next, I hope will learn how to organize my thoughts and writing them in good paragraphs. My job now is taking care of two children, but I cannot help them with their writing homework for school. If I can to learn to write well, I may able to help them. Even more, someday I may able to help my own children with their homework and their writing. Also, writing well could make a big difference in the future, when I finish college and work in an office. I also hope that I will learn how to correct my mistakes in writing. Eventually, I might could learn to avoid these mistakes in the first place. I really hope I could do all of this in this class.

Section Review Practice 4.3

Edit the following passage to correct mistakes.

A Choice to Make

I should have finished college before I started working. Looking back, I'm not sure why I didn't. It must have been because I was tired of school. It must have been because I wanted to start making money—and spending it. It must have been because I got a good job, although it didn't last. That first job was working for my boyfriend. When we broke up, I lost the job. After that, I can never find such a good job again. Now I'm a middle-aged woman with a nine-year-old son. It can be late for me to start something new in my life, especially compared to the young people around me, but I wish it is not too late. I believe that even if it is late, you would try. The problem now is to decide what I would study. I was studying accounting when I dropped out of college before. If I choose accounting again, I can use some of the credits I earned years ago. But I don't want to study accounting. I want to be an elementary school teacher. If I try to do that, it takes much longer, and I can't even go to school full time. I must to keep working to pay the bills. So, accounting or education? I hope I would make the right choice.

Prepositions

Bayonne, France

Introduction to the Topic

Prepositions are words such as *in* and *at* that take noun or pronoun objects. They can have multiple meanings. Some meanings of an English preposition may be the same as a preposition in the learner's first language, while other meanings are different. For this reason, learners often find English prepositions frustrating. In this chapter, you will learn some of the most common uses of the prepositions *in*, *on*, and *at* to give information about location and time.

EXPLORING THE TOPIC

In the following passage from Ernest Hemingway's novel *The Sun Also Rises*, some travelers are in Bayonne, in France. They want to go to Pamplona, in Spain.

Compare the two versions of the passage. The prepositions *in*, *on*, and *at* are in italics. In one version, these prepositions are used correctly; in the other version, they are used incorrectly. Which is the correct version? Is the other version difficult to understand?

In Bayonne (Version 1)

In the morning it was bright, and they were sprinkling the streets of the town, and we all had breakfast *in* a café. Bayonne is a nice town. It is like a very clean Spanish town and it is on a big river. Already, so early *in* the morning, it was very hot *on* the bridge across the river. We walked out *on* the bridge and then took a walk through the town. . . .

We found out *at* the tourist office what we ought to pay for a motor-car to Pamplona and hired one *at* a big garage. . . . The car was to pick us up *at* the hotel *in* forty minutes, and we stopped *at* the café *on* the square where we had eaten breakfast. . . . It was hot, but the town had a cool, fresh, early-morning smell, and it was pleasant sitting *in* the café.

In Bayonne (Version 2)

At the morning it was bright, and they were sprinkling the streets of the town, and we all had breakfast *on* a café. Bayonne is a nice town. It is like a very clean Spanish town and it is *in* a big river. Already, so early *on* the morning, it was very hot *in* the bridge across the river. We walked out *at* the bridge and then took a walk through the town. . . .

We found out *on* the tourist office what we ought to pay for a motor-car to Pamplona and hired one *on* a big garage. . . . The car was to pick us up *in* the hotel *at* forty minutes, and we stopped *on* the café *at* the square where we had eaten breakfast. . . . It was hot, but the town had a cool, fresh, early-morning smell, and it was pleasant sitting *on* the café.

ABOUT PREPOSITIONAL PHRASES

Look again at version 1 of "In Bayonne." Every preposition is followed by a noun with a determiner and/or a modifier. Underline the prepositions *in*, *on*, and *at* and the noun phrases that follow them.

The noun or pronoun that follows a preposition is called the *object* of the preposition. The preposition and its object form a *prepositional phrase*. Some of the prepositional phrases you just underlined are *in the morning, in a café, on the bridge,* and *at a big garage.*

 Location

EXPLORING THE GRAMMAR POINT

Read the following passage from a letter. What is the preposition for each kind of location: countries, states/provinces, cities/towns, streets, addresses? What would you guess are the prepositions for regions of a country and neighborhoods of a city?

Dear Sonya,

I'm in the U.S., in New York, New York! (That means in New York City and in New York State.) I'm staying at 30 West 9th Street. It's my cousin Pavel's place. I saw Irina yesterday. She's living on West 16th Street.

UNDERSTANDING THE GRAMMAR POINT

Use *in* for countries, regions, states, cities, and neighborhoods. Some examples of regions of the U.S. are New England, the Midwest, and the Pacific Northwest. Some examples of neighborhoods of New York City are Chinatown, the Theater District, and Harlem. Use *on* for streets and *at* for building addresses.

> **THE NITTY GRITTY** Use in *with countries, regions, states, cities, and neighborhoods; use* on *for streets; use* at *for addresses of buildings.*

Practice 1.1

Complete the passage with *in*, *on*, and *at*.

Washington or Washington?

When I first lived _____in_____ the U.S. as a child, I confused Washington, D.C.,
                        1

with the state of Washington. When I heard that the president lived _____
                                                                          2

Washington, I thought of Washington State. The fact is that the president lives in the

White House _____ Washington, D.C. Once a person is _____ the right
                  3   4

Washington—Washington, D.C.—the White House is not hard to find. It's _____
                                                                            5

Pennsylvania Avenue, not far from the Washington Monument, which is _____
                                                                          6

15th Street. The White House is _____ 1600 Pennsylvania Avenue, N.W. Next
                                    7

week I'm taking my kids on a trip to Washington and the South. We'll be _____
                                                                            8

Washington (D.C.!) for three days and _____ the South for a week. _____
                                            9   10

Washington, we're staying with my sister _____ the Adams-Morgan neighborhood.
                                              11

EXPLORING THE GRAMMAR POINT

Read the following sentences with *in*, *on*, and *at*. Which preposition is used for enclosed areas? Which is used for surfaces? Which is used to describe a general location which may possibly be inside, outside, or just near something?

1. We had breakfast **in** a café.
2. Bayonne is **on** a big river.
3. We walked out **on** the bridge across the river.
4. The car was going to pick us up **at** the hotel.
5. It was warm **in** the hotel room.
6. We sat **at** a table **on** the sidewalk.

UNDERSTANDING THE GRAMMAR POINT

Use *in* for enclosed areas. Use *on* for surfaces, sides, and edges. Use *at* for general locations. These could be inside, outside, or just near—*at* does not specify.

> **THE NITTY GRITTY** Use in *for enclosed areas; use* on *for surfaces, sides, and edges; use* at *for general locations.*

Practice 2.1

Write *in*, *on*, or *at* next to the illustration that correctly represents the preposition.

1. _____

2. _____

3. _____

Practice 2.2

Complete the text of the comic strip with *in* and *at*.

By permission of Mell Lazarus and Creators Syndicate, Inc.

Writing Assignment 1

The comic strip above was drawn before the advent of cell phones. How have cell phones affected communication between parents and children? Do you think children have more or less freedom because of cell phones? Are parents better informed about their children's activities because of cell phones?

Practice 2.3

Read the following sentences about painting a room. Complete them with *in* or *on*.

1. Before you start painting, you have to mix the paint ___in___ the can.
2. Be careful where you put the lid of the can because there is paint _____ it.
3. As you paint, you put paint _____ your brush, and then _____ the surface you are painting.
4. When you begin, all the paint is _____ the can.
5. As you continue painting, you get paint _____ the outside of the can too.
6. Soon you may have some paint _____ your hands.
7. To avoid this, don't hold the paint can _____ your hand.
8. Put it _____ the floor, _____ an old newspaper or a rag.
9. If you take a break, leave the paintbrush _____ the can, not _____ the can or _____ the newspaper because the paint might begin to dry.
10. When you finish painting, if there is still paint _____ the can, put a small amount of water _____ the can too.
11. Put the lid _____ the can very tightly.
12. Store the can _____ a cool place.

Grammar Point 3 Events

EXPLORING THE GRAMMAR POINT

Some tourists are in Mexico City. The following sentences describe where each person is. Consider the prepositional phrases in boldface type. What do they have in common?

1. The tour guide is at the hotel. He's **at a card game.**
2. Mrs. Ellerbee is **at a dinner party.**
3. The Ling sisters are **at a concert** at the Palace of Fine Arts.
4. Ron Fox is at the national university, **at a film festival**.

UNDERSTANDING THE GRAMMAR POINT

The phrases in boldface type all use *at*, and they all describe events, not locations.

THE NITTY GRITTY   *Use* at *for events.*

Practice 3.1

Enrique is visiting Mexico for his sister's wedding. What is the object of *at* in the following sentences, a location or an event? Underline the prepositional phrases with *at,* and write *L* (for a location) or *E* (for an event).

1. Enrique was tired when he arrived. He actually fell asleep <u>at a family get-together</u> <u>at his brother's house.</u>
      E̲
2. There were a lot of relatives at the rehearsal dinner. It was at a restaurant in San Angel.
3. He met an old friend at the wedding reception, which was held at the same place as the rehearsal dinner.
4. Yesterday he was at an art gallery, at an auction.
5. Next weekend he'll have fun at a dance at the club.
6. Before he leaves, he'll see everyone one more time at a picnic. They're going to have it on one of the boats at the "floating gardens" of Xochimilco.

Practice 3.2

Complete the passage with *in, on,* and *at.*

First Date

I met my wife ____on____ the subway. We both got on the train _____
          1   2

Times Square. It was very crowded _____ the car, and I apologized for bumping
                                  3

into her. We began talking, and then we both got off _____ South Ferry. We stood
                                            4

_____ the platform _____ the station for twenty minutes, just talking.
      5   6

Then we both realized we had to be _____ work. Carol gave me her phone
                                      7

number and I put it _____ my pocket. As soon as I was _____ the office,
                   8   9

I called her and we made a date for the next night. We arranged to go to the movies. We

were going to meet _____ the Clearview Cinema _____ 23rd Street. We
                       10   11

would meet _____ the sidewalk if it was nice. If it was raining, we would meet
                 12

_____ the lobby.
      13

That night, I arrived _____ a taxi and looked for Carol. She wasn't _____
                          14   15

the theater, either outside or inside. I waited and waited. The show started, and still no

Carol. Finally I decided she must have changed her mind. As I was leaving, Carol ran up

to me, breathless. There are two Clearview Cinemas _____ 23rd Street,
                                            16

one _____ Seventh Avenue and one _____ Eighth! She had been
       17   18

_____ the other theater. So I found my wife _____ the subway, but I almost
      19   20

lost her _____ the movies.
      21

 **Time**

EXPLORING THE GRAMMAR POINT

Read the following sentences and underline the prepositional phrases with time expressions.

Which preposition is used for months, seasons, and years? Which is used for days and dates? Which is used for clock time? Which is used for most parts of the day? Which is used for *night*?

1. We were there in 1999.
2. We went in the summer, which was the rainy season.
3. It rained in the morning, afternoon, and evening almost every day.
4. In July, we stayed in an old colonial-style hotel.
5. They served tea at 4:00.
6. Sometimes there was dancing at night.
7. On July 15th, there was a small earthquake.
8. It happened on Thursday, when we were at the beach.

UNDERSTANDING THE GRAMMAR POINT

Use *in* for periods of time such as years, seasons, months (1999, the summer, July), and for most parts of the day (morning, afternoon, and evening, except use *at* for *night*).

Use *on* for dates (July 15th) and days, including days of the week (Thursday)* and holidays (Thanksgiving).

Use *at* for clock time (4:00), for other specific times of day (sunrise, sunset), and for *night*.

 Use *in* for periods of time, including morning, afternoon, and evening. Use *on* for days and dates, including holidays. Use *at* for clock time, including sunrise and sunset, and for *night*.

✳ *It is also correct to refer to days of the week without a preposition: It happened Thursday.*

EXPLORING THE GRAMMAR POINT

Read the following sentences and consider the words in boldface type. How are the correct sentences different from the incorrect ones?

1. a. **Incorrect**: They go to Europe **in every** year.
   b. **Correct**:   They go to Europe **every** year.
2. a. **Incorrect**: I was planning my trip **on all day** Saturday.
   b. **Correct**:   I was planning my trip **all day** Saturday.

UNDERSTANDING THE GRAMMAR POINT

Do not use a preposition before a time expression with *every* and *all*.

 When every *or* all *precedes a time expression, the phrase does not take a preposition.*

Grammar Point 6   *Last*, *This*, and *Next*

UNDERSTANDING THE GRAMMAR POINT

Time expressions often do not take prepositions when they are preceded by *last*, *this*, or *next*.

PAST TIME	
Last	I was in Paris **last night.**

FUTURE TIME	
This	I'm traveling **this weekend.**
Next	We're going to Canada **next month.**

 When last, this, *and* next *precede a time expression, the phrase often does not take a preposition.*

Practice 6.1

Complete the passage with *in*, *on*, and *at* if needed.

Arriving in Ghana

The first foreign country I lived in was Ghana, West Africa. ___In___ 1966, I
_____ took a three-month training program to be a teacher there. My group arrived in Ghana

_____ January, 1967. _____ the dry season, the *harmattan* winds
   2   3

blow red dust down from the Sahara. When we got off the plane _____ four
                                                                  4

_____ the afternoon, the sky was red and the sun was a dim red ball. Also, I
   5

smelled smoke from cooking fires and other scents I didn't recognize. Suddenly I knew I

was a long way from home.

We got there _____ Saturday, and _____ Sunday, _____
                 6   7   8

sunrise, trucks began arriving to take us to our schools. The truck came from my school

_____ the late afternoon. We arrived in the village _____ night, they took
   9   10

me to my house, and I fell into bed and slept. _____ the morning, there was a
                                                    11

staff meeting at the school. _____ the following day, _____ January 16th
                                12   13

_____ 7:00 A.M., I faced my first class as a teacher.
   14

Practice 6.2

Write five true sentences reporting recent experiences or describing future plans.
Use a time expression with one of the following modifiers in each sentence: all, every,
last, this, next.

I was sick all week.

_____

_____

_____

_____

_____

Writing Assignment 2

Think of a time when you found yourself in a place that was new and strange to you. It
could be a new country, city, school, house, or some other place. Why were you there?
When and how did you get there? Describe the sights and sounds that you noticed
immediately and how you felt about them. Describe your first experience(s) there.

Location

> **THE NITTY GRITTY**
> - *Use* in *with countries, regions, states, cities, and neighborhoods; use* on *for streets; use* at *for addresses of buildings.*
> - *Use* in *for enclosed areas; use* on *for surfaces, sides, and edges; use* at *for general locations.*
> - *Use* at *for events.*

Time

> **THE NITTY GRITTY**
> - *Use* in *for periods of time, including* morning, afternoon, *and* evening. *Use* on *for days and dates, including holidays. Use* at *for clock time, including* sunrise *and* sunset, *and for* night.
> - *When* every *or* all *precedes a time expression, the phrase does not take a preposition.*
> - *When* last, this, *and* next *precede a time expression, the phrase often does not take a preposition.*

Review Practice 13.1

Write the correct preposition before each item that needs one. In each case, what is the explanation?

1. There is a poster of Venice _____ the wall _____ my room.
2. I'll see you _____ next weekend.
3. Rob isn't here. He's _____ a ball game _____ Springfield.
4. Edith is _____ the store. She'll be back soon.
5. I love watching the fireworks _____ the Fourth of July.

Review Practice 13.2

Edit the following passage for problems with *in, on,* and *at.*

> ### My Pain-in-the-neck Allergies
>
> My allergies are a pain at the neck. To start with, I have to get shots every week. I
> go to the doctor in every Tuesday afternoon, on the middle of my busy day. The doctor's
> office is at Long Beach, at the busiest part of town. It is in a tall building in Long Beach
> Boulevard with very little free parking nearby. I usually have to park at a parking lot. After
> lunch, the _∧office opens in 2:00 P.M., and I usually have my appointment in 2:30. After
>
> *doctor's*
>
> I stop at the receptionist's desk, I often have to wait for almost an hour at the waiting
> room. It's usually very noisy at there, because everyone is talking in their cell phones.
> I tried to remember to bring my CD player, so I can put on my headphones and listen
> to music, instead of all the noisy patients. After all that aggravation, I get one shot on
> each arm. To make things worse, I have to pay for the shots in every month, and they're
> expensive. Not only are allergies a pain at the neck, they're also a pain in the wallet.

Review Practice 13.3

In the following extract from the story "Tuesday Siesta," by Gabriel García Márquez, two travelers arrive by train at a small town in Colombia. It is the middle of a very hot day. Edit the passage for problems with *in, on,* and *at*.

Arrival

There was no one on the train station. On the other side of the street, at the sidewalk shaded by almond trees, only the pool hall was open. The town was floating at the heat. The woman and the girl got off the train and crossed the abandoned station—the tiles were split apart by the grass growing up between—over to the shady side of the street. It was almost two. In that hour, weighted down by drowsiness, the town was taking a siesta. The stores, the town offices, and the public school closed on eleven and didn't reopen until a little before four, when the train went back. Only the hotel across from the station, with its bar and pool hall, and the telegraph office in one side of the plaza stayed open. The houses, most of them built on the banana company's model, had their doors locked from the inside and their blinds drawn. On some of them it was so hot that the residents ate lunch at the patio. Others leaned a chair against the wall, on the shade of the almond trees, and took their siesta right out at the street.

Review Practice 13.4

Peter Hessler, an American, taught in Fuling, Sichuan Province, China, for two years. He wrote about his experience in his memoir *River Town*. Edit the following passage for problems with *in, on,* and *at*.

Leaving Fuling

I left Fuling at the fast boat to Chongqing. It was a wet, rainy morning on June—the mist was thick in the Yangtze like dirty gray silk. At the morning, I said goodbye to the other teachers, and then I headed down to the docks in a car from the college. The city rushed past, gray and familiar on the rain.

A few of the students came to see me off, along with Dean Fu. I shook hands awkwardly and boarded the boat. Karaoke videos played at the television screen while we sat there on the dock for thirty minutes. I watched the students standing at the rain and wondered what their futures would be like. William was going off to teach on a private school at the eastern province of Zhejiang; Mo Money was looking for business jobs in Fuling; Luke would be married in October, in National Day.

The boat pulled out of the harbor. The students stood perfectly still at the dock. Behind them, the city rose, gray and dirty-looking on the mist. It was hard to believe that for two years this place had been my home. I wondered when I would see it again, and how it would be changed.

Word Forms

Purple loosestrife

Introduction to the Topic

The different kinds of words in a language are called *parts of speech*. The four principal parts of speech in English are nouns, verbs, adjectives, and adverbs. You studied nouns and verbs earlier in *Chapter 1, Sentence Essentials*. In this chapter, you will learn about adjectives and adverbs. You will also learn how to turn one part of speech into another by adding certain word endings.

REFRESHING YOUR MEMORY

Recall what you learned about nouns and verbs in *Chapter 1, Sentence Essentials*. Complete these statements. Write *Nouns* or *Verbs*.

1. _____ express actions, states, or situations.
2. _____ name people, places, things, concepts, or activities.

EXPLORING THE TOPIC

Read the following passage about purple loosestrife. Some of the nouns and verbs are in italics. Circle words that give more information about an italicized noun or verb.

The Purple Invader

Purple *loosestrife* is an invasive *plant* that *arrived* accidentally from Europe in the early *1800s*. It has no natural *enemies* in North America, so its distribution today is from Canada to Mexico. The *plant* is beautiful, with showy *spikes* of purple-pink *flowers* on very tall *stems*. Unfortunately, purple loosestrife provides neither food nor shelter for native *wildlife*. It grows in wet, marshy *areas*, where it *spreads* rapidly and soon *crowds out* native *plants*.

① Parts of Speech

Grammar Point 1 Adjectives and Adverbs

EXPLORING THE GRAMMAR POINT

Read the following sentences. In each sentence, the adjective or adverb in boldface type tells more about a noun or verb in the sentence. Underline that noun or verb.

1. **Adjectives:** a. He wrote a **long** report.
                    b. All of his facts were **correct.**
2. **Adverbs:**   a. He writes **fast.**
                    b. He **always** checks his facts.

UNDERSTANDING THE GRAMMAR POINT

Adjectives and adverbs are *modifiers*. They modify (tell more about) another word. Adjectives modify nouns, and adverbs modify verbs. (Adverbs can also be used to modify adjectives and other adverbs. However, this chapter is concerned only with adverbs that modify verbs.)

In sentence 1a, *long* modifies the noun *report*. It answers the question, "What kind of report?" In sentence 1b, *correct* modifies the noun *facts*, answering the question, "What kind of facts?" In sentence 2a, *fast* modifies the verb *writes*. It answers the question, "Writes how?" In sentence 2b, *always* modifies the verb *checks*. It answers the question, "How often?"

 Adjectives modify nouns. Adverbs modify verbs.

EXPLORING THE GRAMMAR POINT

Read the following sentences and identify the words in boldface type as nouns, verbs, adjectives, or adverbs.

1. Last year it didn't **rain** in June.
2. I hope there will be **rain** in June this rear.
3. After I caught the bird, I wanted to **free** it.
4. She won a **free** trip to Costa Rica.
5. He speaks Spanish very **well**.
6. They get their water from a **well** on their farm.

UNDERSTANDING THE GRAMMAR POINT

Most English words have no endings to identify their part of speech. In most cases, the part of speech of a word is clear because of the context.

In sentence 1, *rain* is a verb; in sentence 2, it is a noun. In sentence 3, *free* is a verb; in sentence 4, it is an adjective. In sentence 5, *well* is an adverb; in sentence 6, it is a noun.

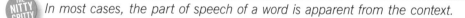 *In most cases, the part of speech of a word is apparent from the context.*

EXPLORING THE GRAMMAR POINT

Read the following sentences and identify the words in boldface type as nouns, verbs, adjectives, or adverbs.

1. We found the **information** on the Internet.
2. I didn't **realize** that she was married.
3. They gave us a **beautiful** rug as a wedding gift.
4. Since the accident, I drive **slowly** and pay attention.

UNDERSTANDING THE GRAMMAR POINT

In the sentences above, *information* is a noun, *realize* is a verb, *beautiful* is an adjective, and *slowly* is an adverb. You may have used the context to identify the words, or you may know the word endings *-ation*, *-ize*, *-ful*, and *-ly*.

Word endings can often be used to determine the part of speech of a word. But more than that, by adding or changing a word ending you can often change the part of speech of a word. For example, the ending -ation can be added to the base word inform (a verb) to change it into a noun: information.

There are exceptions, but in general, words ending in -ation are nouns, words ending in -ize are verbs, words ending in -ful are adjectives, and words ending in -ly are adverbs. You will work with these and other word endings in the next section of this chapter.

> THE NITTY GRITTY
> • The part of speech of many words can be identified by their endings.
> • For many words, changing or adding an ending can change the part of speech.

Practice 3.1

Read the following passage and use context or word endings to identify the words in italics as nouns (n.), verbs (v.), adjectives (adj.), or adverbs (adv.). Circle the word endings that show parts of speech.

Public Speaking

Giving a *talk* [n.] in front of an audience can be *frightening* [adj.] but if you *plan ahead*, you will be *satisfied* with the *results*. Here are some tips to help you give a *successful* talk.

1. Don't let the *walk* to the *front* of the room frighten you. *Walk slowly* and *breathe deeply*. *Turn confidently* toward your audience.

2. If you *panic* at first, take a deep breath and try *again*. The *panic* will go away.

3. If your *talk* is more than five minutes *long*, *request* a glass of water. *Drinking* some water will give you a good *reason* to *pause*, and *pauses* can help you *maintain* your *concentration*.

4. *Trust* your audience. They want you to *succeed*, so give them your *trust* from the start.

5. *Talk* about something you are *truly interested* in. Your *interest* in your topic will *automatically interest* the audience in what you have to say.

6. *Practice* your talk in advance. Be *careful*, but don't worry too much about *mistakes*. *Certainly* don't *apologize!* Everyone makes *mistakes*.

Writing Assignment 1

Think of a time when you spoke or performed in public, or for your family or friends.
What was the occasion? How did you feel about it? How did it go? How did the
experience affect you?

2 Common Word Endings

Grammar Point 4 | **Changing Verbs to Nouns**

EXPLORING THE GRAMMAR POINT

Read the sentences below. Which words in boldface type are nouns? Which are verbs?
Circle the word endings that change one part of speech to the other.

1. I am not a good **gardener**, but I love to **garden**.
2. I always get good **production** with tomatoes.
3. One tomato plant can **produce** dozens of tomatoes in a summer.
4. Tomatoes **require** little care.
5. One **requirement** is plenty of sunlight.

UNDERSTANDING THE GRAMMAR POINT

In the example sentences, *garden*, *produce*, and *require* are verbs. The endings *-er*, *-tion*,
and *-ment* change them to nouns. The chart on the next page includes these and other
endings that change verbs to nouns.

Complete the chart with verbs from the box. Write each verb in the left-hand column of the chart next to the appropriate ending. Then use the ending to turn the verb into a noun. Adding word endings sometimes requires spelling changes in the base word.

VERBS

~~assign~~	attend	counsel	differ
discuss	motivate	require	reserve

VERBS TO NOUNS

Verb	+ Ending	= Noun
agree	**-ment**	agreement
assign		assignment
accept	**-ance/-ence**	acceptance
prefer		preference
educate	**-tion/-sion/-ation**	education
comprehend		comprehension
inform		information
erase	**-er/-or**	eraser
educate		educator

 Certain word endings can be used to change some verbs to nouns. These endings include -ment, -ance, -ence, -tion, -sion, -ation, -er, and -or.

Practice 4.1

Complete the following passage with the correct noun forms of the verbs in parentheses.

My Former Instructor, Mrs. Albelo

Mrs. Albelo was one of the best (instruct) _____instructor_____ I have ever had.
                                                        1
She won the (admire) _____ of most of her students. For one thing,
                              2
her style of classroom (manage) _____ was effective. She required
                                         3
regular (attend) _____ . She stressed coming to class on time and
                        4
handing in all (assign) _____ on their due date. Also, she always
                               5
announced (examine) _____ a week ahead of time. Second, she was an
                             6
expert in (motivate) _____ . For example, she always made (discuss)
                            7
_____ interesting, and the (inform) _____ she
         8   9
presented often came within humorous stories. These stories encouraged us to use our
(imagine) _____ , which added to our (enjoy) _____
                  10   11
of the class. Third, Mrs. Albelo made it clear that she cared for all her students.
She often stayed after class for (converse) _____ . This attitude
                                                    12
made a big (differ) _____ to us. I'm really glad that my (counsel)
                          13
_____ recommended Mrs. Albelo to me. She made getting an (educate)
        14
_____ a pleasure.
        15

Grammar Point 5 | Changing Adjectives to Nouns

EXPLORING THE GRAMMAR POINT

Read the sentences below. Which words in boldface type are adjectives? Which are nouns? Circle the word endings that change one part of speech to the other.

1. Not all **mature** trees are naturally **full** and symmetrical.
2. Tree farmers prune (or cut) the branches to encourage **fullness**.
3. At **maturity**, a well-pruned tree brings a higher price than an unpruned one.

UNDERSTANDING THE GRAMMAR POINT

Full and *mature* are adjectives. The endings *-ness* and *-ity* change them to nouns. The chart below also includes a third ending, *-ism*.

Complete the chart by turning each adjective from the box into a corresponding noun, using the appropriate ending.

ADJECTIVES					
able	elite	equal	ideal	~~playful~~	ugly

ADJECTIVES TO NOUNS		
Adjective	**+ Ending**	**= Noun**
kind	**-ness**	kindness
sleepy		sleepiness
playful		playfulness
secure	**-ity**	security
real		reality
parallel	**-ism**	parallelism
active		activism

> **THE NITTY GRITTY** *Certain word endings can be used to change some adjectives to nouns. These endings include* -ness, -ity, *and* -ism.

Practice 5.1

Complete the passage with the correct noun forms of the adjectives in parentheses.

The Children in the Yard Next Door

The kids next door inspire me when I watch them playing in their yard. When they

shout and run out onto the grass in the morning, their (loud) _____loudness_____
                                                                       1

---

does not bother me. Instead, I appreciate their sounds of joy and (happy)

_____ . They ignore the (ugly) _____ in the
2   3

street and focus on the beauty and (pleasant) _____ of their own
                                                          4

world. The children's attitude inspires me to think about how I can put more (playful)

_____ into my own life. Their (active) _____ inspires
5   6

me to be more energetic. And their (curious) _____ makes me
                                                      7

want to find out more about the world around me. At the end of the day, I notice the

children's (tired) _____ , and I recognize my own need for rest. I am
                        8

also grateful because these wonderful children have helped me remember the (ideal)

_____ that I almost left behind in childhood.
9

Grammar Point 6 ## Changing Nouns to Adjectives

EXPLORING THE GRAMMAR POINT

Read the sentences below. Which words in boldface type are nouns? Which are adjectives? Circle the word endings that change one part of speech to the other.

1. It was a **rainy** day. After walking for a couple of hours, we went to a flower show to get out of the **rain**.
2. The flowers were **beautiful** to look at, but the real **beauty** was their smell.
3. Unfortunately, I began sneezing as soon as we got there. It was an **allergic** reaction to some of the flowers. I never had an **allergy** before.

UNDERSTANDING THE GRAMMAR POINT

Rain, beauty, and *allergy* are nouns. The endings *-y, -ful,* and *-ic* change them to adjectives. The chart on the next page includes these and other endings that change nouns to adjectives.

Complete the chart by turning each noun from the box into a corresponding adjective, using the appropriate ending. Some of the nouns can take more than one ending.

NOUNS

artist	base	boy	count	element	fool	humor	limit
~~luck~~	moment	nerve	noise	person	power	sleep	success

NOUNS TO ADJECTIVES

Noun	+ Ending	= Adjective
sun	**-y**	sunny
luck		lucky
nation	**-al**	national
universe		universal
child	**-ish**	childish
girl		girlish
danger	**-ous**	dangerous
mystery		mysterious
revolution	**-ary**	revolutionary
honor		honorary
optimist	**-ic**	optimistic
class		classic

use	**-less**	useless
end		endless
beauty	**-ful**	beautiful
wonder		wonderful

> **THE NITTY GRITTY** *Certain word endings can be used to change some nouns to adjectives. These endings include* -y, -al, -ish, -ous, -ary, -ic, -less, *and* -ful.

Practice 6.1

Complete the following passage with the correct adjective forms of the nouns in parentheses.

Interviewing My Classmate Loc

Loc Nguyen and I are in the same ESL class at Rancho Santiago College. At first I was (nerve) _____nervous_____ about interviewing him, although I knew that was (fool) _____ . In any case, his (boy) _____ smile
quickly made me feel comfortable. After I found out some (base) _____
information about Loc, he told me (count) _____ (humor)
_____ stories about his first few months in the U.S. For example,
at first he worked three jobs and was always (sleep) _____ . Once he
went to the home of a new girlfriend for dinner—and fell asleep at the table! It was a
(moment) _____ nap, but it made a (power) _____
impression on her parents. Later, I asked him more (person) _____
questions, such as how he likes the U.S. Loc said he feels (luck) _____ to
be in this country. He feels the opportunities here are almost (limit) _____ .
Here he can pursue his (artist) _____ interests. He is a dancer and hopes
to have a career in dance someday. Right now he is teaching dance in an after-school
program at an (element) _____ school. I'm sure that Loc will be

---

(success) _____ in his future in this country, and I am glad that I had the
                    15
chance to interview him.

Writing Assignment 2

Interview a classmate. You do not have to get the person's whole life story, but try to
find out something interesting. Write a report about what you learn.

Grammar Point 7 ▸ **Changing Verbs to Adjectives**

EXPLORING THE GRAMMAR POINT

Read the sentences below. Which words in boldface type are verbs? Which are
adjectives? Circle the word endings that change one part of speech to the other.

1. Gardens **attract** deer and rabbits.
2. Many gardeners have **considerable** trouble with these animals.
3. Between the two, deer and rabbits **consider** almost everything in a garden
   to be **attractive** food.
4. No garden plants are actually **repellent** to deer and rabbits.
5. To **repel** them, the best thing is a fence.

UNDERSTANDING THE GRAMMAR POINT

Attract, *consider*, and *repel* are verbs. The endings *-ive*, *-able* and *-ant* change them to
adjectives. The chart below includes these and other endings that change verbs to adjectives.

Complete the chart by turning each verb from the box into a corresponding adjective,
using the appropriate ending.

VERBS						
~~conserve~~	effect	excel	please	return	talk	wash

VERBS TO ADJECTIVES		
Verb	**+ Ending**	**= Adjective**
attract	**-ive/-ative**	attractive
conserve		conservative

urge	**-ant/-ent**	urgent
repel		repellent
understand	**-able**	understandable
agree		agreeable

> **THE NITTY GRITTY** *Certain word endings can be used to change some verbs to adjectives. These endings include* -ive, -ative, -ant, -ent, *and* -able.

Practice 7.1

Complete the following passage with the correct adjective forms of the verbs in parentheses.

Overly Talkative Salespeople

Salespeople are not always helpful when a person is trying to decide on a purchase. The other day I was shopping for a jacket, and I found an (attract)

_____attractive_____ one. I liked it because it was (conserve) _____
1   2
in color and style. It was also (wash) _____ , and I travel a lot.
                                              3
Furthermore, the price was (excel) _____ and it was (return)
                                          4
_____ if I changed my mind. I decided to buy it.
        5
    Just then a salesperson came over to me. She was very (please)

_____ , but she talked so fast that she wasn't (understand)
        6
_____ . This almost made me change my mind about buying the jacket.
        7
I asked her to let me think for a minute, and she was (agree) _____ .
                                                                        8
In the end, I decided for the second time to buy the jacket.

EXPLORING THE GRAMMAR POINT

Read the following extract from a traditional Irish legend. Underline three *-ing* or *-ed* verb forms that are used as adjectives in the passage. Circle the nouns they modify.

An Irish Legend

One day the king took his elder son with him on a long trip. After several hours, he said to his son, "Son, shorten the road for me." The son had no idea what to do, and the disappointed king turned around and returned home with his son.

Some time later, the king took his younger son on a trip and made the same request. Right away, the young man began to tell his father a long and entertaining story. The king became so interested in the story that he never noticed the length of the journey.

UNDERSTANDING THE GRAMMAR POINT

The *-ing* form of a verb is called the *present participle*. The *-ed* form, as you know, is both the past tense and the *past participle* of regular verbs. In certain circumstances, both participles can be used as adjectives.

In the passage, *disappointed* modifies *king*. The king hoped that his older son would entertain him on the journey. When the son did not understand, the king was disappointed. In another sentence, *interested* modifies *king*. It was a good story, so the king was interested in it. *Entertaining* modifies *story*.

A present participle (*-ing*) describes an *event* that causes a reaction. The younger son's story caused a reaction in the king. The story (an event) was interes*ting*. A past participle (verb + *-ed*) describes a *reaction* to an event. The king had a reaction to his younger son's story. The king was interes*ted*.

The older son did not understand what his father wanted. This situation was disappoint*ing*. The king was disappoint*ed*.

> **THE NITTY GRITTY** *Present participles (verb + -ing) and past participles (verb + -ed) are often used as adjectives. Use a present participle to describe an event that causes a reaction. Use a past participle to describe a reaction to an event.*

Practice 8.1

Circle the correct adjectives.

1. I flew to Canada. It took twenty-two hours. The flight was *tiring / tired*.
2. I always get motion sickness, so I couldn't read during the flight. I was *boring / bored*.

3. It took two hours to go through Immigration. I was *exhausting / exhausted*.

4. When I arrived, my sister was waiting for me. The arrival was *exciting / excited*.

5. At first everything was new and different. I was *fascinating / fascinated*.

6. Later, everything seemed strange and difficult. Living in Canada was *frustrating / frustrated*.

7. My English wasn't very good, and it was hard to go places and do things. I often felt *confusing / confused*.

8. Now things are easier, and I am getting used to my new life. I am feeling more *relaxing / relaxed*.

Practice 8.2

Write six sentences about your life and experiences, three with *-ing* adjectives and three with *-ed* adjectives. You may select adjectives from this list, but you are not limited to the list.

ADJECTIVES			
amazing	amazed	exhausting	exhausted
amusing	amused	frightening	frightened
annoying	annoyed	frustrating	frustrated
boring	bored	inspiring	inspired
confusing	confused	interesting	interested
depressing	depressed	puzzling	puzzled
disappointing	disappointed	relaxing	relaxed
disgusting	disgusted	satisfying	satisfied
embarrassing	embarrassed	shocking	shocked
encouraging	encouraged	surprising	surprised
entertaining	entertained	tiring	tired
exciting	excited		

My brother's room is dirty and disgusting.

I was amazed when my father bought a motorcycle.

EXPLORING THE GRAMMAR POINT

Read the sentences below. Identify the words in boldface type as verbs, adjectives, or adverbs. What word ending marks the adverbs? What ending marks the verbs?

1. Many people do not **realize** that bonsai are **real**, natural trees that are grown and shaped in very small pots.
2. The Japanese art of bonsai requires **patient** effort over many years.
3. Much of bonsai culture is just waiting **patiently** for time to do its work.

UNDERSTANDING THE GRAMMAR POINT

Patient and *real* are adjectives. *Patiently* is an adverb and *realize* is a verb; -*ly* marks adverbs and -*ize* marks verbs. The chart below also includes nouns that change to verbs with the addition of -*ize*.

Complete the following chart. Turn each adjective and noun from the box into the corresponding adverb or verb, using the appropriate ending.

| clear | correct | modern | perfect | slow | summary |

+ LY

Adjective + ly	= Adverb
careful	carefully
clear	clearly

+ IZE

Noun/Adjective + ize	= Verb
emphasis	emphasize
real	realize

- *Some adjectives can be changed to adverbs with the ending -ly.*
- *Some nouns and adjectives can be changed to verbs with the ending -ize.*

Practice 9.1

Complete the following passage with the correct verb or adverb forms of the words in parentheses.

> **A Great Day**
>
> Last weekend I (priority) _____ prioritized _____ my homework so that I had some
> 1
> time to relax on Sunday. I really enjoyed the time off. Then today, Monday, my ESL class
> was especially satisfying. We handed in our writing assignments at the beginning of
> class. I (real) _____ that some of the students were having problems
> 2
> finishing the assignment. The instructor asked me to (summary) _____
> 3
> my paper for the class, and I did. I (emphasis) _____ my topic and
> 4
> supporting ideas, and for once, I was (perfect) _____ comfortable
> 5
> in front of the class. Next, the instructor explained the new grammar lesson (slow)
> _____ and (clear) _____ . I did the exercises
> 6   7
> (careful) _____ . (Final) _____ , we had a quiz, and I
> 8   9
> answered all the questions (correct) _____ . What a great day!
> 10

Writing Assignment 3

Write about one of these topics.

1. Write about a time when you grew something in a garden or a container. What did you grow and why? Were you successful? What did other people think of your effort? How did the experience affect you?
2. Write about a plant or a garden that has impressed or interested you. Describe it. What was special about it? How did the experience affect you?

Parts of Speech

- *Adjectives modify nouns. Adverbs modify verbs.*
- *In most cases, the part of speech of a word is apparent from the context.*
- *The part of speech of many words can be identified by their endings.*
- *For many words, changing or adding an ending can change the part of speech.*

Common Word Endings

- *Certain word endings can be used to change some verbs to nouns. These endings include -ment, -ance, -ence, -tion, -sion, -ation, -er, and -or.*
- *Certain word endings can be used to change some adjectives to nouns. These endings include -ness, -ity, and -ism.*
- *Certain word endings can be used to change some nouns to adjectives. These endings include -y, -al, -ish, -ous, -ary, -ic, -less, and -ful.*
- *Certain word endings can be used to change some verbs to adjectives. These endings include -ive, -ative, -ant, -ent, and -able.*
- *Present participles (verb + -ing) and past participles (verb + -ed) are often used as adjectives. Use a present participle to describe an event that causes a reaction. Use a past participle to describe a reaction to an event.*
- *Some adjectives can be changed to adverbs with the ending -ly.*
- *Some nouns and adjectives can be changed to verbs with the ending -ize.*

Review Practice 14.1

1. For each of the following words, identify its part of speech and the base word it is derived from.

	Part of Speech	Base Word
a. attendance	_____	_____
b. heroic	_____	_____
c. kissable	_____	_____
d. slowly	_____	_____
e. sweetness	_____	_____
f. theorize	_____	_____

2. What is a present participle? Write a sentence in which a present participle is used as an adjective.

Review Practice 14.2

Complete the second sentence so that it means the same (or almost the same) as the first sentence.

1. It's hard for me to be careful when I write. I am a _____ writer.
2. It is very easy to love her. She is very _____ .
3. Everyone felt encouraged by your words. Your words were _____ .
4. I noticed that he was kind. I noticed his _____ .
5. Her voice was sweet. She sang _____ .
6. The job requires a driver's license. One _____ of the job is a driver's license.
7. He always looked at the world with humor. His view of the world was always _____ .
8. They dance well. They are good _____ .
9. He is able to accept difficulties in life. He is _____ of difficulties.
10. He was not allowed to be very active after his surgery. His _____ was limited.
11. She enjoyed being active in local politics. She enjoyed her _____ .
12. We could not understand him. He was not _____ .

Review Practice 14.3

Edit the following paragraph for problems with word forms.

Organization

Recent my teacher told me that my biggest problem in writing is organizing my ideas effective. This was surprised because I thought my biggest problem was grammar. However, this realization has been very help for me. When I did my last writing assign, I gave a lot of attention to organize. I was supposed to reaction to a short magazine article. After the topic sentence, I summarization the writer's main ideas briefly. Then I gave my own reactions to the article and emphasis my strongest point. In the conclude, I generalized about the effective the article may have had on others like me. I think it is my best compose so far. I am pleasing with the results.

Review Practice 14.4

Edit the following paragraphs for problems with word forms.

Dutch Elm Disease

A hundred years ago, most North American towns and cities were full of tall, grace American elms. The trees lined both sides of shade streets. Even modest neighborhoods looked welcome because of their beauty elms.

Then, around 1930, the elms began to die of a new disease. The cause was a fungus that entered this country accidental from Europe. Beetles spread the fungus when they colony the elms. The fungus quick blocks the disease trees' circulatory systems so that they cannot get water. Today, no American city has all its original elms, and most cities have none, or nearly none.

The disease is called Dutch elm disease because it initial arrived in elm wood from Holland. A few American elms are natural able to resistance Dutch elm disease. Scientists are trying to maximum this natural resist through select breeding. Only time will tell if this strategy can save the American elm.

Final Do's and Don'ts

Introduction to the Topic

This chapter discusses a number of distinct grammar points that frequently cause problems for developing writers. Your instructor may select points that you particularly need to work on, or may choose to cover all of the points. In either case, you can return to this chapter to refresh your memory when you have difficulties with these grammar points in your writing.

ABOUT DIRECT AND INDIRECT OBJECTS

In the sentences below, *direct objects* are in regular boldface type; *indirect objects* are in boldface italics. Direct objects answer the question "What?" For example, in sentence 1, the question is "What can Eddie say?" Indirect objects answer the question "To whom?" For example, in sentence 2, the question is "Whom did Eddie's mother tell?"

1. Little Eddie can say **the alphabet**.
2. Eddie's mother told ***me* the news**.
3. I said **she should leave**.
4. I told ***Reina* she should leave**.

Indirect objects can be nouns, noun phrases, or pronouns. Direct objects can be nouns, noun phrases, pronouns, or noun clauses.* This Grammar Point is concerned with noun clauses as direct objects (as in sentences 3 and 4).

EXPLORING THE GRAMMAR POINT

Read the following sentences with *say* and *tell*. Underline the direct objects and circle the indirect objects. Which verb (*say* or *tell*) can take a noun clause as a direct object? Which verb is followed by both an indirect and a direct object?

5. I said that it was OK.
6. He always says he will take care of it.
7. I told John that it was OK.
8. He always tells me he will take care of it.

UNDERSTANDING THE GRAMMAR POINT

The direct objects are *that it was OK* (sentences 5 and 7) and *he will take care of it* (sentences 6 and 8). The indirect objects are *John* (sentence 7) and *me* (sentence 8).

Both *say* and *tell* can take noun clauses as direct objects. *Tell*, however, needs an indirect object as well. So, if you want to mention who was spoken to, use *tell*. If you do not want to name the listener, use *say*.

> **THE NITTY GRITTY**
> - *Both* say *and* tell *can take a noun clause as a direct object.*
> - Say *needs only a direct object* (say + *direct object*).
> - Tell *needs both an indirect object and a direct object*
>   (tell + *indirect object* + *direct object*).

✱ *For more about noun clauses, see* Chapter 12, *Hope and Wish.*

Practice 1.1

Complete the following sentences with *said* or *told*.

1. My aunt once _____told_____ me that most problems exist only in our imaginations.

2. The guru _____ his followers that people can change their lives by changing their attitude toward life.

3. Someone _____ that laughter translates into any language, but jokes do not.

4. Graham Greene _____ that in human relationships, kindness and lies are worth a thousand truths.

5. The speaker _____ us that storms make trees grow stronger roots.

6. My accountant _____ me that a fool and his money are soon parted.

7. Someone _____ that when one teaches, two learn.

8. Thomas Edison _____ somebody that he never did a day's work in his life. He _____ it was all fun.

Writing Assignment 1

Choose one of the statements in Practice 1.1 and comment on it. You may agree or disagree. Give at least one detailed example to support your view.

Grammar Point 2 *Another*

EXPLORING THE GRAMMAR POINT

Read the following sentences. In which sentence(s) is *another* an adjective? In which is it a pronoun? What does *another* mean in sentence 1a? The meaning of *another* is not clear in sentences 2 and 3. Why not?

1. a. I gave my computer to my niece because I bought **another** one.
   b. I wanted **another** computer because the old one was too slow.
   c. I hope I won't have to buy **another** for a few years.

2. Some people can't accept **another**.

3. Jerry didn't know about **another**.

UNDERSTANDING THE GRAMMAR POINT

In sentences 1a and 1b, *another* is an adjective. It means *one additional*. *Another + one* is an especially common and useful combination. In sentences 1c, 2, and 3, *another* is a pronoun. In sentence 1c, it means *one additional computer*.

In sentences 2 and 3, however, we do not know what *another* means because there is no context to tell us. The sentences do not relate to sentences 1a–c, and they do not tell us what noun is referred to. When using a pronoun, you must make sure that the context shows what noun it refers to.

Another *means* one more. *It can be used as an adjective to modify a singular noun. It can also be used as a singular pronoun.*

Grammar Point 3 *Other* and *Others*

EXPLORING THE GRAMMAR POINT

Read the following sentences. In which sentence(s) is the boldface word an adjective? Are the nouns it modifies singular, plural, or noncount? In which sentence(s) is the boldface word a pronoun? Are the pronouns singular or plural?

1. I priced a desk chair at a store on Third Avenue. Later I saw **other** desk chairs that I liked at Dekkon.
2. I need some **other** furniture too.
3. I saw some nice dining room chairs at Farmingdale's. Then I saw **others** at Reco that were cheaper.

UNDERSTANDING THE GRAMMAR POINT

Other is an adjective. It means *additional*. Like any adjective, it has only one form. In sentence 1, it modifies a plural noun (chairs); in sentence 2, it modifies a noncount noun (furniture). *Some + other* is a common and useful combination.

Others is a plural pronoun. In sentence 3, it means *additional chairs*.

- Other *means* additional. *It is an adjective. It can modify a plural noun or a noncount noun.*
- Others *means* additional ones. *It is a plural pronoun.*

Practice 3.1

Complete the passage. Write *another*, *other*, or *others*.

Careers in Photography

Many people have careers in photography. Some take pictures for movies. Some

run television cameras. _____Other_____ people operate X-ray machines. Still
                              1

_____ photograph weddings or _____ celebrations. There are
         2   3

many _____ jobs in photography besides taking pictures, though. One is
              4

developing film. _____ is selling cameras and supplies. Camera repair is
                          5

_____ related job. Many people also work in large manufacturing facilities
         6

that make photo paper, film, and _____ photographic supplies.
                                            7

Grammar Point 4 ▶ *The Other* and *The Others*

EXPLORING THE GRAMMAR POINT

Read the following sentences. In which sentence(s) is *the other* an adjective? In which
is it a pronoun?

1. a. I have two printers at home. When one doesn't work, I use **the other printer.**
   b. . . . I use **the other one.**
   c. . . . I use **the other.**
2. a. We have five old printers at the office. With our limited budget, we can replace
      only three of them now. Next year we can replace **the other printers.**
   b. . . . we can replace **the other ones.**
   c. . . . we can replace **the others.**

UNDERSTANDING THE GRAMMAR POINT

In sentences 1 and 2, a and b, *the other* is an adjective (modifying *printer/printers* and
one/ones) that means *the remaining*. In sentence 1c, *the other* is a singular pronoun. It
means *the remaining printer*. *The others*, in sentence 2c, is a plural pronoun. It means
the remaining printers.

Practice 4.1

Complete the quiz questions with *the other* or *the others*. You do not have to answer the questions, but see page 253 for the answers.

Quiz: The Former Soviet Union

1. Russia and Ukraine are the largest states of the former USSR.

   Can you name ___the others___ ?

2. Latvia and Lithuania are two of the three Baltic republics.

   Can you name _____ ?

3. Lenin was the first leader of the USSR. Gorbachev was the last.

   How many of _____ can you name?

4. St. Petersburg has had three names since it was founded by Peter the Great.

   One of _____ names was Petrograd. Do you know _____ ?

5. Eleven different seas border Russia. The Baltic Sea is one of them.

   Can you name _____ ?

Grammar Point 5 ▷ Noun Adjectives

EXPLORING THE GRAMMAR POINT

Read the following correct sentences and the incorrect forms that follow them. What makes the incorrect forms incorrect? How can you explain this?

1. **Correct:**   Our ESL class had two **big** parties at the end of the semester, one in class and the other at my house.

   Incorrect: two **bigs** parties

2. **Correct:**   I bought a lot of **paper** plates.

   Incorrect: **papers** plates

3. **Correct:** After the party, I recycled 18 **soda** bottles.
   Incorrect: sodas bottles

UNDERSTANDING THE GRAMMAR POINT

In the sentences above, *big* is an adjective. As you know, English adjectives have only a singular form. There is no such word as *bigs*. *Paper* and *soda* are nouns. However, in these sentences, they are functioning as adjectives and are called *noun adjectives*. Adjectives are never plural.

 Nouns can be used as adjectives to modify other nouns. Like every other adjective, a noun adjective has no plural form.

Grammar Point 6 ## Numerical Noun Adjectives

EXPLORING THE GRAMMAR POINT

Read the following correct sentences and the incorrect forms that follow them. What makes the incorrect forms incorrect?

1. **Correct:** I have a **six-burner**, **two-oven** stove in my kitchen.
   Incorrect: six-burners, two-ovens

2. **Correct:** Everyone in my family helped with the party, even my **five-year-old** son.
   Incorrect: five-years-old

UNDERSTANDING THE GRAMMAR POINT

You can say "my stove has six burners," but it is a *six-burner* stove. The son is five years old, but he is the writer's *five-year-old* son. *Six-burner* and *five-year-old* are called *numerical noun adjectives*. Even when a noun adjective contains a number greater than one, it has only one form, and that form is singular.

 Numerical noun adjectives, like all adjectives, have no plural form.

Quiz Answers (For Practice 4.1, page 252)
1. Belarus, Lithuania, Latvia, Estonia, Moldavia, Georgia, Armenia, Azerbaijan, Turkmenistan, Uzbekistan, Kazakhstan, Kyrgyzstan, Tadzhikistan.
2. Estonia
3. Stalin, Malenkov, Khruschev, Brezhnev, Andropov, Chernenko
4. Leningrad
5. White Sea, Barents Sea, Kara Sea, Laptev Sea, East Siberian Sea, Bering Sea, Sea of Okhotsk, Caspian Sea, Sea of Azov, Black Sea.

Practice 6.1

As a young man, the writer Roald Dahl worked for the Shell Oil Company. Complete the sentences with numerical noun adjectives.

1. First he had a ____twelve-month____ training period. (of twelve months)

2. The management wanted to send him on a _____ assignment to Egypt. (of three years)

3. They eventually sent him for a _____ stay in East Africa. (for three years)

4. It was a _____ journey to get there. (of two weeks)

5. He received a _____ salary. (of fifteen thousand dollars)

6. When he went to East Africa, he was a _____ businessman. (twenty years old)

Practice 6.2

Complete the following sentences describing an expensive home. Use the information in parentheses to create noun adjectives and numerical noun adjectives.

1. They have a _____two-story house_____ (house with two stories) near two _____golf courses_____ (courses for playing golf).

2. It's a _____ (house with four bedrooms) on a _____ (lot of three acres).

3. The first floor has _____ (ceilings that are thirty feet high) and an _____ (fireplace that is eight feet wide).

4. There are many _____ (gardens of flowers) and a big _____ (garden for growing vegetables).

5. There is also a separate _____ (house for guests).

6. They have three cars and a _____ (garage for three cars).

7. On the patio, there's a _____ (grill for cooking with charcoal), and a _____ (table for picnics).

EXPLORING THE GRAMMAR POINT

Notice the use of *almost*, *most*, *most of*, and *almost all* in these sentences. Why is *almost* incorrect?

1. **Incorrect:** **Almost** students wear uniforms in Korea.
   Correct: **Most** students wear uniforms in Korea.
   Correct: **Almost all** students wear uniforms in Korea.

2. **Incorrect:** **Almost** sand is silica.
   Correct: **Most** sand is silica.
   Correct: **Almost all** sand is silica.

UNDERSTANDING THE GRAMMAR POINT

Almost is not an adjective, so it cannot modify a noun like *students* or *sand*. *Most* is an adjective used with plural and noncount nouns. *Almost all* is an adverb + an adjective, also used with plural and noncount nouns. *Almost all* indicates a larger number than *most*.

When *most* is used before a noun with a determiner, use *of* before the determiner.

3. **Correct:** **Most of my** friends in Korea didn't like their uniforms.
4. **Correct:** **Most of the** sand on this beach is silica.

> **THE NITTY GRITTY** Almost *cannot modify a noun; use* most *or* almost all. *If the noun has a determiner, use* most of.

Practice 7.1

Complete the statements with *almost all* or *most (of)* + a plural or noncount noun. Write statements that you think are true.

1. _Almost all of my friends_____ have cars.

   or

      _Most of my friends_____ have cars.

2. _____ like ice cream.
3. _____ eat *kim chi*.
4. _____ need sunshine to grow.
5. _____ have homework to do.
6. _____ falls in winter.
7. _____ drink milk.
8. _____ cause pollution.

EXPLORING THE GRAMMAR POINT

Read the following sentences. All are grammatically correct. Which one is not logical?

1. I'm happy because my son makes **too much** money.
2. I have **too much** homework, so I'm going to drop a class.
3. Rachel has **too many** books. She should get rid of some of them.

UNDERSTANDING THE GRAMMAR POINT

Too much means *beyond some acceptable limit*. It expresses dissatisfaction. Sentence 1 is not logical. If the writer is happy about his son's money, then he is satisfied, not dissatisfied.

Sentence 2 is logical. The writer feels that the amount of homework is beyond a limit that is acceptable to her. She is dissatisfied.

The choice between *a lot* and *too much/many* is often subjective. It depends on the writer's point of view. The writer of sentence 3 has an opinion about Rachel's books. He thinks there are too many of them. However, Rachel herself may not agree. She might say that she has a lot of books, but not too many.

Use *too much* with noncount nouns. Use *too many* with plural nouns. Use *a lot of* with either noncount or plural nouns. If the context makes the reference clear, it is not necessary to use the noun with these expressions. (Without a noun, use *a lot*, not *a lot of*.)

4. My son has a very good job. I'm happy because he makes **a lot**.
5. My homework is driving me crazy. I have **too much**, so I'm going to drop a class.
6. Rachel never throws a book away. She has **too many**. She should get rid of some of them.

> • Too much/many *means* beyond some acceptable limit. *It expresses dissatisfaction.* A lot *means* a large amount or quantity. *It does not say anything about satisfaction or dissatisfaction.*
> • *Use* too much *with noncount nouns. Use* too many *with plural nouns. Use* a lot of *with either noncount or plural nouns.*
> • Almost *cannot modify a noun; use* most *or* almost all. *If the noun has a determiner, use* most of.
> • Too much, too many, *and* a lot *can be used without a noun if the context makes the noun clear.*

Practice 8.1

Complete the following statements with *too much/many* or *a lot*, according to your personal standards.

1. There's a one-bedroom apartment near the school. The rent is $1400. That's _____ too much _____ . *or* That's ___ a lot of money ___ .

2. A friend of mine is taking seven courses this semester. That's _____ .

3. My physics textbook cost $75. That's _____ .

4. A family in my town has twelve children. That's ___ _____ .

5. The cheapest ticket to the play is $44. That's _____ .

6. Mr. Ogden has seventeen cats. That's _____ .

7. I had to do six hours of homework last night. That's _____ .

8. My nephew drinks about ten cans of soda a day. That's _____ .

Writing Assignment 2

Think of a time when you paid too much for something, accepted too much responsibility, took too much time to do something, or had some other experience that was just too much. Describe the situation and what happened as a result. Give plenty of details to make your account interesting to your readers.

Grammar Point 9 *After* and *Afterwards*

EXPLORING THE GRAMMAR POINT

Read the following five examples. Four of them mean the same thing. Which one has a different meaning from the others?

1. I took a shower **after** I played soccer.
2. **After** I played soccer, I took a shower.
3. I played soccer. **Afterwards**, I took a shower.
4. I played soccer. I took a shower **afterwards**.
5. I played soccer **after** I took a shower.

UNDERSTANDING THE GRAMMAR POINT

Sentences 1–4 mean that the writer played soccer first and took a shower second. Sentence 5 means that the writer took a shower first and played soccer second.

Adding commas to sentence 5 does not change the meaning; it just creates a run-on sentence.

6. **Incorrect:** I played soccer, **after**, I took a shower.

Breaking the sentence into two by adding a period and a capital letter results in a sentence fragment:

7. **Incorrect:** I played soccer. **After** I took a shower.

Both *after* and *afterwards* are used to show the order in which events happen. *After* is a subordinator. It begins a dependent clause and joins it to an independent clause to make a complex sentence. The action in the *after* clause happened first. The action in the main clause happened second. Either clause can begin the sentence.

Afterwards means *after that*. It is a *transition word*: It shows a relationship between two sentences. The action in the first sentence happened first. The action in the *afterwards* sentence happened second. *Afterwards* can come at the beginning or the end of its sentence. If at the beginning, follow it with a comma.

> **THE NITTY GRITTY**
> - After *joins a dependent clause to an independent clause. It means that the action in the independent clause followed the action in the dependent clause.*
> - Afterwards *is a transition word. It means* after that. *It shows that the action of its sentence followed the action of the previous sentence.*

Practice 9.1

Rewrite these pairs of sentences as one sentence (with *after*) or two sentences (with *afterwards*). Use the words in parentheses to indicate the order in which the events happened. Write logical sentences. It may be necessary to reverse the order of the sentences given.

1. I went home and went to bed early. I had dinner with a friend. (after)

   After I had dinner with a friend, I went home and went to bed early.

2. I worked for a few hours in the evening. I felt tired. (afterwards)

   _____

3. I brushed my teeth. I went to bed. (after)

   _____

4. I slept well. I set the alarm clock for 7:00. (afterwards)

   _____

5. I visited the campus. I decided to find out about my local community college. (after)

   _____

6. I filled out an application. I took the English and math placement tests. (afterwards)

   _____

7. She helped me apply for financial aid. I spoke to a counselor. (after)

_____

8. I went to my first class and bought my textbooks. I registered for classes. (afterwards)

_____

Grammar Point 10 ▸ *During* and *While*

EXPLORING THE GRAMMAR POINT

Read the following correct sentences. What follows *during*: a noun phrase or a clause? What follows *while*?

1. a. Jesse stays with the kids **during** his wife's night class.
   b. He works **during** the day.
2. a. Jesse takes care of the kids **while** his wife goes to her night class.
   b. She stays home with them **while** Jesse is at work.

UNDERSTANDING THE GRAMMAR POINT

Both *during* and *while* mean that something takes place at the same time as something else. These words are used differently, however.

During is a preposition, so it begins a prepositional phrase. It is followed by a direct object,* which can be a noun or noun phrase.

While is a subordinator, so it begins a dependent clause.

> **THE NITTY GRITTY** During *is a preposition. It is used in prepositional phrases with a noun or noun phrase.* While *is a subordinator. It is used to begin dependent clauses.*

Practice 10.1

Complete the sentences with *during* or *while*.

1. Jesse watches the kids _____ while _____ his wife goes to her night class.
2. He fixes dinner _____ the kids watch TV.
3. Sometimes they all watch TV _____ dinner.
4. Usually, though, Jesse and the kids talk _____ they eat.
5. _____ most of the week, Jesse works overtime.
6. He's usually working _____ the kids and his wife are having dinner.
7. But on Tuesdays, _____ his wife's class, Jesse gets to know his children better.
8. Now he looks forward to Tuesday _____ the whole week.

✱ *For more about direct objects, see Grammar Point 1 at the beginning of this chapter.*

EXPLORING THE GRAMMAR POINT

Read the following sentences, with the words *sometimes* and *sometime* in boldface type. Which word refers to an indefinite time in the future? Which word means *from time to time* (a frequency between *usually* and *seldom*)?

1. **Sometimes** I think about Korea.
2. I **sometimes** think about Korea.
3. I think about Korea **sometimes**.
4. **Sometime** I'd like to go back for a visit.
5. I'd like to go back for a visit **sometime**.

UNDERSTANDING THE GRAMMAR POINT

Sometimes is a frequency adverb like *always*, *never*, and *usually*. It means *from time to time*—a frequency between *usually* and *seldom*. It can go at the beginning or end of a sentence, or between the subject and the verb. With the verb *be*, it goes at the beginning or end of a sentence or after the verb.

6. I am **sometimes** homesick for Korea.

Sometime refers to an indefinite time in the future. It can go at the beginning of a sentence or at the end.

> **THE NITTY GRITTY**
> • Sometimes *is a frequency adverb. It means* from time to time.
> • Sometime *is a time adverb. It means* at an indefinite time in the future.

Practice 11.1

Complete the sentences with *sometimes* or *sometime*.

1. I _____ sometimes _____ fall asleep in class.
2. _____ I'll tell you about your Uncle Rob.
3. I hope I can see the Taj Mahal _____ .
4. _____ I don't know the answer.
5. I am _____ late for class, but not often.
6. I forget what I'm doing _____ .
7. _____ I want to learn to play the piano.
8. I'd like to take my family to Ireland _____ .

UNDERSTANDING THE GRAMMAR POINT

Special is an adjective. It goes before a noun or noun phrase, or after a stative verb.

1. A birthday is **a special day.**
2. I **feel special** on my birthday.

Specially is an adverb. It is often used to modify a past participle that is being used as an adjective. It is also used in verb phrases with *be + specially +* past participle.

3. I always get a few **specially wrapped** presents.
4. The birthday cake **is specially made** by my grandmother.

Especially is an adverb. It is often used in the middle of a sentence, to introduce an example. *Especially* can also mean *very* or *more than usual* when it is used before an adjective.

5. Everyone has a good time, **especially me.**
6. I feel **especially happy** when I make a wish and blow out all the candles.

> **THE NITTY GRITTY**
> - Special *is an adjective. It goes before a noun (or noun phrase) or after a stative verb like* be *or* feel.
> - Specially *is an adverb. It is often used (1) before a participle used as an adjective, and (2) in verb phrases with* be + specially + *past participle.*
> - Especially *is an adverb. It is often used in the middle of a sentence, to introduce an example.*
> - Especially *can also mean* very or more than usual *when it is used before an adjective.*

Writing Assignment 3

Write about one of your favorite days of the year. It might be a birthday, anniversary, holiday, or some other occasion. What makes it special? Explain and give details and examples so that your readers can understand your enthusiasm.

Practice 12.1

Complete the passage with *special*, *specially*, and *especially*.

Special Resource Center

El Camino College has a _____special_____ program to assist students with
1

disabilities. The staff is _____ trained to help disabled students,
2

_____ those with physical and learning disabilities, the deaf and
3

hard of hearing, and the visually impaired. The center houses _____
4

equipment, such as large-print typewriters, talking computers, and reading machines.

The center's high-tech lab makes computers accessible to disabled students through

_____ designed equipment that helps students input, process, and
5

output information. The curriculum includes _____ classes in English,
6

math, and career preparation. _____ useful are the adaptive physical
7

education classes, _____ created for disabled persons needing an
8

individualized exercise program. All of these services are offered on a relatively small,

flat campus that has been _____ constructed to meet the needs of
9

students with physical disabilities.

Grammar Point 13 *For Example*

UNDERSTANDING THE GRAMMAR POINT

In the middle of a sentence, *for example* can introduce one or more specific examples.
If there is more than one example, separate them with commas.

1. Dr. Potter has students from all over the world; **for example, Korea, Russia,
   Nigeria, and Chile.**

For example can also be a transition word to connect a general statement in one
sentence with a specific example in the next sentence. The second sentence begins
with *for example*.

2. Dr. Potter likes to have his students share their background and experience
   with the class. **For example, he recently asked Boris to talk about primary
   education in Russia.**

For example is always followed by a comma. In the middle of a sentence, *for example* is also preceded by a comma.

Do not begin a sentence with *For example* and follow it with nothing more than a list of specific examples. This produces a sentence fragment.

3. **Incorrect:** Dr. Potter gives his students many opportunities to work together in class. For example, group presentations, interviews, and cooperative reading.

4. **Correct:** Dr. Potter gives his students many opportunities to work together in class. For example, my group planned and researched a project on slavery and presented it to the class.

> THE NITTY GRITTY
> • *For example* is often used in the middle of a sentence to introduce one or more specific examples.
> • *For example* can also be a transition word to connect a general statement in one sentence with a specific example in the next sentence. The second sentence begins with For example.

Practice 13.1

Complete these sentences with examples. Use *for example* to introduce a list or a sentence. Remember commas and periods.

1. There are some good restaurants in my neighborhood , for example, the Flea Market, Paprika, Esashi, and Madras Café.

2. My friend loves to cook special dishes from our country _____

3. It isn't easy to find ingredients for some dishes in American supermarkets _____

4. Sometimes my recipes don't work out _____

5. I enjoy cooking together with friends _____

6. Some of my favorite foods are not very good for you _____

7. When I'm at a good restaurant, I like to order something I would never make at home _____

8. When I travel, I like to try the local foods _____

Grammar Point 1 *Say* and *Tell*

- *Both* say *and* tell *can take a noun clause as a direct object.*
- Say *needs only a direct object* (say + direct object).
- Tell *needs both an indirect object and a direct object* (tell + indirect object + direct object).

Grammar Point 2 *Another*

- Another *means* one more. *It can be used as an adjective to modify a singular noun. It can also be used as a singular pronoun.*

Grammar Point 3 *Other* and *Others*

- Other *means* additional. *It is an adjective. It can modify a plural noun or a noncount noun.*
- Others *means* additional ones. *It is a plural pronoun.*

Grammar Point 4 *The Other* and *The Others*

- The other *can be an adjective. As an adjective, it means* the remaining. The other *can also be a singular pronoun. As a pronoun, it means* the remaining (one).
- The others *is a plural pronoun. It means* the remaining (ones).

Grammar Point 5 *Noun Adjectives*

- *Nouns can be used as adjectives to modify other nouns. Like every other adjective, a noun adjective has no plural form.*

Grammar Point 6 *Numerical Noun Adjectives*

- *Numerical noun adjectives, like all adjectives, have no plural form.*

Grammar Point 7 *Almost, Most (of),* and *Almost All*

- Almost *cannot modify a noun; use* most *or* almost all. *If the noun has a determiner, use* most of.

Grammar Point 8 *Too Much / Many* vs. *A Lot*

- Too much/many *means* beyond some acceptable limit. *It expresses dissatisfaction.* A lot *means a large amount or quantity. It does not say anything about satisfaction or dissatisfaction.*
- *Use* too much *with noncount nouns. Use* too many *with plural nouns. Use* a lot of *with either noncount or plural nouns.*
- Almost *cannot modify a noun; use* most *or* almost all. *If the noun has a determiner, use* most of.
- Too much, too many, *and* a lot *can be used without a noun if the context makes the noun clear.*

Grammar Point 9 *After* and *Afterwards*

- After *joins a dependent clause to an independent clause. It means that the action in the independent clause followed the action in the dependent clause.*
- Afterwards *is a transition word. It means* after that. *It shows that the action of its sentence followed the action of the previous sentence.*

Grammar Point 10 *During* and *While*

- During *is a preposition. It is used in prepositional phrases with a noun or noun phrase.* While *is a subordinator. It is used to begin dependent clauses.*

Grammar Point 11 *Sometimes* vs. *Sometime*

- Sometimes *is a frequency adverb. It means* from time to time.
- Sometime *is a time adverb. It means* at an indefinite time in the future.

Grammar Point 12 *Special, Specially,* and *Especially*

- Special *is an adjective. It goes before a noun (or noun phrase) or after a stative verb like* be *or* feel.
- Specially *is an adverb. It is often used (1) before a participle used as an adjective, and (2) in verb phrases with* be + specially + *past participle.*
- Especially *is an adverb. It is often used in the middle of a sentence, to introduce an example.*
- Especially *can also mean* very *or* more than usual *when it is used before an adjective.*

Grammar Point 13 *For Example*

THE NITTY GRITTY

- For example *is often used in the middle of a sentence to introduce one or more specific examples.*
- For example *can also be a transition word to connect a general statement in one sentence with a specific example in the next sentence. The second sentence begins with* For example.

Review Practice 15.1

Answer the questions.

1. If you want to mention the person you spoke to, which verb do you use: *say* or *tell*? Write an example sentence.

2. Of the words and phrases below, which are adjectives and which are pronouns? Of the pronouns, which are singular and which are plural?

    another   other   the other   others   the others

3. If you have a car with four doors, how can you describe the car?

4. Why is this sentence wrong? Correct it.

    Almost children like ice cream.

5. What is wrong with this statement? Correct it.

    The party was perfect. Too many people were there.

6. Why is the second sentence wrong? Correct it.

    He graduated from college last year. After, he got his first full-time job.

7. Which word begins a dependent clause: *during* or *while*? Write an example sentence.

8. Which word means *at an indefinite time in the future*: *sometime* or *sometimes*? Write an example sentence.

9. Circle the correct phrase in boldface type:

    She told **a special** / **a specially** / **an especially** good joke.

10. What is wrong with the following statement? Correct it.

    We read some difficult books in college. For example, *Remembrance of Things Past*, by Proust.

Review Practice 15.2

Edit the following groups of sentences for problems with the grammar points that were discussed in this chapter.

1. Sometimes I wonder if I will ever figure out what I want to do with my life. Others times, it doesn't seem like a problem.

2. My sister sent me some of her special cookies. She made them especially for me.

3. One reason is that it would be too expensive. The other reason is that it would take too much time. Another reason is that I don't want to. Those are my three reasons.

4. I said them they were wrong. They said I was crazy.

5. Most of children like ice cream, but my 7-years-old brother is crazy about it, for example, a quart of Double Dutch Chocolate ice cream all by himself. After he got sick.

6. Eloise always eats popcorn during the game. She ate two bowls of it during the last one. I never eat during I'm watching TV, but I drank six cans of diet soda.

7. I keep the registration in the gloves compartment of the car.

8. Sometimes while I'm in New York next month, I especially want to see the Statue of Liberty. I have already seen almost of the others sights.

9. Some people are afraid to take chances in life. The others take chances all the time. I am one of the others—somewhere in the middle.

10. There were too many people on the subway this morning. I could hardly breathe.

SECTION 5 REVIEW

Chapter 13 **Prepositions**

Chapter 14 **Word Forms**

Chapter 15 **Final Do's and Don'ts**

REFRESHING YOUR MEMORY

Answer the following questions based on what you learned in Chapters 13–15.

1. Complete the sentences with *in*, *on*, or *at* if needed. What guidelines explain your answers?

   a. We live _____ Lake Street.

   b. Put that _____ the table, please.

   c. We met _____ a dance.

   d. Judy is _____ work right now.

   e. I was _____ home all day.

   f. We moved here _____ 2001.

   g. I'll see you _____ Sunday.

2. The box below lists some common parts of speech. Complete statements a–g by indicating the part of speech to which the boldface word belongs; the type of base word from which it derives; and the word ending.

a noun   a verb   an adjective   an adverb   a present participle   a past participle

   a. It doesn't make any **difference** to me.

   This is an example of changing _____ to _____ by adding _____ .

   b. It is hard to find job **security** these days.

   This is an example of changing _____ to _____ by adding _____ .

   c. The band is going to have a **national** tour.

   This is an example of changing _____ to _____ by adding _____ .

   d. There is an **urgent** message for you.

   This is an example of changing _____ to _____ by adding _____ .

   e. He told one **boring** story after another.

   This is an example of using _____ as _____ .

f. She answered 82 percent of the questions **correctly**.

This is an example of changing _____ to _____

by adding _____ .

g. He **emphasized** that it was important.

This is an example of changing _____ to _____

by adding _____ .

3. What is the difference between the expressions in each pair?

a. *other* and *the other*

b. *too much* and *a lot*

c. *during* and *while*

d. *say* and *tell*

Section Review Practice 5.1

Edit the following passage to correct the mistakes.

A Perfect Marriage

My older brother and his wife may have a perfect marriage. They met on a high school basketball game. Afterwards, were always together. They got married in the same day they graduated from high school. Some people said the marriage would never last because they were too young. But other, like me, said it would. Afterwards high school, they both went to college and got degrees in history. Now my brother teaches high school history and June has a consulting business. Ron and June seem like they were special made for each other. June loves Ron's kindness and considerate. She also admires his limit patience with his students. Ron appreciates June's optimist and her humor attitude toward life. Neither of them is perfectly, and they know it, but each of them feels accepting by the others.

There are some things they do to make their marriage work. The most importance thing they do is priority the marriage—nothing else comes first. Other thing is that they spend too much of their free time together, but they make sure they have time apart too. They never go to bed mad, and they say each other "I love you" on every day. I hope sometimes I will find a relationship as good as Ron and June's.

Section Review Practice 5.2

The following passage is based on a student composition. Mistakes have been added for practice. Edit the composition to correct the mistakes.

Two Heads Are Better Than One

"Two heads are better than one." This saying means that working together is more effect than working alone. I agree with this saying. In work a few years ago, my boss used a new network system to connection all the computers on the office. After she completed the install, some of the computers worked, but other did not. At first, my boss tried to figure out what was wrong by herself. She worked slow and careful, but she couldn't find the problem. Finally she said me that she could not find it and asked me to help her. When my boss showed me how she had connected the computers, I noticed that the order of the steps was incorrectly. When I told her about my discover, we both made the necessary changes. After, all the computers on the network worked perfect. This experience showed me that sometime two people can solve a problem better than one person working alone, specially if they cooperation well. It's important to cooperative and work as a team so that more talents and skills can be applied in any situation.

APPENDIX A

COMMONLY CONFUSED WORDS

1. **an**   article
  and   coordinator

  I wrote **an** essay **and** a poem in my English class.

2. **accept**   verb
  except   preposition

  The teacher will **accept** a composition in any color ink **except** red.

3. **advice**   noncount noun
  advise   verb

  I **advise** you to get some **advice** before you choose your classes.

4. **buy**   verb
  by   preposition

  When you **buy** your textbooks, you can pay **by** credit card.

5. **breath**   noun
  breathe verb

  When I saw the price of my chemistry book, it took my **breath** away.
  When I found a used copy, I could **breathe** again.

6. **fell**   verb, past tense of *fall*
  felt   verb, past tense of *feel*

  I **felt** like a fool when I **fell** walking into the lab.

7. **firstable** incorrect – not a real word
  first of all introductory phrase

  First of all, we need to get organized.

8. **for**   preposition
  four   4

  I paid $206 **for four** textbooks.

9. **he's**   *he is*
  his   possessive

  Where's Professor Brown? **He's** in **his** office.

10. **hear**   verb
   here   adverb

  Listen! You can **hear** air escaping **here**.

11. **hole**   noun
   whole adjective

  A **hole** in a rubber tube ruined my **whole** chemistry experiment.

12. **is**   third person singular, present tense of *be*
     it's   *it is*
     its   possessive

If the lab equipment **is** poor, **it's** hard to do a good experiment.
Its results will be unreliable.

13. **know**   verb
     now   adverb

Now I **know** how to organize a lab report.

14. **loose**   adjective, *not tight*
     lose   verb

If a tube is **loose**, it will **lose** pressure.

15. **nobody**   pronoun
     no body   *no* + noun

Nobody can work on a cadaver today because we have **no body**.

16. **quiet**   adjective, *not noisy*
     quite   adverb, *very*

When I write, I am **quite** happy if the room is **quiet**.

17. **than**   comparative conjunction
     then   adverb
     that   relative pronoun

I know **that** I should write my papers early in the morning because
then it is quieter **than** in the evening.

18. **there**   adverb, opposite of *here*
     there   filler subject
     their   possessive
     they're   *they are*

I like to study in the library because **there** are a lot of reference books **there**.
They're easy to consult and **their** information is reliable.

19. **thorough**   adjective, *complete*
     though   subordinator, *although*
     thought   verb, past tense of *think*
     threw   verb, past tense of *throw*
     through   preposition
     thru   informal, short form of *through*, incorrect in formal writing

Though I made a **thorough** search **through** all my magazines, it turned out that my
roommate **threw** out the one I was looking for. He **thought** I was finished with it.

20. **to**   preposition
    to   first part of an infinitive verb
    too   adverb
    two   2

    I try **to** go **to** the library for at least **two** hours every day. My wife does **too**.

21. **were**   verb, past tense of *be*
    where   adverb

    Where were you during lab today?

22. **who's**   *who is*
    whose   possessive

    Who's the student **whose** poem was published in the paper?

23. **worse**   comparative
    worst   superlative

    The C is **worse** than the B, but this F is the **worst** grade I've ever gotten.

24. **you're**   *you are*
    your   possessive

    You're going to have **your** last chemistry quiz on Friday.

APPENDIX B

COMMON IRREGULAR VERBS

BASE FORM	PAST TENSE	PAST PARTICIPLE
be	was/were	been
beat	beat	beaten
become	became	become
begin	began	begun
bite	bit	bitten
break	broke	broken
bring	brought	brought
build	built	built
buy	bought	bought
catch	caught	caught
choose	chose	chosen
come	came	come
cost	cost	cost
cut	cut	cut
do	did	done
drink	drank	drunk
drive	drove	driven
eat	ate	eaten
fall	fell	fallen
feel	felt	felt
fight	fought	fought
find	found	found
fly	flew	flown
forget	forgot	forgotten
get	got	gotten
give	gave	given
go	went	gone
grow	grew	grown
have	had	had
hear	heard	heard
hold	held	held

BASE FORM	PAST TENSE	PAST PARTICIPLE
hurt	hurt	hurt
keep	kept	kept
know	knew	known
leave	left	left
lend	lent	lent
let	let	let
lie*	lay	lain
lose	lost	lost
make	made	made
mean	meant	meant
meet	met	met
pay	paid	paid
put	put	put
quit	quit	quit
read	read**	read**
ride	rode	ridden
run	ran	run
say	said	said
see	saw	seen
sell	sold	sold
send	sent	sent
show	showed	shown
sing	sang	sung
sit	sat	sat
sleep	slept	slept
speak	spoke	spoken
spend	spent	spent
stand	stood	stood
steal	stole	stolen

* *The irregular verb is* lie *as in* lie down. *The other verb* lie, *meaning to tell an untruth, is regular.*

** *The past tense and the past participle are pronounced the same, but not the same as the base form. They sound the same as the color* red.

BASE FORM	PAST TENSE	PAST PARTICIPLE
swim	swam	swum
take	took	taken
teach	taught	taught
tell	told	told
think	thought	thought
throw	threw	thrown
understand	understood	understood
wear	wore	worn
win	won	won
write	wrote	written

Credits

ART

ILLUSTRATION CREDITS

Kathryn Adams: 76, 216
Matt Collins: 67, 108, 123
Jerry Zimmerman: 1, 15, 51, 141, 181, 247

54 Mother Goose and Grimm by Mike Peters. Reprinted by permission: Grimmy, Inc./King Features Syndicate
92 Hi and Lois by Brian and Greg Walker. Reprinted by permission: King Features Syndicate
190 © The New Yorker Collection 2005 Frank Cotham from cartoonbank.com. All Rights Reserved.
200 Crock by Rechin and Wilder. Reprinted by permission: North American Syndicate
217 Momma by Mell Lazarus. Reprinted by permission: Creators Syndicate.

PHOTOGRAPHY CREDITS

4 ©Hulton Archive/Getty Images
31 ©Corbis
35 ©Time & Life Pictures/Getty Images
43 ©Corbis
87 ©Corbis
105 ©AFP/Getty Images
110 ©Corbis
131 ©Getty Images
144 ©Getty Images
159 ©Tony Savino/The Image Works
163 ©Lisa Quinones/BlackStar/News.com
195 ©Les Stone/News.com
204 ©Michael Newman/PhotoEdit
213 ©Corel/Fotosearch
227 ©ageFotostock
231 ©Corbis
261 ©Getty Images

Thank you to the following reviewers for their insights:

Deedee Myers, Tallahassee Community College
Ellen Bittner, Montana State University
Grace Tomlinson, Los Angeles City College
Melina Rubinstein, Essex County College
Audrey Short, Bronx Community College
Darcy M. Meijer, Maryville College

Index